Georgia
& the Carolinas

Jeremy Gray
Jeff Davis
China Williams

LONELY PLANET PUBLICATIONS
Melbourne • Oakland • London • Paris

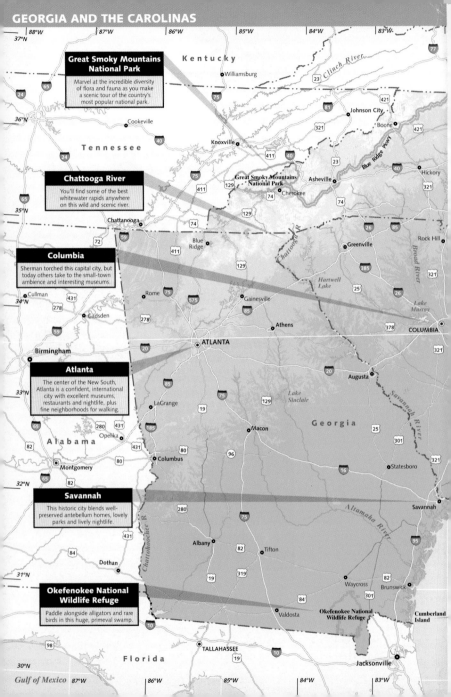

Great Smoky Mountains National Park

Marvel at the incredible diversity of flora and fauna as you make a scenic tour of the country's most popular national park.

Chattooga River

You'll find some of the best whitewater rapids anywhere on this wild and scenic river.

Columbia

Sherman torched this capital city, but today others take to the small-town ambience and interesting museums.

Atlanta

The center of the New South, Atlanta is a confident, international city with excellent museums, restaurants and nightlife, plus fine neighborhoods for walking.

Savannah

This historic city blends well-preserved antebellum homes, lovely parks and lively nightlife.

Okefenokee National Wildlife Refuge

Paddle alongside alligators and rare birds in this huge, primeval swamp.

SOUTH GEORGIA   233

SOUTH CAROLINA   248

NORTH CAROLINA   318

4 Contents

MAP INDEX

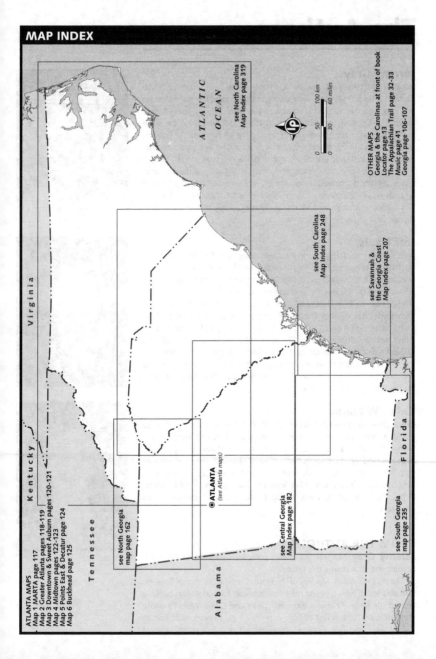

Virginia

Kentucky

Tennessee

Alabama

Florida

ATLANTIC OCEAN

see North Carolina
Map Index page 319

see South Carolina
Map Index page 248

see Savannah &
the Georgia Coast
Map Index page 207

see North Georgia
map page 162

◉ATLANTA
(see Atlanta maps)

see Central Georgia
Map Index page 182

see South Georgia
map page 235

0   50   100 km
0   30   60 miles

The Authors

Jeremy Gray

A native of Shreveport, Louisiana, Jeremy knew he'd return to North Carolina after learning to square dance in the Pisgah National Forest far too long ago. He studied literature at the University of Texas before moving to Germany on scholarship in 1984, and next thing he knew Jeremy was translating plumbing orders for the US Air Force. In England he survived a hurricane and a stint at a headhunting agency to become a news journalist, and got a rush out of having bigwigs around Europe avoid his telephone calls. While freelancing in Holland for the *Financial Times*, Jeremy discovered Lonely Planet, and since 1998 he has worked on titles including *Germany, France, The Netherlands* and *USA*, as well as LP's guides to *Munich* and *Montreal*. 'Home' usually means the coffee-stained desk of his Amsterdam flat.

Jeff Davis

Born in Alabama, Jeff grew up mostly in Columbus, Georgia. He would like to state, one more time, for the record, that he is *not* named after the president of the Confederacy. He attended college in Illinois and studied music, chemical engineering and writing. As an environmental engineer, Jeff has recently traveled the USA preparing oil spill prevention plans for truck stops (alas, none of these made the cut for this book). He took up travel writing in an effort to appear more interesting to his friends (they didn't buy it). Jeff now lives in Cincinnati, Ohio, with his wife and a lot of dead house plants (no connection implied!). He previously worked on the Panama chapter of Lonely Planet's *Central America on a Shoestring* and claims to be hard at work on the Northwest Territories and Nunavut for the 8th edition of *Canada*.

China Williams

China grew up in Aiken, South Carolina, but high-tailed it up north to attend a small liberal arts college in Annapolis, Maryland. Next came a term in the nation's capital as an editor for an itty-bitty geology magazine, followed by a teaching job in northeast Thailand. She now works as an editor in Lonely Planet's Oakland office and lives in San Francisco with her husband, Matt. Traces of her Southern upbringing can still be found in her love of sweet iced tea, talking to strangers and drawling when necessary.

FROM THE AUTHORS

Jeremy Gray My sections of this book are dedicated to Petra, for keeping me sane during this project.

Thanks to Christine Mackey of the North Carolina Division of Tourism, Film and Sport, who plugged me into hospitable folks at visitors bureaus around the state. Fellow authors Jeff Davis and China Williams wrote their socks off for this first edition, and were a joy to work with. Editors Robert Reid and Erin Corrigan provided wit and judgement when I needed them most, and cartographers Annette Olson and Tessa Rottiers get kudos for crafting fine maps from my crude dots and arrows.

Jeff Davis Thanks to the many Georgians and fellow travelers who helped me during my journey. Special thanks go to my Georgian relatives who gave me shelter and insider hints: my mother Tina Davis in Columbus and Jakin (population 157); Geri and Bill Chambers in Chickamauga; and Lola and Jerry McGuffey in Conyers, outside Atlanta. A special 'hello' to my grandmother Clara Watters Myers in my birthplace of Troy, Alabama. I'm grateful to Lonely Planet for the opportunity to see more of Georgia in a few weeks of travel than in all my years of growing up there. Extra thanks to Kate Hoffman, who introduced me to travel guidebook writing and had the good sense to avoid mentioning the rigors of the job before I became addicted. Jeremy Gray and Erin Corrigan struggled through my early drafts – many thanks to them. Most of all, thanks to my wonderful wife Rina, who caught my most embarrassing mistakes.

China Williams Big thanks to Matt for heroically tolerating my absence (to research this book) following our wedding. To my family, who kindly cleaned up allergy-inducing cat hair at the SC homestead. Susan Fox, Stan Gray and the folks at Bed, No Breakfast extended the famous Charleston hospitality. Bill Chambers gave an applaudable guerilla-style tour of Beaufort. Thanks to John Williams (my brother) and Gordon Williams (no relation) for recommending Columbia's best beef and beer joints. Jenny Shaw and her bonfire pit crew managed to steer me in the right direction in Greenville. Thanks also to the waitstaff, bartenders, hotel clerks, visitor bureaus and gas station attendants for tips and chit-chat. This good looking book is also thanks to co-authors Jeremy Gray and Jeff Davis, and to Robert Reid, Erin Corrigan, Annette Olson, Tessa Rottiers and all the talented folks at LP's Oakland office.

This Book

This first edition of *Georgia & the Carolinas* was produced in Lonely Planet's Oakland office. It was edited by Erin Corrigan and Susannah Farfor (on loan from Oz). A whole heap of people helped Erin proof the book, including Kevin Anglin, Wade Fox, David Lauterborn, Susan Shook Malloy and Pelin Thornhill. Oversight and assistance came from Wade, Robert Reid and Kate Hoffman.

The maps were drawn by many many people, but mostly by Tessa Rottiers, Laurie Mikkelsen and Graham Neale. They were assisted by Sean Brandt, Justin Colgan, John Culp, Matthew DeMartini, Rachel Driver, Molly Green, Mary Hagemann, Patrick Huerta, Kimra McAfee, Andrew Rebold and Ed Turley. The senior cartographers were Annette Olson and Tracey Croom. As always, Alex Guilbert was king of all mapworld.

This lovely book was laid out by Gerilyn Attebery and Margaret Livingston. Jen Steffey designed the cover. Gerilyn chose the color photos. Justin Marler provided the new illustrations (including the Music Map, with help from Annette), and Justin and Beca Lafore coordinated all the illustration aspects of the book. Illustrators included Justin, Mark Butler, Hugh D'Andrade, Hayden Foell, Shelly Firth and Laura Sox Harris.

And last but never least, the index was created by Ken Della Penta.

Foreword

ABOUT LONELY PLANET GUIDEBOOKS

The story begins with a classic travel adventure: Tony and Maureen Wheeler's 1972 journey across Europe and Asia to Australia. Useful information about the overland trail did not exist at that time, so Tony and Maureen published the first Lonely Planet guidebook to meet a growing need.

From a kitchen table, then from a tiny office in Melbourne (Australia), Lonely Planet has become the largest independent travel publisher in the world, an international company with offices in Melbourne, Oakland (USA), London (UK) and Paris (France).

Today Lonely Planet guidebooks cover the globe. There is an ever-growing list of books, and there's information in a variety of forms and media. Some things haven't changed. The main aim is still to help make it possible for adventurous travelers to get out there – to explore and better understand the world.

At Lonely Planet we believe travelers can make a positive contribution to the countries they visit – if they respect their host communities and spend their money wisely. Since 1986 a percentage of the income from each book has been donated to aid projects and human-rights campaigns.

Updates Lonely Planet thoroughly updates each guidebook as often as possible. This usually means there are around two years between editions, although for more unusual or more stable destinations the gap can be longer. Check the imprint page (usually following the color map at the beginning of the book) for publication dates.

Between editions up-to-date information is available in two free newsletters – the paper *Planet Talk* and email *Comet* (to subscribe, contact any Lonely Planet office) – and on our Web site at www.lonelyplanet.com. The *Upgrades* section of the Web site covers a number of important and volatile destinations and is regularly updated by Lonely Planet authors. *Scoop* covers news and current affairs relevant to travelers. And, lastly, the *Thorn Tree* bulletin board and *Postcards* section of the site carry unverified, but fascinating, reports from travelers.

Correspondence The process of creating new editions begins with the letters, postcards and emails received from travelers. This correspondence often includes suggestions, criticisms and comments about the current editions. Interesting excerpts are immediately passed on via newsletters and the Web site, and everything goes to our authors to be verified when they're researching on the road. We're keen to get more feedback from organizations or individuals who represent communities visited by travelers.

Lonely Planet gathers information for everyone who's curious about the planet – and especially for those who explore it first-hand. Through guidebooks, phrasebooks, activity guides, maps, literature, newsletters, image library, TV series and Web site we act as an information exchange for a worldwide community of travelers.

Research Authors aim to gather sufficient practical information to enable travelers to make informed choices and to make the mechanics of a journey run smoothly. They also research historical and cultural background to help enrich the travel experience and allow travelers to understand and respond appropriately to cultural and environmental issues.

Authors don't stay in every hotel because that would mean spending a couple of months in each medium-size city and, no, they don't eat at every restaurant because that would mean stretching belts beyond capacity. They do visit hotels and restaurants to check standards and prices, but feedback based on readers' direct experiences can be very helpful.

Many of our authors work undercover; others aren't so secretive. None of them accept freebies in exchange for positive write-ups. And none of our guidebooks contain any advertising.

Production Authors submit their raw manuscripts and maps to offices in Australia, the USA, UK or France. Editors and cartographers – all experienced travelers themselves – then begin the process of assembling the pieces. When the book finally hits the shops, some things are already out of date, we start getting feedback from readers and the process begins again...

WARNING & REQUEST

Things change – prices go up, schedules change, good places go bad and bad places go bankrupt – nothing stays the same. So, if you find things better or worse, recently opened or long since closed, please tell us and help make the next edition even more accurate and useful. We genuinely value all the feedback we receive. A well-traveled team reads and acknowledges every letter, postcard and email and ensures that every morsel of information finds its way to the appropriate authors, editors and cartographers for verification.

Everyone who writes to us will find their name listed in the next edition of the appropriate guidebook. They will also receive the latest issue of *Planet Talk*, our quarterly printed newsletter, or *Comet*, our monthly email newsletter. Subscriptions to both newsletters are free. The very best contributions will be rewarded with a free guidebook.

We may edit, reproduce and incorporate your comments in all Lonely Planet products, such as guidebooks, Web sites and digital products, so let us know if you don't want your comments reproduced or your name acknowledged.

Send all correspondence to the Lonely Planet office closest to you:

Australia: Locked Bag 1, Footscray, Victoria 3011
USA: 150 Linden St, Oakland, CA 94607
UK: 10a Spring Place, London NW5 3BH
France: 1 rue du Dahomey, 75011 Paris

Or email us at: talk2us@lonelyplanet.com.au

For news, views and updates, see our Web site: www.lonelyplanet.com

HOW TO USE A LONELY PLANET GUIDEBOOK

The best way to use a Lonely Planet guidebook is any way you choose. At Lonely Planet, we believe the most memorable travel experiences are often those that are unexpected, and the finest discoveries are those you make yourself. Guidebooks are not intended to be used as if they provided a detailed set of infallible instructions!

Contents All Lonely Planet guidebooks follow roughly the same format. The Facts about the Destination chapters or sections give background information ranging from history to weather. Facts for the Visitor gives practical information on issues like visas and health. Getting There & Away gives a brief starting point for researching travel to and from the destination. Getting Around gives an overview of the transport options when you arrive.

The peculiar demands of each destination determine how subsequent chapters are broken up, but some things remain constant. We always start with background, then proceed to sights, places to stay, places to eat, entertainment, getting there and away, and getting around information – in that order.

Heading Hierarchy Lonely Planet headings are used in a strict hierarchical structure that can be visualized as a set of Russian dolls. Each heading (and its following text) is encompassed by any preceding heading that is higher on the hierarchical ladder.

Entry Points We do not assume guidebooks will be read from beginning to end, but that people will dip into them. The traditional entry points are the list of contents and the index. In addition, however, some books have a complete list of maps and an index map illustrating map coverage.

There may also be a color map that shows highlights. These highlights are dealt with in greater detail in the Facts for the Visitor chapter, along with planning questions and suggested itineraries. Each chapter covering a geographical region usually begins with a locator map and another list of highlights. Once you find something of interest in a list of highlights, turn to the index.

Maps Maps play a crucial role in Lonely Planet guidebooks and include a huge amount of information. A legend is printed on the back page. We seek to have complete consistency between maps and text and to have every important place in the text captured on a map. Map key numbers usually start in the top left corner.

Although inclusion in a guidebook usually implies a recommendation, we cannot list every good place. Exclusion does not necessarily imply criticism. In fact there are a number of reasons why we might exclude a place – sometimes it is simply inappropriate to encourage an influx of travelers.

Introduction

The Southeast – our shorthand for Georgia and North and South Carolina – is a gorgeous and unpredictable patchwork encompassing the Blue Ridge Mountains, fertile Piedmont plains and wildly seductive beaches and islands bathed in warm Gulf Stream waters. Lodged between the Deep South and the mid-Atlantic states, this region lures visitors with discriminating tastes: for the hospitality and colonial heritage the South is famous for, but also for the great outdoors – camping, shooting the rapids or scaling a mountain face. Here you can as easily go clubbing as clamming, with few pretensions in between. Somewhere between steamy, slow-moving Louisiana and hyperactive New York, the Southeast relishes the best of both worlds – without getting stuck-up about it.

In some minds, this part of the map is inescapably Old South, where hoopskirts, mint juleps and Scarlett O'Hara remain defining features. You can indulge this Old South fantasy in Savannah or Charleston, where the streets are lined with antebellum mansions and shaded by live oaks dripping Spanish moss. Look at the cotton gins churning across the vast plains of the Piedmont – just as they did a century ago – and the anachronism seems complete. Yet nearly half of Georgia's population lives in Atlanta, a shiny cosmopolitan hub where dim sum or *kofta* are as available as grits or collard greens. The fast-growing capital has skyscrapers that house CNN, Coca-Cola and Delta Airlines, and remember when that Georgian peanut farmer ran the White House?

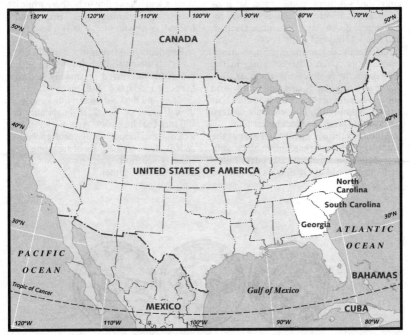

13

What South Carolina lacks in size, it makes up for in spunk. The 'Sandlappers' pushed for independence from Britain, then from the Union – and the state became the first to secede on the eve of the Civil War. More recently, it incensed civil rights groups by keeping the Confederate banner flying at the legislature (about the same time, Georgia quietly deleted this symbol from the state flag). While the past still lingers, the Southeast is moving toward the future: Listen to the African-American rhythms of the ancient Gullah language on the South Carolina coast and then, further inland, to the German accents at BMW's $900 million plant outside Greenville.

Arguably the least Southern of the three states is North Carolina. Historically the state had strong economic and patriotic ties to the North and – though it was committed to slavery before the Civil War – a relatively liberal stance on race issues. Thousands of jobs are created every year in sectors that ain't too Southern in heritage, such as finance (Charlotte, Winston-Salem), research and development (Raleigh, Durham and Chapel Hill) and cutting-edge manufacturing. But every year the multitudes are attracted to a much different story in the Appalachians – bluegrass festivals, folk dance and top-quality arts and crafts. And good stories are never lacking in the fun port city of Wilmington, Hollywood's eastern outpost that produces blockbuster films.

Mother Nature is possibly *the* star of the Southeast. While she can put on airs – well-groomed paths, mileposts and safety rails – such niceties end at Georgia's Okefenokee Swamp, which is about as primordial a spot as you could imagine. Alligators lurk in its brutal subtropical goop, and the blackwater here is so acidic that few bacteria can call it home. The fabulous beaches of the Atlantic Coast are in relatively unspoiled, protected areas; set off to camp on a barrier island, and days might elapse before you hear a cellular telephone. Secluded views abound in the Blue Ridge Mountains, which sprawl through the Carolinas into the northern tip of Georgia (don't miss the blaze of fall colors).

The booming '90s pumped money into cultural projects, so visual and performing arts in the Southeast, particularly top-notch music gigs, are sizzling. The populations of towns such as Chapel Hill, Durham, Macon and Athens swell during the summer festivals, while Atlanta's buzz of concerts and events never seems to stop. Hip-hop or pop, gospel or grunge, reggae or retro-jazz – the top talents launch their careers in these venues, and it's exciting to be there while it's happening. Organizing your visit around a festival, or a chain of events, is a smart way to start out.

Residents in Atlanta or Charlotte crack jokes about unbridled development, but few seem interested in slowing it down. Make no mistake, the pace of life in Georgia and the Carolinas is quickening, although good ol' Southern hospitality can still turn the clock back. As a matter of fact, a chat with a friendly local – preferably over an ice cold beer or a plate of steaming Lowcountry seafood – can make you forget about time altogether.

Facts about Georgia & the Carolinas

HISTORY

The Southeast has been many things to many people: first it was a tiny corner of an indigenous American civilization; then a backward patch of British Empire; then a section of a proud but ultimately defeated Confederacy. Most recently it has borne the stamp of the prosperous 'New South,' with a degree of justification. Yet the present is peeled away in an instant, at the next Confederate fort, plantation or colonial-era home. 'New' means 'modern,' in mentality as well as wealth, so Southerners generally don't mind holding up their history for inspection – even if some periods throw strange and disturbing shadows.

Native American Nations

The decline of the native Indian civilizations began after European contact in the mid-15th century. Europeans brought epidemics – smallpox, diphtheria, scarlet fever and measles among them – that wiped out entire tribes. Survivors were dominated by the groups that became known as the 'Five Civilized Tribes' – the Cherokee, Choctaw, Chickasaw, Creek and Seminole – so named by Europeans for their sophisticated agriculture, political organization and adoption of Christianity.

The Cherokee Nation was centered in the Appalachian Mountains, with strong communities in western North Carolina and northern Georgia. Similar in culture but more antagonistic, the Choctaws occupied the area from Tennessee to northern Mississippi. The Creek Confederacy stretched from the Atlantic Coast across Georgia into western Alabama. The Seminoles broke away from the Creek ('seminole' is Creek for 'runaway' or 'separatist') and settled in Georgia and southern Alabama along the Chattahoochee River before they were pushed farther south into Florida.

Over the three hundred years following European contact, the southeastern Indian nations were conquered by Europeans with an insatiable desire for new land on which many hoped to grow cotton. At first these nations were able to play off rival traders from English, Spanish and French territories, but after the Europeans abandoned their claims to the new United States, the Indians were faced with a precarious situation.

Some groups were conquered by military might, but most were defrauded by economic pressure. The US government's strategy (originally devised by Thomas Jefferson) was to establish trading posts among the Indians, encourage a dependence on European goods, allow the Indians to fall into debt and then force them to cede lands as repayment. Treaties sealed the deal. The cultural fabric of Indian nations also came under attack from missionaries, government agents and 'mixed bloods,' whose combined efforts forged a new policy of accommodation with the whites.

The final assault on the remaining tribes came in the 1830s. President Andrew Jackson, a South Carolinian (although often claimed by Tennessee), issued an ultimatum: Move voluntarily to Indian Territory out west or be 'removed' by force. Of all the southeastern Indians, the Cherokee fought the most determined legal battle against removal. In 1827, they formalized their own sovereignty as the Cherokee Nation by adopting a constitution based on the US model. In 1829, the state of Georgia passed legislation annexing a large portion of Cherokee territory and declaring Cherokee law null and void. The Cherokee appealed all the way to the Supreme Court, and in *Cherokee Nation v Georgia* (1831), Chief Justice John Marshall found the Georgia laws unconstitutional. Nonetheless, in contempt of the authority of the Supreme Court, President Jackson is reported to have said 'John Marshall has rendered his decision, now let him enforce it.' In 1838, the US Army along with local militias forced 18,000 Cherokee off their land and sent them west with little more than the clothes on their backs; 4000 Cherokee died en route.

Besides the Choctaw and Cherokee, other southeastern nations were similarly banished and forced along routes that came to be remembered as Trails of Tears. Survivors established communities in what is now Oklahoma, and their descendants remain there still.

Isolated Native American communities managed to remain in the southeast; some were eventually granted trust land. The 16,500-member band of the Eastern Cherokee has built a reservation in western North Carolina, thanks largely to summer tourism and year-round casino dollars. Other Native American communities remain distributed throughout the region without trust land.

Native American traditions and powwows are celebrated on reservations and at historic sites throughout the region, and some of their ancient burial grounds have been preserved as historical sites. The Etowah Mounds near Cartersville, north Georgia, are one of the most important archeological sites in North America.

European Exploration

The first encounter with Europeans probably took place in 1521, when the Spanish expedition of Francisco Cordillo poked around the Carolina coast. Five years later, a Spanish judge named Lucas Vásques de Ayllón attempted to found a colony at the mouth of the Cape Fear river and then on Winyah Bay in South Carolina, but disease, poor weather and starvation ended the venture a year later.

Gaining a foothold would prove a difficult undertaking. In 1540, Spanish explorer Hernando de Soto landed with an army of 900 soldiers and hundreds of horses in the New World, but immediately set off in search of gold to rival the looting of Peru's Inca empire. His route led from Georgia through South Carolina to the mountains of western North Carolina and on to the Mississippi River, where he turned south to the Gulf of Mexico. Though he charged through the southeast on the attack, the greatest damage he wrought was not in brutal en-

counters with the Indians but by exposing the indigenous populations to devastating diseases. De Soto himself died of fever during the journey and his body was interred in the Mississippi River.

Several other European expeditions met with tragedy over the next decades. In 1563 a group of French Huguenots set up camp at Port Royal Sound in South Carolina, but pulled out after their supplies were destroyed by fire. A few years later a Spanish contingent arrived from Florida and established Fort San Filipe; they endured for 20 years, convinced of their claim to this virgin territory until Sir Francis Drake's raid on nearby St Augustine reminded them of the existence of armed rivals. No mistake, the English were coming, and they would push back the Spaniards and French over the next two centuries.

The Lost Colony

The next curious, largely clueless, Europeans came in 1584, when Sir Walter Raleigh dispatched two ships to establish a colony in the New World. They landed at Roanoke Island, at a bay inside the northern end of the Outer Banks. The first governor, Ralph Lane, wrote of the 'huge and unknown greatness' of the American continent and that the native Indians, probably of the Hatteras or Yamassee tribes, were 'courteous and very desirous to have clothes' and were invited on board ship. However, the party spent more time searching for riches than planting crops, and stores ran low by wintertime. By chance, Sir Francis Drake's ships retrieved the luckless colonists and returned them to England.

A second shipload of 100-odd settlers arrived in 1587, this time with women and children on board, to populate this strange, limitless expanse of dense vegetation and staring inhabitants. A few months later the first English child, Virginia Dare, was born in North America with little fanfare. Unfortunately, they had arrived too late to plant crops, and the new head of the colony, John White, sailed for England to fetch supplies. War had broken out with Spain, however, and White – Virginia's grandfather – was unable to return to Roanoke until 1590. The only trace he found of the colony was the word 'Croatan' carved in a tree trunk, which probably referred a nearby Indian tribe. Later searches along the coast for this 'Lost Colony' proved fruitless; it's generally believed that they either died in attacks by the native inhabitants or intermarried and lived happily ever after.

The English tried again at Jamestown, Virginia, where a lasting settlement was established in 1607. Generations of American schoolbooks would wrongly imply that it was in Virginia that Europeans gained their first foothold in the New World.

Proprietary Business

By the 1630s the English had successfully colonized the Albemarle region along the North Carolina coast. In 1663 and '65, Charles II granted a huge expanse of land between Virginia and northern Florida to eight proprietors, or royal landowners, for development. Although the proprietors had the final say in their regions, local governments emerged and the colony of Carolina was founded in 1670. The fields of rice and indigo were tended by workers brought in from Barbados. As the settlement grew, the proprietors founded Charles Town (later Charleston) and appointed a colonial governor to administer from there, with a deputy for the northern territory. Complications with the Indians, local legislators and simple distance soon led to a split of the colony into North and South Carolina in 1712; the proprietors sold out altogether in 1729.

Georgia remained almost untouched by Europeans during this period, controlled by the Creek and a number of smaller tribes. Here, the first permanent town was established in 1733, when a group of English investors led by General James Edward Oglethorpe won a charter for a colony meant to act as a buffer against Spanish interests in Florida. Oglethorpe's company had a strict code in the beginning – no slaves, liquor or Catholicism, and even land ownership was forbidden. Early stabs at agriculture yielded modest results, but plantings of rice, cotton and indigo were more successful after the ban on slavery was lifted in 1750. Plantations dotted the coastal plain all the way to North Carolina, and their owners formed the monied classes that prevailed through the Civil War.

Road to Revolution

After a long, expensive war in French Canada, the British began to turn the tax screws on the colonies in the 1760s. Duties were placed on goods such as sugar, coffee and paper, but these levies proved difficult to enforce. In North Carolina, the assembly enacted a poll tax to pay for the new governor's palace in New Bern, and this led to the formation of a grassroots group called the Regulators, who vowed to rebel against usurious British tax schemes. In 1771 some 2000 Regulators clashed with crown militia, and although the Tories scored an easy win, the battle sparked the creation of organized militias – later, the basis of a major revolt against British sovereignty.

In the early stages, groups in the Southeast were divided over how to react to the British 'tyranny.' Many of the settlers were of Anglo-Saxon origin – British, but also Irish, German and Swiss – and while most resented the heavy taxes being imposed, sentiment wasn't running high enough to support a war.

The Boston Tea Party of 1773 tipped the scale. On the North Carolina coast, some aristocratic women – including the confident wife of the state's agent to the crown – held their own little tea party, and were satirized in the English press as 'Edenton's female artillery.'

After that, the Carolinas helped to lead the charge, although funding for military activity was scarce. In 1775, Charlotte became the first city to declare itself independent from Britain. The same year, the patriots stormed and took Fort Charlotte in South Carolina; delegates from all three colonies signed the Declaration of Independence the same year.

The British attacked Charleston in the early days of the war but were repulsed, and were preoccupied for four years before they could return. Under the command of Lord

Pirates of the Atlantic Coast

In the late 17th century, piracy started as your standard smuggling – trying to avoid tariffs levied by the British on goods shipped to America. During Queen Anne's War (1701–13), pirates began to plunder vessels on the high seas, which was fine with the British as long as targets were French or Spanish. Problem is, they kept it up after the war, and the Atlantic Coast was terrorized with increasingly brazen hit-and-run tactics. The stakes were so high that even some highly respected sailors turned to piracy; the notorious Captain William Kidd was commissioned by New York's colonial governor as a legal privateer in 1689 before he went 'bad.'

However, the very worst scoundrels were Stede Bonnet and Edward Teach (aka Blackbeard), who hid in the numerous sounds and bays along the Outer Banks. In the summer of 1718, four ships under Teach's command anchored outside Charleston harbor, took hostages and held them for a ransom of medical supplies. When Bonnet – who was called the 'Gentleman Pirate' because of his background as an educated planter in Barbados – pulled the same stunt, Charleston sounded the alarm. A military search party was dispatched, and Bonnet and his men were captured, tried and summarily hanged. For more about Bonnet's illustrious 'career,' see 'The Gentleman Pirate' in the South Carolina chapter.

A giant of a man who braided his long locks for maximum effect, the restless Blackbeard – who for a short period managed to settle with a wife in Bath, North Carolina – met his grisly end a few months later. On November 21, 1718, two Royal Navy ships under the command of Lt Robert Maynard slipped into Ocracoke Inlet and staged a dawn raid on Blackbeard's sloop. After a fierce battle, Blackbeard and half of his crew were slain, and the pirate's head was stuck on the bow of Maynard's ship for the voyage back to Virginia.

With the demise of Bonnet and Blackbeard, the heyday of piracy was finished, but vestiges of the era survived. Even in the 20th century, regular navy crews still held rights to prizes for captured enemy ships; the US abolished the practice only in 1904, after Admiral Dewey was denied prize money for ships he'd captured in Manila Bay.

Cornwallis, British forces launched a major offensive against George Washington's Continental Army in 1780. After gaining virtual control over Georgia, Cornwallis assembled his troops in Savannah and began to zigzag towards Virginia, first taking the town of Beaufort and then Charleston. Cornwallis' men had hoped to garner volunteer support along the way, but committed a major blunder by slaughtering a group of patriots while they were attempting to surrender at Lancaster, South Carolina. Backwoods folk, aghast at the behavior of

their potential allies, turned squarely against the soldiers, whose ranks were thinned by guerilla skirmishes on their trek north.

The hit-and-run tactics of the rebels would take their toll, slowly but surely. The battle at Camden, South Carolina in the summer of 1780 was the last sound British victory in the entire war; their weakened forces only just managed to take Charlotte, which the general described as a 'hornet's nest of rebellion' due to the sniper fire, arson and terrorist tactics to which his troops were subjected. After just 17 days of occupation, a miffed Cornwallis pulled up stakes and abandoned the city.

From late 1780 onwards, British forces were taking a beating throughout the colonies. A clash at Guilford Courthouse near Greensboro in January 1781 left almost one-quarter of Cornwallis' troops wounded – although the general was quick to claim victory and announce that North Carolina was safely under Parliament's control. From there he led his troops south to the port city of Wilmington, where he spent months cogitating and amassing reinforcements. From there, Cornwallis resumed his trek up the east coast towards Yorktown, where surrender to Washington awaited on October 18, 1781.

King Cotton

Long after the cities of the North were transformed by the Industrial Revolution, the Southeast maintained its old, measured agricultural way of life. The majority of the farms were small, owner-operated properties growing mostly subsistence crops, but large-scale plantations dominated the economy and politics of the region. Rice

Different Worlds

Immigration to the New World increased sharply in the early 18th century, and settlers of older colonies turned their eyes to the Southeast for opportunities. Anglo-Saxon groups, mainly Scotch-Irish and Germans, loaded up their wagons and headed for the lush valleys of the Appalachians and the Piedmont. Most were Protestant minorities – Moravians, Presbyterians and Quakers – and shared few interests with the rich plantation owners of the east. This led to clear political and socio-economic divisions between the folks of the Backcountry and Lowcountry (in South Carolina, the common terms are Upcountry and Lowcountry). The split persists to a certain extent today, and depending on where you are, making cracks about hillbillies or city slickers is a time-honored pastime.

and indigo were grown along the coast, but the biggest money-spinner of them all was cotton, especially in South Carolina and Georgia. Farther north the mainstay was tobacco, which still drives North Carolina.

So predominant was the white, fluffy product that it was matter-of-factly referred to as 'King Cotton.' The climate and soil, enriched by the alluvial sediments in the coastal plains, were ideally suited for growing cotton, and in the 18th and 19th centuries textile factories in Europe acquired a habit for it. Stretching across hundreds of acres of dark fertile soil, plantations in the Southeast were the domain of a privileged class of planters with immense political clout. It was a system – and a way of life – that would prove resistant to change.

Toward the end of the 18th century, cotton profits began to lag, and its production might have waned if not for the cotton gin, which was invented by Eli Whitney in 1793. Gins mechanized the laborious task of separating seeds and hulls from cotton fibers, thus making production much more efficient, and soon they were installed on plantations throughout the Southeast.

Even with the new technology, cotton was labor-intensive and not particularly profitable if those who labored over it were paid a fair wage. But, of course, the big-time planters didn't have that problem.

Slavery

Planters failed to recognize the inhumanity of slavery. Exhibiting an impressive faculty for self-deception, slave owners of the Southeast shared a common perception that their slaves were merely a docile lot, content to remain in servitude for their entire lives. Planters frequently boasted that their slaves were the 'happiest people on earth' – and seemingly believed it.

The unhappy reality was that, in addition to being denied the most basic human liberties, slaves were not allowed to maintain African or Haitian cultural practices, many were prohibited from learning to read, some masters sexually exploited female slaves, and all too often slaves experienced painful separations as family members, even children, were sold to other plantations.

South Carolina in particular was the scene of untold barbarity, as Charleston was the main port of entry for thousands of slaves, who were put to work almost as soon as they climbed from the holds of incoming ships. While some slaves rose in stature by learning trades or becoming house servants, the great majority were field workers whose legal status was hardly greater than that of domestic animals. After removing its initial ban on slavery, Georgia quickly caught up and surpassed South Carolina in terms of numbers of slaves; by contrast, the preponderance of small farms in North Carolina made it less thirsty for slave labor.

The runaway slave's chance of achieving freedom was slim. Punishment, if a runaway was caught, was always severe – sometimes it was death – and slave hunters and their hounds were not so easily eluded. But many slaves were willing to take these risks. Some escapees hoped to find refuge in self-sufficient runaway colonies in remote corners of the wilderness, but many more headed to the North via the Underground Railroad.

Meanwhile, many planters enjoyed a comfortable lifestyle modeled on the traditions of European aristocracy. The wealthiest planters inhabited impressive Greek Revival mansions with household servants attending to domestic needs, including cooking, craftwork, child-raising and even wet-nursing. In this rarified atmosphere, an elitist code of ethics was maintained, upholding values like chivalry and honor that by that time might well have seemed old-fashioned to most Northerners.

Calhoun & the Secessionists

One by one, Britain and other European powers abolished the slave trade in the early part of the 19th century, and the abolitionist movement in the North demanded the same thing. Ironically, it was the issue of tariffs that initially sparked talk of secession – just as Britain's colonial taxes had served as a catalyst for the Revolutionary War.

Beginning in 1816, tariffs were imposed on imported goods with the aim of protecting American industry. The levies benefited the industrial North, but forced Southerners to pay higher prices for manufactured goods. In 1830, a brilliant, irascible statesman from South Carolina named John C Calhoun, then vice-president to Andrew Jackson, informed the nation that if the tariffs were not repealed, the states had the right to 'interpose their sovereignty' and declare the law null and void – a theory he called Nullification. The tariffs stayed, South Carolina made good on its threat and Jackson sent warships into Charleston harbor to enforce the law. The Senate negotiated a compromise by lowering the tariffs, but Calhoun resigned the vice-presidency to join the Senate as a defender of South. Georgia and North Carolina um'd and ah'd but failed to support nullification. However, the topic of secession was firmly on the agenda in the next decades.

By the mid-19th century, slavery was illegal in half of the states that then formed the US, and a figurative line had already been drawn between the 'slave states' and the 'free states.' Put simply, to the south of the line, the prevailing argument was for preserving the balance of power as the nation grew – for each new free state admitted to the rapidly expanding Union, Southern lawmakers wanted a new slave state admitted.

Naturally, South Carolina was at the forefront of this movement. Calhoun was doing everything possible to preserve the 'peculiar institution' of slavery, and he had become the clear voice of the Secessionists. As the Northern states garnered support for the bill known as the Compromise of 1850, which, among other things, admitted new territories into the Union without a provision for legal slavery, a deathly ill Calhoun showed up to the Senate to argue that two separate nations already existed in the US, and should part ways. The bill passed, but Calhoun's political writings laid the philosophical groundwork for the Confederacy. His last words were: 'The South, the poor South.'

The Confederacy

The conflict over slavery came to a head in the election of 1860. Republican candidate Abraham Lincoln was an unlikely frontrunner, being a soft-spoken, ungainly man who frequently dared to be candid about controversial subjects. He'd made public his feelings that slavery was morally wrong, and he boldly summarized the state of the Union: 'I believe this government cannot endure permanently half slave and half free.' With the pro-slavery Democrats divided, Lincoln won the election.

Within a month of the presidential ballot, South Carolina statesmen gathered at the First Baptist Church in Columbia to draw up the Ordinance of Secession, which was unanimously adopted on December 20, 1860. Six other Southern states had seceded from the Union before Lincoln took office in January 1861. It wasn't easy for many states to make the decision to secede, and divisions within the Confederate borders would last until the Civil War (also known as the War between the States) was over. In the upland areas, there were few plantations, and small farmers and workers opposed slavery. North Carolina – whose inland and mountain areas were largely pro-Union – became the last state to join the Confederacy, and only did so after Lincoln requested troops to quell the rebellion.

Provoked by Lincoln's decision to resupply troops at Fort Sumter in South Carolina, Jefferson Davis sent orders to his 'fire-eaters' in the provisional government to fire the first shot of what would prove the bloodiest war in US history. Most of the lowlands and coastal plains of Georgia and the Carolinas were occupied by the summer, although the port cities of Charleston, Savannah and Wilmington teetered on the edge of Confederate control as Union gunboats attempted to choke off supplies. Wilmington hung on until 1865, earning the nickname from Robert E Lee as 'lifeline of the Confederacy.'

Sherman's March The Southeast was spared from serving as a major battleground until May 1864 – and then all hell broke loose. As Union general Ulysses S Grant advanced into Tennessee, he called on William Tecumseh Sherman to 'create havoc and destruction of all resources that would be beneficial to the enemy.' Perhaps the first exponent of total warfare, Sherman carved a swath of devastation 60 miles wide and 250 miles long through eastern and central Georgia on his infamous 'March to the Sea,' with soldiers and civilians alike fleeing in his path.

Atlanta was taken on September 2 after a protracted siege, and although much of the city was destroyed, the damage approached obliteration when retreating Confederates blew up their own munitions, including 81 railway cars filled with explosives. Sherman ordered the evacuation of the civilian population, and when his troops left in November they burned the city to a crisp. The red-headed Ohioan later said, 'The same reason which caused me to destroy Atlanta will make it a great city in the future' – but he was probably thinking of its strategic location.

Savannah was reached in December, but that town was mercifully spared as a 'Christmas present' to Lincoln. Then Sherman's war machine rolled into South Carolina, where the only forces to oppose his 62,000 men were a motley collection of militia and under-age reserves. In February 1865, Columbia was dealt with particularly harshly and two-thirds of the city was destroyed; many Federal troops harbored a special hatred for South Carolina because they felt the state had been responsible for starting the war. Too late to make much of a difference, General Joseph E Johnston was given command of all remaining Confederate forces in North Carolina and concentrated his 21,000 effectives at a bloody battle on March 19 at Bentonville, near Durham. Outflanked by Sherman's reinforcements, Johnston was forced to retreat and the war was definitively lost. On April 7, 1865 General Lee signed the articles of surrender at Appomattox Courthouse in Virginia.

One week after that, President Lincoln was assassinated in Washington, DC, by

John Wilkes Booth, an avowed white supremacist. For many Americans, the world seemed to come to an end.

Reconstruction

At the end of the war, the Southeast lay in ruins and an entire generation of white men was spent. Huge tracts of soil had been laid to waste by advancing and retreating armies. Homes had been looted and torched, fields had been plundered and left fallow, and families had been decimated. Southern blacks – now free – faced a decidedly uncertain future. Lincoln had not arrived at a coherent plan for bringing the South back into the fold, and after his death his successor, Andrew Johnson of North Carolina, fumbled with the issues of Reconstruction.

Establishing pro-Union governments in the South proved tricky. Radical Republicans, who favored complete emancipation and suffrage for freed slaves, held sway in Congress but were deeply unpopular in the former Confederacy. With voting restricted to loyalists, the way was paved for opportunists from the North, who headed South and assumed an influential political role. Known as 'carpetbaggers' – many had arrived with their clothes packed in traveling bags made of carpet, which were popular at the time – these outsiders represented a bitter pill for the South to swallow.

Emancipation – and everything it implied – proved not so easy to sort through either. Blacks amounted to 40% of the South's population, but in states such as South Carolina they constituted a majority. In 1867, Congress passed the Reconstruction Acts, which granted blacks the right to vote and divided the South into military districts. Yet little changed for many slaves, who continued to work the plantations as they had before the war. Only now, as paid laborers, they were required to pay rent and for supplies and food. A sharecropper system gradually developed, in which field hands relied on the landowners for supplies and were constantly in debt. A large number of blacks soon became part of a migrant workforce with a limited range of opportunities before them.

Southern Unionists who took political posts were derogatorily known as 'scalawags,' who along with freed blacks were elected with the support of newly enfranchised black voters. Some progressive policies were introduced, but generally these legislatures were inefficient and grossly corrupt, imposing confiscatory taxes and repressive measures against a resentful white community. All in all, Reconstruction probably did more to foster hatred of Yankees than the war itself.

One by one, the Unionist carpetbagger regimes of the Southeast fell. In 1870, the Democrats scored an early post-war victory in North Carolina by impeaching Republican governor William Holden, who had willfully imposed martial law. Georgia's state legislature returned to the Democrats in 1871 but South Carolina's scalawags hung on until 1877, when President Rutherford B Hayes declared Reconstruction to be over. After that, major political

The Real Jim Crow

At one time, 'Jim Crow' was used to describe African Americans, much as 'Mick' referred to Irish Americans, and its sense was either derogatory or patronizing. It later came to describe the legal separation of the races, as in 'Jim Crow laws.'

The origins of the term are hazy and we are left with unlikely stories. But it is known that the term was popularized by a white minstrel entertainer, Thomas 'Daddy' Rice, who performed a black-face routine under the name Jim Crow. Rice said he'd met a slave named Jim whose master's surname was Crow, but this explanation is generally discredited. It's more probable that wordplay brought together 'Jim' (being, like 'Joe' or 'Buddy,' a name used when a man's given name wasn't known) and 'Crow' (referring to the color black).

posts throughout the Southeast tended to be occupied by former Confederates.

Post-War Realities

With the emancipation of blacks, the pretense of paternalism vanished and deepseated hatreds rose to the surface. Emancipation was followed by white resistance to black suffrage; blacks gaining the right to vote led to efforts to limit eligibility and intimidate black voters. 'Jim Crow' restrictions, which maintained racial segregation of transportation modes, waiting rooms, hotels, restaurants and theaters, were enforced. Separate public institutions were created, including schools and hospitals, and 'white' and 'colored' signs began to appear over doorways and drinking fountains throughout the region.

In 1896, the Supreme Court's decision in *Plessy v Ferguson* solidified institutionalized racism. The court ruled that separation of the races was within the bounds of the Constitution as long as equal accommodations were made for blacks, underpinning the 'separate-but-equal' doctrine for decades.

Meanwhile, whites frequently acted outside the law in order to reinforce discriminatory standards. Formed in Tennessee after the war, the Ku Klux Klan (KKK) quickly spread to the Carolinas and Georgia with the aim of opposing the perceived excesses of Reconstruction. It officially disbanded in 1870, when ugly racist overtones led to a federal crackdown. But it returned in 1915 after the release of the film *Birth of a Nation,* based on Thomas Dixon's novel *The Clansman.* By this time, the KKK's unambiguous mission was to keep blacks down. (It also targeted Jews, Catholics and foreigners.)

The Klan, a terrifying force, reached peak membership in the 1920s. Riding horseback at night, wearing hoods to obscure their identities (many were prominent citizens), Klansmen harassed targeted individuals and groups without legal consequence. Rampant violence led the Klan to lose public favor, and membership fell drastically in the 1930s. But the KKK would rear its ugly head again during the Civil Rights movement.

Economic Stirrings

Most of the South languished for decades after the Civil War. The majority of farmers were sharecroppers who tilled small patches of cotton – far too much of it, as it turned out, and prices spiraled downward. Leading industrialists took advantage of the cheap fiber and built textile mills in towns across the Piedmont, luring thousands of workers off the land and into the factories.

Another boost was provided by tobacco. The large-leafed plant was nothing new per se – Sir Walter Raleigh had taken seeds back to England some three centuries earlier – but the end product was improved. In the final days of the war, soldiers of both armies converged on Durham, North Carolina, where they discovered a warehouse filled with cured tobacco. This Brightleaf became a popular smoke, and easier to consume following the invention of the cigarette-rolling machine in 1881. Tobacco factories sprung up alongside the textile mills, and soon the fortunes of the Duke and Reynolds families were running on autopilot. Furniture became a leading commodity as well, particularly around the hardwood and pine forests of North Carolina and northern Georgia.

To a certain extent these new crops and their accompanying industries enabled the region to avoid the abject poverty felt elsewhere in the South. By their sheer remoteness, however, the highlands failed to benefit from this development, a pattern which would repeat itself again and again.

The Civil Rights Movement

For most Americans, the Civil Rights movement began on May 17, 1954, when the US Supreme Court handed down its decision in the *Brown v Board of Education* case outlawing segregation in public schools. However, Southern states did not accept this ruling, and the next 11 years saw demonstrations, protests and civil action aimed at desegregation and increased black political representation. Numerous incidents occurred in the Southeast, although the centers of activity were usually in the Deep South states such as Mississippi or Alabama.

On December 1, 1955, in Montgomery, Alabama, 42-year-old seamstress Rosa Parks refused to surrender her bus seat to a white passenger and was arrested for violating the segregation laws. The black community mobilized a citywide boycott galvanized by the leadership of Dr Martin Luther King Jr, who had grown up in Atlanta's Sweet Auburn district. The boycott of the city's bus companies that few expected to last a week continued 13 months before the Supreme Court affirmed a lower court's ruling outlawing segregation of public transit.

The Civil Rights movement gathered steam, but still moved far too slowly for the taste of some. In 1960, black students in North Carolina organized a pivotal 'sit-in' at a Woolworth's lunch counter (see 'The Greensboro Sit-Ins' in the North Carolina chapter). The next big protest was a 'Freedom Ride,' organized by activists intending to ride buses from Washington, DC, to New Orleans to challenge segregation laws in public facilities. The federal government had outlawed segregation in interstate travel in 1955, yet riders of this bus were beaten in South Carolina and subjected to various abuses at other spots along the journey. As elsewhere, early civil rights demonstrations in the Southeast were peaceful affairs, but the marches and rallies grew more vigorous as time went on. One such example was a mass rock-hurling that took place during a gathering in Albany, Georgia in early 1962.

From the Brown decision until the passage of the Voting Rights Act in 1965, the US experienced more social change, court decisions and legislation in the name of civil rights than in any other decade of US history. Many advocates for change were committed to nonviolence, yet it's still the relatively few violent clashes that stick in people's minds, such as the Orangeburg Massacre of 1968, when police officers shot and killed three students and wounded 27

others at the town's only bowling alley, five blocks from the South Carolina State College campus.

President Lyndon B Johnson signed into law the Voting Rights Act of 1965, despite vigorous opposition from conservative statesmen such as Sam Ervin Jr (North Carolina), Strom Thurmond (South Carolina) and Richard B Russell (Georgia). The act required all or part of seven states – Alabama, Georgia, Louisiana, Mississippi, Virginia and the Carolinas – to have every change in their local or state election laws approved by the US Justice Department or federal courts in Washington, DC. The law banned literacy tests as a prerequisite to voting and other obstacles designed to block the black franchise. Enforcing the act has led to sweeping changes in the American political process; by 1992, there were more than 5000 African-American elected officials in those seven states, compared to only 300 in the entire nation in 1965.

However, the act was no cure-all, and some stalwart segregationists remained entrenched in the political scene until the 1970s. Lester Maddox, who had brandished a pistol to keep demonstrators outside of his whites-only eatery in Atlanta, squeaked into the Georgia governor's office in 1966. Maddox introduced no major changes during his tenure, and integration of the schools remained on track despite his occasional outbursts against civil-rights activists. A re-election bid in 1974 met with failure – Georgia voters had decided to move on.

The New South
The idea of a 'New' South has been around since Reconstruction, but it never seemed so much a reality in the Southeast until recently. Gleaming skyscrapers grace the skylines of cities such as Atlanta, Charlotte, and Raleigh; 'clean' industries in manufacturing, finance and research now stand alongside fields of the old standbys, cotton and tobacco; and the US military bases founded in WWII boost the local economies. Unfortunately, the new wealth isn't evenly distributed and poverty still exists in the marginal

counties of the Appalachians and the 'Black Belt' of southern Georgia. Many textile workers face a difficult transition to other jobs, if any, as some foreign companies have become a direct threat since the passage of the North American Free Trade Agreement (NAFTA), which nearly eliminated trade restrictions between the US, Canada and Mexico.

The region's social profile has altered dramatically and will likely continue to do so with the prosperity of coming decades. As a result, the stereotypes that may have applied in the past are looking decidedly tarnished. Georgia and the Carolinas used to suffer from periodic emigration, but nowadays well-educated people from all over the world are moving to the region to take up skilled occupations. 'New Southerners' could as easily be of Asian or Hispanic descent as white or African American, and California fusion cuisine has become about as popular as fried chicken. Race relations are not nearly as fragile as in the past, and visitors expecting to sight droves of Bible-thumping fundamentalists are likely to be disappointed.

In short, this is a region in flux, but that's not to say that the old charms have faded. Wherever you go, good old-fashioned Southern hospitality can still be sampled, and in generous helpings.

GEOGRAPHY

From the Appalachian highlands to the Piedmont plateau to the coastal estuaries, the three zones of Southeastern landscape capture all the colors of the topographical map.

Of the three states, North Carolina is the most mountainous, with the Blue Ridge and Great Smoky ranges to the west sporting peaks over 6000 feet. The Appalachians also poke up through the northern and western extremes of South Carolina and Georgia, before the land begins its inexorable slide to the sea. Waterfalls abound in the highlands, sparkling expressions of erosive forces. Between the mountains and the sea lies the Piedmont, a relatively low-lying plateau that extends from Virginia to northern

Alabama. Its most prominent features are rivers, pine forests and rich farmland.

The coastal plains are dotted with swamps, marshes and tidal rivers, some of them startlingly wild and primitive. Georgia's Okefenokee Swamp on the Florida border is the largest freshwater wetland habitat in the US. Many of the boggy lowlands along the coast have been drained for agricultural use but a good bit of muck remains, much of it now valuable wildlife and nature reserve. The barrier islands are a curious feature, as storms and ocean currents can change their shape overnight. The 1000-plus miles of Atlantic shoreline offer plenty of dunes, sea oats and, of course, white sandy beaches. Unlike elsewhere in the South, there are no bayous.

A string of lakes, some of them quite large and deep, and mostly man-made, stud the coastal plain. The many rivers run ice-cold with Appalachian run-off, and distinctive ones include the Edisto in South Carolina, the longest blackwater river east of the Mississippi with a white sandy bottom. The upper part of the lengthy Savannah River, which marks the border between South Carolina and Georgia, forms a chain of freshwater lakes and rivers for which the region is famous.

GEOLOGY

The Appalachians were formed nearly half a billion years ago, and at the time were the tallest peaks in the world, towering over 40,000 feet. As the mountains rose, the reverberations caused tectonic plates in the even older Piedmont to crack and buckle, creating the rolling landscape we see today. The bits of exposed plate opened up opportunities for mine shafts, of which 100 were sunk in the Piedmont during the 1800s.

North Carolina is the most geologically diverse state in the region, and the richest in minerals. The world's largest granite quarry is in Mt Airy, near the Virginia border, and large gold deposits were hauled from the earth in the early 19th century. The New River running through the northern mountains is the oldest river in the US, and second-oldest in the world after the Nile.

Across all three states, the Appalachians offer fascinating networks of caves and caverns; examining the deposits is akin to counting the rings on a tree trunk.

The soils of the Piedmont, which extends from Virginia to northern Alabama, consist of sandy loam and red clay. These foothills constitute the Fall Line, the point where waterfalls, rivers and streams descend sharply on their long journey to the sea. South of the Piedmont in Georgia, a strip called the 'Black Belt' – so-called for its sticky, black calcareous clay soil – stretches all the way to Texas.

The coastal swamps and bogs of the Southeast are cushioned by layers of peat thousands of years old. The Atlantic Ocean lapped over this region until the last Ice Age ended, leaving sands and marine sediments. Compared to the rest of the region, the barrier islands of the Carolinas are geological youngsters, formed only 15,000 years ago when the sea level dropped and the wind whipped up sandbars.

CLIMATE

Varied landscape and altitudes mean the Southeast is guaranteed four distinct seasons. In general, spring and fall have very pleasant weather, with seasonal blossoms and colors a highlight in the mountain regions. In the lower plains of the Piedmont and southern Georgia, spring tends to be fleeting and finishes by late May.

Temperatures for the region as a whole range from about 20° to 93° F (-4° to 34° C), with the mountains cooler and the plains and coast clearly warmer. In the mountains, temperatures seldom go above 80° F during

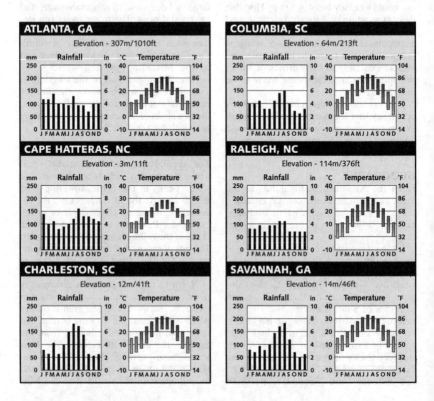

the summer, while the mercury in the coastal plains and southern Georgia often moseys up into the 90s. Humidity makes it feel a lot hotter, and drippier, but sea breezes tend to keep things cooler along the shoreline. The extreme south of Georgia is considered sub-tropical, with mild winters of around 50° F and long steamy summers.

Hurricane season is from June to November, with peak strikes in August and September. North Carolina ranks third among the states receiving the most hurricanes (tying with Louisiana, after Florida and Texas); South Carolina ranks fifth. Georgia can have tornadoes, and while we're on natural disasters, all three states suffer periodic droughts and flooding.

Average precipitation is nothing out of the ordinary: between about 40 and 75 inches per year, with higher amounts in the mountains. Normally only the Appalachians see any real snow, and two to four inches is normal, but the winter of 2000 brought blizzards and snow drifts to the Piedmont – and

Big Blows

The hurricane season in the eastern US is from June to November, with most activity occurring in August and September. Hurricanes can also appear outside the official season but are much less common. While the annual average is only about five hurricanes per year, the frequency can vary greatly from year to year.

Hurricanes are defined as storms that originate in the tropics and have winds in excess of 120 km/hr (74 mph). Those that hit the Southeast form off the coast of Africa and whip in a westerly direction across the Atlantic. The winds of these hurricanes revolve in a counterclockwise direction around a center of lower barometric pressure, picking up energy from warm waters and moisture as they approach the Caribbean.

The first stage of a hurricane's approach is called a tropical disturbance. The next stage is a tropical depression. When winds exceed 64km/hr (39 mph), the system is upgraded to a tropical storm and is usually accompanied by heavy rains. The system is called a hurricane if wind speed exceeds 120km/hr (74 mph) and intensifies around a low-pressure center called the eye of the storm.

The strength of a hurricane is rated from one to five. The mildest, a Category 1 hurricane, has winds of at least 120km/hr (74 mph). The strongest and rarest hurricanes, the Category 5 monsters, pack winds that exceed 250km/hr (150 mph); Hurricane Mitch, which killed more than 10,000 people in Central America in late 1998, was a rare Category 5 hurricane. Hurricanes travel at varying speeds, from as little as 10km/hr (6 mph) to more than 50km/hr (30 mph).

If you are caught by an approaching hurricane, stay calm and follow local warnings. Hotels are typically of concrete and steel construction capable of withstanding strong winds with minimal damage. However, in low-lying areas ocean swells can also pose a hazard – if you have an ocean-front room it's a wise precaution to relocate to a unit farther inland. The flooding caused by storm surge has been known to completely cover outlying barrier islands. Most hurricane injuries are the result of flying debris, so don't be tempted to venture outside in the midst of a storm. If a hurricane warning is announced, stay sober. A hurricane is no time to be partying. You'll need your wits about you both during and after the storm.

Hurricanes are tracked by the US National Hurricane Center in Miami. Satellite weather forecasts provide advance warning, but it is difficult to predict a storm's path. For current weather information, you can visit The Miami Herald's website (www.herald.com) and scan the menu for hurricane and storm information. Another excellent place to find current English- and Spanish-language tropical-storm information is the National Hurricane Center's Tropical Prediction Center Web site (www.nhc.noaa.gov/), maintained by the US National Oceanic and Atmospheric Administration.

even the barrier islands were dusted with a pretty white coat.

ECOLOGY & ENVIRONMENT

The environmental ravaging of America's natural riches is legendary. Exploitation of the Southeast has continued almost unabated since colonial times. Even today, vestiges of a near-feudal mentality among politicians and industrialists remain, encouraging a system of patronage that allows predominant industries to go about their business with little oversight from local authorities.

By the early part of the 20th century, poor land management of the singly important cotton crop had exhausted the soil – Piedmont blues artists sung about 'pickin' cotton low' because plants didn't have the strength to grow higher. Vital wetlands were being drained or filled for agricultural development and jetties built along the Atlantic caused extensive erosion as ocean currents were redirected (an oft-repeated sin even today).

During this same period, timber companies swooped in and cleared whole regions of forest, destroying habitats and further eroding the soil in their wake. In the 1930s, the Civilian Conservation Corps – 'Roosevelt's Tree Army' to detractors – performed restorative work by replanting trees and establishing erosion controls, in addition to building recreation areas such as those in the Great Smoky Mountains.

This did little to stop the destruction. As the 20th century progressed, the Army Corps of Engineers dammed rivers for reservoirs – practically all the large lakes in the Carolinas were made this way – and paper mills ate away huge chunks of mountain hardwood forest. In fact, of all wetlands destruction in the nation – saltwater and fresh – the Southeast has been hardest hit.

Environmental advocates have now begun to speak out and defend the region's natural resources more vigorously, though state governments continue to accommodate polluting industries. The power stations of the Tennessee Valley Authority, for instance, are a prime source of air pollution in North Carolina. But even mass deaths in the Appalachians of red spruce – which serve as the 'coal-mine canaries of the woods' because of their sensitivity to impure air – haven't brought about sufficient political pressure to take significant steps.

The many container ships that pass the shoreline as they travel the Intracoastal Waterway may represent a greater threat of spills – with their loads of chemicals – but so far there have been no major accidents (which is incredible, as dredging on some waterway sections is near negligent).

Natural disasters such as hurricanes wreak periodic havoc on the coast. Hurricane Hugo drove ashore in 1989, causing $8.5 billion in damage (and a whopping $5 billion alone in South Carolina); several other major hurricanes have struck in the '90s, including Fran and Floyd. The hurricane cycle is an argument for keeping coastal development of housing and industry to a minimum, but this logic routinely goes unheeded.

There are few silver linings in this cloud, except that environmental organizations are now on guard and have teamed up with local advocates vocal in their opposition to any offense to their land. Properties that have become protected, and habitats that have been restored, if only on a small scale, represent major miracles.

FLORA & FAUNA

The diversity of plant and animal life is a chief draw for many visitors. From the autumn valleys bursting with color, to larks swooping low over fields of bowing wildflowers, to alligators lurking in dark, squelching swamps – the wilds of the Southeast offer something for just about everybody.

Flora

As a meeting place of northern and southern varieties, the Southern Appalachian forest has more tree types than in all of Europe (130 vs 85), including towering maples and hickories, elms and poplars. At higher altitudes are forests of Fraser fir and red spruce. The land south of the mountains (northern Georgia) was once covered in forest, but was mostly cleared for agriculture and cotton plantations.

As in other leafy expanses of the US, forest fires are a recurring problem. More than 7000 acres of Appalachian forest burned in 2000, with the biggest blaze occurring in the Pisgah National Forest in North Carolina. Haze and a smell of smoke were discernible in Charlotte, more than 100 miles away.

On the Piedmont plateau, varieties such as ash, black locust, wild cherry and American elm thin as you go south and as the forest makes a transition from the deciduous northern varieties to rough southern conifers, pine and cedar. In coastal areas, bald cypress, black gum and sweet gum trees give way to maritime forests of oak, cedar and holly, with salt marsh and palmetto palms growing in the subtropical latitudes – South Carolina is the Palmetto State.

The Southeast is well known for many flowering species of trees, shrubs and flowers. Gardening is big here, and landscape architects plan their arrangements as if with an artist's brush and palette. From the blooming of the first tender crocuses in late January until the last patches of yellow witch hazel in December, blossoms can be seen throughout most of the year. Some of the common flowering species include southern and Fraser magnolias, azalea, rhododendron, mountain laurel, dogwood, redbud, wax myrtle and hydrangeas. Introduced by millionaire George Vanderbilt, the lavender blooms of the Paulownia hang over the back roads in the Appalachian foothills. Jasmine and honeysuckle sweeten the air in the South Carolina Lowcountry, especially around Charleston.

And then there are the wildflowers, which tumble off the highway medians and mountain shoulders in seemingly endless varieties. The Blue Ridge Parkway is really *the* place to feast your eyes on trillium, Indian pipe, bee balm and lady's slippers.

In the coastal areas you'll glimpse a strange plant long associated with the romantic South: wispy tendrils of Spanish moss draped from the broad limbs of a live oak. However, despite its name, Spanish moss is neither moss nor Spanish. Related to the pineapple, the flowering plant is an epiphyte: It sucks all its daily nutrition from the air. The plant's name was supposedly derived from its resemblance to a Spaniard's beard.

More exotic are the insect-eating pitcher and trumpet plants, as well as the celebrated Venus Flytrap – so named because its early observers believed its spiked 'jaws' came from another planet. Many of these species are native only to the boggy Cape Fear coast, and they attract their kill with a sticky sweet secretion, which also serves as digestive fluid.

Another common sight is the unstoppable kudzu (KUD-zoo) vine, which seems to shroud whole forests along interstate byways, choking growth and killing native species. It was originally imported from Japan in the early 19th century for erosion control (for more, see 'Kudzu' in the Facts about Georgia chapter).

Fauna

Reptiles & Amphibians The Okefenokee Swamp in southern Georgia teems with over 200 varieties of reptiles and amphibians. The American alligator is an almost certain sighting in the creeks and lowland marshes along the coast – even the USS *North Carolina* battleship has its own pet 'gator' named Charlie. Once hunted to dwindling numbers for its valuable hide, the alligator has made a comeback due to the protection provided by the Endangered Species Act.

Freshwater turtles are abundant (the soft-shelled variety is considered the most tasty and is marketed commercially), but sea turtles, some of which are endangered, are seen only rarely. In wetlands, there are snapping turtles and many varieties of frog, toad and newt.

Poisonous snakes are present but are rarely encountered. Water moccasins – called 'cottonmouths' for the white lining they reveal when extending their jaw – live in the coastal plains. Copperheads and rattlesnakes are found at the higher elevations.

Birds The Atlantic Coast is one of the four flyways across the North American continent. Migratory birds stop over at wetlands, many of which have been declared national wildlife reserves. Dozens of duck species, herons, Canada geese, pelicans and egrets can be spotted year-round. The magnificent Tundra swan winters in marshes and lakes along the Carolina coast, and North Carolina's Lake Mattamuskeet hosts as many as 100,000 at one time.

In the woodlands you'll hear many songbird varieties, including warblers, sparrows, mockingbirds, cardinals and thrashers. Shorebirds include gulls, terns, brown pelicans and several dozen species of sandpiper and plover. Owls, hawks and golden eagles are the main raptors, with the once-endangered American bald eagle making a comeback. Many home gardens attract ruby-throated hummingbirds to special hanging feeders.

The wild turkey is one of the most popular native game birds, along with the quail and dove.

Fish The Atlantic Coast has a cornucopia of varieties that frequently turn up on local menus, including flounder, drum, sea bass, mackerel, whiting and spot. Mullet was an important food source through the 19th and early 20th centuries, and you'll see plenty of Mullet Ponds, Mullet Points etc. Bass, white perch, bream, sunfish and catfish are common inhabitants of the freshwater lakes. In the mountain-cooled rivers, speckled and brown trout are prized catches.

Mammals White-tailed deer are by far the most common large mammal of the Southeastern forests. The primary food source for generations of Native American inhabitants, deer is still prized game for local hunters. But what you'll see most frequently are the smaller mammals, primarily raccoon, opossums (called 'possum'), rabbits, squirrels, bats and the occasional woodchuck.

Many visitors are thrilled to see black bears, several hundred of which inhabit the Great Smoky Mountains National Park. Some of the critters look positively cuddly, but feeding is strongly discouraged as it disrupts their instincts and can make them aggressive – not a good idea for a creature that can weigh up to 300 lbs. In 2000 there was the first documented case of a black bear killing a human, and the big female (as well as its nearly full-grown young) was immediately killed.

Nocturnal wild boar also number about 2000 in the park and compete with the bears for food. These primitive-looking tusked creatures with a wiry coat are descendants of the animals that escaped from a hunting reserve in 1912.

Off the Atlantic Coast, bottle-nosed dolphins can often be seen accompanying deep-sea fishing boats or passing freighters. Otters are found in the Okefenokee and some other protected areas.

Insects The Southeast has many varieties of huge and colorful butterflies, which are drawn to the region's abundant flowering plants; indeed, some gardens are specially designed to attract butterflies. Dragonflies inhabit the wetlands, and katydids and crickets chirp through the night along the lower shores.

Mosquitoes are the most feared wildlife in the region, especially along the marshy coast; listen for the soft drone in the still air of early evening that signals their emergence. You'll also make the acquaintance of nuisance gnats, so small they're called 'no-see-ums' but with gargantuan appetites.

Huge brown winged cockroaches are another pest; they grow up to three inches long, live both indoors and out, and will even fly in your face if you get too close.

Endangered Species Dozens of species are on the endangered list in the Southeast, although it must be acknowledged that some of them have been brought back from the brink of extinction.

At one time red wolves roamed the hills from the Atlantic Coast to Texas, but their numbers had sunk to less than 100 by 1970;

these animals have been reintroduced with success to three habitats in North Carolina, including the Great Smoky Mountains National Park and the Abermarle. Beavers have returned to the park but you'll be lucky to see one.

Larger predators such as the eastern cougar once ranged from Canada to South Carolina alongside herds of elk and bison. Today there are only scattered sightings of the eastern cougar in forested areas of the Appalachians.

The piping plover now breeds in scattered locations along the Atlantic beaches and lakeshores. The endangered red-cockaded woodpecker thrives in the Sandhills and the Okefenokee. Cooper's hawk, snowy egrets and loggerhead shrike are among those earmarked on the Special Concern list throughout the Southeast.

Five species of sea turtles, including the loggerhead, are also under threat, as human traffic on the beaches disturbs their nesting grounds. Georgia has a high proportion of endangered fish species, including four kinds of dasher.

National Parks

Federal sites overseen by the National Park Service (NPS) in Georgia include the Okefenokee National Wildlife Refuge, the Cumberland Island National Seashore, the Chattahoochee River National Recreation Area, the Chickamauga & Chattanooga National Military Park and several National Historic Sites, including Jimmy Carter in Plains and Martin Luther King Jr in Atlanta.

In North Carolina, the NPS is responsible for maintaining the Blue Ridge Parkway, the Great Smoky Mountains National Park, the National Seashores of Cape Hatteras and Cape Lookout and a host of Historic Sites, including Guilford Courthouse at Greensboro, Moore's Creek near Wilmington, and the Carl Sandburg Home south of Asheville as well as the Wright Brothers Memorial and Fort Raleigh on the Outer Banks.

In South Carolina, NPS maintains the Congaree Swamp National Monument,

Charles Pinckney National Historic Site, Cowpens National Battlefield, Fort Moultrie National Monument, Fort Sumter National Monument and Kings Mountain National Military Park. The larger refuges here are administered by the Fish and Wildlife Service, including Cape Romain National Wildlife Refuge and Pinckney Island National Wildlife Refuge.

For a complete list or for more information on these national parks, visit www .recreation.gov or www.gorp.com. For state parks and national forests, see individual state chapters.

The Appalachian Trail Known to thru-hikers as the 'long green tunnel,' the Appalachian National Scenic Trail (AT) stretches 2158 miles from Springer Mountain in Georgia to Mt Katahdin in Maine, passing through 14 states and within a day's drive of about two-thirds of the US population. The AT runs along the crest of the Appalachian Mountains parallel to the Atlantic coast, much of it through protected areas, including two national parks, two national recreation areas and 60 state parks, including Georgia's Amicalola Falls State Park, which is the access point to the trailhead.

Easy access draws more than three million people a year to the AT, most of whom are day hikers or weekend backpackers. Each year, more than 2000 hardy souls set out to hike the entire AT, but fewer than 200 actually complete the trail in one season. For information on this long hike, contact the Appalachian Long Distance Hikers Association, 10 Benning St, Box 224, West Lebanon, NH, O3784.
Web site: www.aldha.org

More information on accessing the AT, including outfitters, is found in the regional chapters, particularly North Georgia.

GOVERNMENT & POLITICS

For most of the 20th century, the political image of the South was largely negative, marked by institutions such as Jim Crow segregation, the one-party system and disfranchisement (the denial of one's right to

THE APPALACHIAN TRAIL

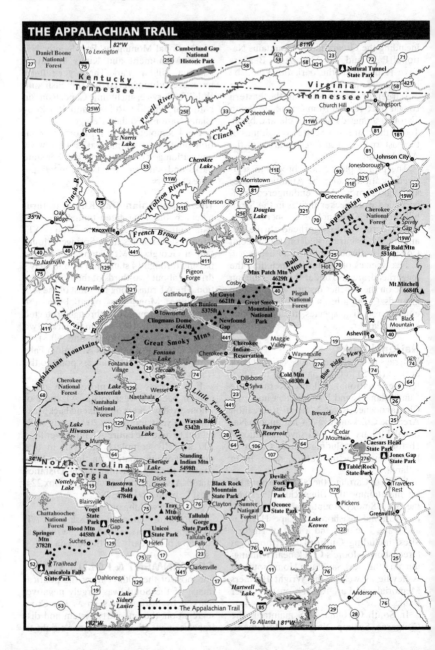

•••••• The Appalachian Trail

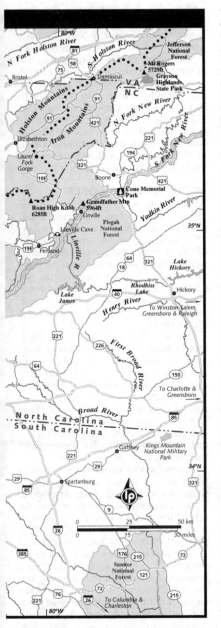

vote). But with two Southern presidents elected in the last quarter-century – Jimmy Carter from Georgia and Bill Clinton from Arkansas – Southern political practices have won new respect and come closer to resembling the national norm. The entire country has moved to the right, and a Southern platform that appeared extremely conservative 20 years ago now seems more mainstream.

The South traditionally has been Democratic because, after the Civil War, Southern whites shunned the Republican party of Abraham Lincoln. However, as the 20th century progressed the Democratic party became more closely aligned with Lincolnian (liberal) principles. This created a region of 'Dixiecrats' – whites on the Democratic rolls whose conservative voting records departed from the increasing liberalism of the rest of the party. In the last 10 years, even old-line Dixiecrats have changed camps and 'come out' as Republicans, joining the party that, today, is more consistent with their beliefs and values. Two long-serving Republican senators who embody old-school conservatism come from the Southeast – Jesse Helms and Strom Thurmond (once a Democrat), from North and South Carolina respectively.

Party lines are influenced by geography in the Southeast. The post-Civil War division in affiliations between the mountains (mainly poor, conservative Republican voters) and the plains (Democratic landowners and industrialists) persists to a certain extent today.

Although there's no clear formula, Democratic and Republican factions are frequently split along racial lines, with this tendency strongest in Georgia. African Americans in the South historically aligned with the Republican party of Reconstruction, but the civil rights efforts of Kennedy's Democratic administration caused many to register as Democrats.

ECONOMY

Agriculture is the economic mainstay of the Southeast, although diversification since WWII has brought many new industries.

Crops such as tobacco, cotton, corn and peanuts account for roughly half of the region's income. Peaches are big business, and few outsiders know that South Carolina produces more of the fuzzy fruits than Georgia, the Peach State. The coastal seafood industry peaked a few years back, but continues to make its contribution. Lumberers and paper processors remain leading local employers in the Carolinas; North Carolina is the largest maker of furniture in the country.

All three states have developed manufacturing zones that are proving to be job-making machines. Atlanta, the Greenville-Spartanburg corridor in South Carolina and the Research Triangle in North Carolina are booming centers of activity, attracting household names such as BMW, IBM and Northern Telecom, and advertising agencies have sprung up in their wake. Banking has grown enormously in recent years and Charlotte is exceeded only by New York in financial volume. Atlanta is the most economically diverse hub, home to a wide spectrum of industries and high-profile tenants such as Coca-Cola and Bell-South.

In recent decades, tourism has become a major industry in the mountains and coastal areas, particularly in the Carolinas, but it has had relatively little impact on the agricultural areas of the Piedmont and rural Georgia.

Thanks to King Cotton, the Southeast was a leading textile center after the Civil War, but this industry has declined sharply over the past decade. For many years the anti-union South was a haven for manufacturing businesses eager to relocate from the pro-union North. The 1996 passage of the North American Free Trade Agreement (NAFTA) caused many businesses to look to foreign countries as a cheaper alternative to the South. Many of these businesses have begun to leave the US entirely, stranding thousands of textile workers with skills not readily adaptable to other industries.

The tobacco industry has also suffered as successful billion-dollar class-action suits against big cigarette manufacturers paint a bleak picture for the future. States have es-tablished funds to help tobacco farmers switch to other crops, a process which has found increasing favor in North Carolina, where dependence on the crop is greatest.

The influx of new corporations has brought new capital to the Southeast, although the trickle-down to the general population has been uneven. In 1999, Georgia had an average per-capita income of $27,340, placing 13th in the US ranking but below the national average of $28,542. North Carolina had crawled up the ranking to 37th, but South Carolina remained near the bottom of the list, at No 45.

POPULATION & PEOPLE

Approximate state populations are as follows: Georgia 8.2 million, North Carolina 8 million and South Carolina 4 million. These populations can be broken down into distinct demographic groups, but it should be noted that there has also been much cultural and racial intermixing over the past 200 years, and racial categories and definitions are often not as sharp as they appear, though white people are still the majority in the Southeast.

Obviously, there's a big cultural difference between the heritages of whites in the mountain and urban areas and of blacks along the coast. The inland areas were settled by Anglo-Saxon Protestants from the Piedmont areas of the Atlantic Coast states of Virginia and Pennsylvania. While these white populations may appear homogeneous compared to other racial groups, they come from historically distinct cultures that can still be distinguished today.

The majority of blacks in the Southeast today are descended from the African slaves who were brought to the Americas to work on plantations. That's in line with the rest of the South, where the majority of blacks in the US continue to live. In 1900, 35 years after the Civil War, over 90% of African Americans in the US lived in the states that had made up the Confederacy. Beginning around WWI and continuing into the 1950s, millions of African Americans migrated north to escape economic hardship and entrenched racism. Significantly,

African Americans are now relocating back to the South in record numbers. Today, the Southeastern states still have a large proportion of blacks: 30% in South Carolina, 29% in Georgia and 22% in North Carolina.

Hispanics now account for about 4% of the region's population, and the numbers of Asians are on the rise as well.

As is true everywhere in the US, the Southeast has been home to Native Americans from prehistory to the present, and the Etowah Mounds of AD 1000–1550 form the best preserved site of the Mississippian culture in the Southeast. However, disease, war and forcible removal wiped out many of the local Native American tribes in the 18th and 19th centuries, and the percentage of people of Native American heritage now in the area hovers around 1% to 2%.

Native American communities live on reservations across the continent. In North Carolina, the federal reservation of the Eastern Cherokee on the edge of the Great Smoky Mountains has 16,500 residents, the descendents of the Cherokee who escaped forced relocation on the Trail of Tears.

A number of smaller tribes who lived in isolated, economically marginal lands were never pressured to move. Among them were the Lumbees, the largest native group east of the Mississippi River and today the largest unrecognized tribe in the US. Their ancestry is obscure but might derive from the Cherokee, the Tuscarora and the eastern Sioux; some historians contend they mixed with survivors of the Lost Colony that left Roanoke Island by 1590. Despite active lobbying they were never granted trust lands by the government, and over 40,000 Lumbee live in south-eastern North Carolina today, mostly as tobacco farmers.

The majority of the remaining Catawba Indians live on a small state reservation near Rock Hill, South Carolina. Other groups without homelands are dotted along the coast of North Carolina, including Haliwa, Coharie and Waccamaw.

EDUCATION

Schools throughout the South became a hotbed of civil rights activity after the Supreme Court outlawed segregation in its *Brown v Board of Education* ruling in 1954. Many white politicians fought desegregation in the following decade.

In 1960, Greensboro became the seat of social reform when four black students staged a sit-in at a local Woolworth's lunch counter and triggered sit-ins across the country. White resistance to integration dragged on until the early 1970s, when federal agents, the press and local activists pushed for compliance with the court directive. By the early 1980s, racial issues had taken a back seat to the quest for quality at all levels of education.

Secondary education in the Southeast continues to be marked by poor funding and a lack of resources, but state programs and initiatives have started to make up for lost ground. South Carolina, the weakest link in the region on matters educational, has developed a network of regional technical schools that work with businesses to retrain former mill workers in more skilled industries.

In educational achievement rankings, Georgia and the Carolinas have improved in recent years and now fall in the upper lower-half (ie, below national averages) for per capita government expenditures on education and for percentages of the population earning a bachelor's degree. The vast majority of pupils complete high school, but scores on college-entrance exams such as the SAT remain low, showing that much remains to be done.

Distinguished universities in North Carolina include Wake Forest, the multi-campus University of North Carolina (UNC) and North Carolina State; UNC is consistently among the top-ranked public universities and Duke University's medical school in Durham is recognized to be world-class. Clemson University in South Carolina has a well-respected agricultural college. Standout Georgia institutions include Emory, which has among the best law and medical schools in the country, Georgia Tech, with a renowned engineering school, and the University of Georgia, the oldest state university (1785).

ARTS
Literature

The legacy of literature of Georgia and the Carolinas is best understood in the context of Southern literature, with a dose of mountain lore thrown in. All influences have their distinct flavors, but all draw on the age-old traditions of oral storytelling – tales told on the porch swing or under the family's live oaks on balmy summer evenings. Many state-specific books and writers are discussed under the Arts section of the state chapters.

19th Century Arguably the most famous Southern writer of the 19th century, Edgar Allan Poe (1809–1849) made his reputation while a journalist in northern cities. As a young man, Poe was stationed in the army on Sullivan's Island, off the coast of Charleston, where he set his eerie tale of buried treasure in *The Gold Bug*. The characters are all Southern stereotypes.

In *Look Homeward Angel* and *You Can't Go Home Again,* Thomas Wolfe (1900–1938) effectively chronicles events in his native Asheville in its headlong tumble towards tourism. The picture that emerges is awash in the contrasts of western North Carolina; during his upbringing, Wolfe was conscious of the grinding poverty of the mountains but also of the promise offered by rich guests streaming through town. Human suffering and the will to endure were recurring themes in his work. Although his reputation may have faded in recent years, William Faulkner ranked Wolfe as one of the nation's greatest writers.

William Sydney Porter (1867–1910) is much better known under his pen name O Henry (said to derive from his calling out 'Oh Henry' to the family cat). While working at a bank in Austin, Texas, Porter was imprisoned for embezzlement and began to write. His more than 300 short stories are realistic and based on his experiences in New York, Texas and his native North Carolina (he grew up in Greensboro). The tales followed a standard formula, dealing with commonplace events in the lives of ordinary people and arriving at a surprise ending through coincidence. *The Gift of the Magi* is his most famous work; for glimpses of North Carolina, read *The Fool Killer* or *Let Me Feel Your Pulse*.

Mary Boykin Chesnut (1823–86), a prominent Columbian, kept personal diaries of the Civil War, which have been collected in *The Civil War Diary of Mary Boykin Chesnut*. It's a volume spiced with wit and intelligence, and is acknowledged by some as the finest literary work of the Confederacy. Historian C Vann Woodward edited the diaries in an effort that earned him the Pulitzer Prize.

Appalachian Literature Early 'pioneer' literature was led by writers who sought to emulate James Fenimore Cooper's historically flawed but moving *The Last of the Mohicans*. In the late 19th century writers such as Mark Twain, George Washington Harris

---

Johnny Reb

The strongest Confederate icon to survive is Johnny Reb, a figure idealized after the Civil War as a defender of morality, dignity and just about everything that was 'good' about the South. Henry Timrod (1829–67), a South Carolinian and the unofficial poet laureate of the Confederacy, cemented this picture in the minds of Southerners after 1866, when elaborate rituals were begun for Confederate Memorial Day. Timrod composed this moving 'Ode' for the first decoration of war graves in Charleston:

> Sleep sweetly in your humble graves,
> Sleep, martyrs of a fallen cause!
> Though yet no marble column craves
> The pilgrim here to pause.

From the 1880s onwards, the character of Johnny Reb was cast in the warm glow of nostalgia, and has been used to depict a doomed (but justified) struggle against overwhelming odds. Curiously, the image of Johnny came to resemble that of Billy Yank around the same time – both patriotic figures fighting for American idealism.

and Davy Crockett exploited the stereotypes and romantic notions of the region with backwoods humor, tall tales and romanticism. This was followed by a group of writers whose works were romantic and written largely in dialect; Mary Noailles Murfree's stories set in the Great Smoky Mountains are a good example. Typical motifs included feuding, the Civil War and moonshine. In the '30s larger, more universal themes appeared from the pens of Jesse Stuart, James Still, Harriette Simpson Arnow and others.

The 1950s saw the advent of younger, more socially conscious writers such as Harry Caudill *(Night Comes to the Cumberlands)* and Jack Weller *(Yesterday's People),* who trained attention on the prevailing political and economic issues of the day. The tradition is carried on in periodicals such as the *Appalachian Journal* and *Foxfire,* whose contributors of poetry, essays and short stories include Fred Chappell, Lee Pennington, James B Goode, George Scarbrough and Gurney Norman.

Local Color *Oxherding Tales,* by sociologist Charles Johnson (1893–1956), is an evocative yet entertaining story about a mulatto slave who is educated in the classics, sold to a sex-crazed female plantation owner, escapes and passes into white society with a slave catcher close at his heels.

Paul Green (1894–1981) is best known for the historical drama *The Lost Colony* (1937), which gives an interesting guess about the fate of the Roanoke Island settlement. It also provided the basis for North America's longest-running outdoor drama.

Red Hills and Cotton by Ben Robertson is an autobiographical story of a family living at the foot of the Blue Ridge Mountains in the early 20th century. The story is lyrical and sentimental, and captures the Southerner's great affection for the land.

Julia Peterkin (1880–1961), from the Murrells Inlet-Pawleys Island area, wrote *Scarlet Sister Mary,* the 1928 Pulitzer-Prize–winning novel about a Gullah woman working on a coastal plantation. Peterkin

was well-qualified: She learned to speak Gullah before she did English.

Popular for the TV series *On the Road,* Charles Kuralt (1934–98), a native of Wilmington, North Carolina, also authored several books on his travels, including *Southerners: A Portrait of a People* (1986) and *Charles Kuralt's America* (1996), which became a best-seller.

For something offbeat, *South Carolina: The WPA Guide to the Palmetto State* was written in 1941 under the government-funded writers' program. It's an interesting read for history and colorful tales, such as the story of a notorious thief who was known to sing the following song:

> Barnwell District, Aiken Town;
> O Lord in Mercy do look down!
> The land is poor, the people too;
> If they don't steal, what will they do?

Southern Renaissance As the rest of the US began to enjoy 20th-century prosperity, the South lagged far behind in terms of education, race relations and nutrition – not to mention high art and literature. Yet, sometime early in the century, this region of storytellers came alive with great literature.

Perhaps the phenomenon was a result of a long period of regional self-analysis brought about by military defeat and Reconstruction; or maybe it was a result of lingering guilt over the treatment of African Americans. In any case, the generation of Southern writers who emerged in the early and mid-20th century remains among the most well regarded in world literature.

The contributions of writers from Georgia and the Carolinas to this pool of literature have been considerable, although more major Southern writers came from other Southern states such as Louisiana, Mississippi and Tennessee.

Flannery O'Connor (1925–64) was perhaps the greatest short story writer of the 20th century. A native of Savannah, O'Connor graduated from the Georgia State College for Women in Milledgeville. She was diagnosed with lupus (a type of autoimmune disorder) in 1950 and moved to her mother's farm where she finished the novel *Wise Blood*. A collection of short stories, *A Good Man is Hard to Find,* appeared in 1955 to widespread acclaim. She died in 1964, a year before her final collection, *Everything That Rises Must Converge,* came out. O'Connor's characters and themes are traditionally Southern, although seen in a religious framework – no other writer has achieved this to the same degree.

Carson McCullers (1917–67) employed the modern South in all of her major fiction. Born in Columbus, Georgia, McCullers achieved fame early with her first novel, *The Heart is a Lonely Hunter* (1940), which documents the social conditions of a mill city during the Depression. Oddly, she tackled a Gothic novel next, *Reflections in a Golden Eye* (1941), a bizarre sexual tale set on a US army base. Her life was marked by illness and depression, and though she labored for a decade on *Clock Without Hands* (1961), it failed to match the level achieved in *Heart*.

The works of Thomas Dixon (1864–1946) straddle several generations. Born in the Piedmont of North Carolina just before the Civil War ended, Dixon lived to see the end of WWII. In the last four decades of his life, Dixon published 22 novels (often in trilogy form) and a host of screenplays, dramas and short stories. His Klan trilogy – including *The Clansman* (1912), on which the movie *Birth of a Nation* is based – depicts racial conflict as an epic struggle. Dixon was against slavery, but argued against social equality for blacks because, he said, it would lead to miscegenation and societal breakdown. Not surprisingly, his works were condemned during the Civil Rights era and are seldom read today.

Margaret Mitchell (1900–49) tried writing short stories in the 1920s without success, but went on to compose *the* Southern novel of all time, *Gone With the Wind*. See the Facts About Georgia chapter for details on Mitchell and a wealth of other writings.

Contemporary Writing Two-bit Gothic romances and law thrillers come and go but thankfully, Southeastern fiction (and nonfiction) has more to offer posterity.

A native of Atlanta, James Dickey (1923–1997) had been writing for two decades before his blockbuster *Deliverance* was published in the early '70s. The novel, which has achieved a kind of cult status in recent years, focuses on a familiar clash of backwoods and urban cultures, with city boys getting their comeuppance in startlingly brutal fashion. Dickey, who taught at the University of South Carolina, also wrote interviews, screenplays and prize-winning poetry.

Erskine Caldwell (1903–87) trained his crosshairs on moral injustice in the South – not exactly as a crusader or muckraker, but with enough power to prick consciences. In well-known novels such as *Tobacco Road* (1933), Caldwell decried the lot of the struggling tenant farmer. Together with Faulkner, Caldwell, a native of Coweta County in Georgia, helped to establish some of the best-known literary types of the Depression era.

South Carolina's most prolific modern writer is Pat Conroy. A love affair with the Lowcountry has inspired many of his novels, including *The Great Santini* (1976), about a domineering marine pilot and his family who have just moved to Beaufort. Conroy's best book is the autobiographical *The Water is Wide* (1972), about his experiences as a teacher on the once-isolated Daufuskie Island, near Hilton Head.

Josephine Humphries wrote *Rich in Love,* a novel which portrays a young woman's coming of age in Mount Pleasant, a Charleston suburb. Heaping helpings of Southern-style humor are served in William Price Fox's *Southern Fried,* which has recently been re-released with six additional stories under the title *Southern Fried Plus Six*.

Fred Chappell's *I Am One of You Forever* (1985) is a delightful collection of regional short stories by North Carolina's reigning poet laureate.

Architecture

The architectural style most commonly linked to the South is the neoclassical antebellum plantation house. The former plantation regions along the coasts and southern plains of the Piedmont hold the greatest concentrations; Wilmington, Charleston and Beaufort on the coast and the area around Athens are prime examples. Ideal places to see examples of the region's traditional architecture are re-created towns and plantation settlements – at Raleigh's Mordecai Park or Stone Mountain near Atlanta, for example. Numerous log cabins, slave communities and the historic homes of the wealthy are also open for viewing.

Sometimes the grandeur of the antebellum era comes off a bit exaggerated. Stone Mountain includes a romantic reconstruction of an 1850s plantation that was reassembled from period buildings moved from around the state; the home of the fictional overseer was in fact the main house at Allen Plantation, not far from Kingston.

Many antebellum mansions are open to public tours. Houses are carefully restored and decorated, both by local historical societies and by individuals, with elaborate interior furnishings in period style; many display the furnishings of the original residents. On guided tours, you'll find that each piece has a story to tell, and the history of the family is at least as important as the house (if not more so). Often, the original architectural craftwork was done by slaves, and a few antebellum houses retain their original slave cabins.

The humble houses of the working class also make a striking impression. In the poorest areas, neighborhoods often called slums, you can still find the proverbial 'shotgun shack,' typically with a rusty corrugated roof, paper-thin walls and about an arm's length to one just like it next door. Their rooms are lined up one after another – behind the small porch there's a living room, then a bedroom, then a kitchen – affording little privacy for whole families. You could stand on the front porch and shoot straight through the back door – hence the term. You'll also notice that many families in poorer communities live out of trailers and keep a 'swept lawn' in the dirt apron out front.

Gardens

Meticulously sculpted gardens, often accompanied by waterfalls, terraces, statuaries and sculptures, are a famous feature of the Southeast. Fine examples of this are the Biltmore Estate Gardens, just outside Asheville, with hundreds of thousands of tulips, azaleas and rhododendrons and a number of carefully-conceived European gardens. Magnolia Plantation in Charleston has a horticultural maze, topiary and a biblical garden. The most famous landscape architect who worked in the Southeast was Frederick Law Olmsted, who designed New York's Central Park before he set to work on plans for Biltmore.

Visual Arts

The arts generate a fair amount of support in the monied Piedmont, and one result is a collection of fine museums of contemporary and classic works in Atlanta, Raleigh, Winston-Salem, Chapel Hill and Greenville, South Carolina. (See the individual chapters for details.) Many emphasize American paintings, though there's a strong regional appetite for European masters.

Locally produced artwork is very distinctive and worth seeing in its native context. Folk arts, for example, express the self-taught artistry of Appalachian or Piedmont craftspeople and reflect their connection to the landscape. Many works explore local themes and rural scenes in self-styled media – blankets, recycled metal, wood scraps and other found objects.

The region is also renowned for its crafts, especially pottery, glasswork and wood carvings made from native materials. The quirky potters of Edgefield, South Carolina, and Seagrove, North Carolina, churn out face jugs of astonishing wit and imagination. The Folk Art Center, located on the Blue Ridge Parkway just outside of Asheville, is perhaps the best place to pick up Appalachian arts and crafts. However, hundreds of artisans and craftspeople sell their wares directly, from roadside shops, mountain cabins or urban galleries. Dilliard, Georgia, has one of the Southeast's leading creative arts centers.

MUSIC OF THE SOUTHEAST

The music of the Southeast is as rich and varied as its mountains-to-swamp geography. Folk music (particularly bluegrass and country) predominates in the Appalachians, while the strains of R&B, alternative rock, hip-hop, soul and dozens of hybrid forms permeate the plains of Piedmont. The Carolina coast prides itself on its relaxed beach music, as performed in the legendary dance halls of Myrtle Beach.

Bluegrass The Appalachian music that's most familiar to contemporary audiences is bluegrass. It's actually a form of country music that originated from Grand Ole Opry star Bill Monroe and his Blue Grass Boys from the 1940s onward. Many of the first bluegrass stars came from outside the mountains – Lester Flatt was from central Tennessee, and Earl Scruggs hailed from the North Carolina Piedmont – but bluegrass was forged primarily in Nashville.

Like country music after WWII, bluegrass was aimed at farm workers and families, and found its origins in dance, traveling theater and religious traditions of the rural South. When it coalesced in the late 1940s, bluegrass was seen as old-fashioned 'backwoods' music, but by the '70s, many players had 'gone electric' and the genre had begun to flirt with rock and pop. Bluegrass became primarily festival music, with fiddle conventions and contests in Kentucky, Tennessee and North Carolina.

Many bluegrass bands still rely on acoustic string instruments – banjo or guitar, string bass and fiddle with vocals is a common lineup. Tunes tend to be pitched high, include alternating solos (as in jazz) and are generally faster than other types of country music.

One of its leading lights is Arthel 'Doc' Watson, from Deep Gap, North Carolina. Born blind, Watson grew up on a farm and was oriented toward religion and music. He played guitar and a banjo of hickory, maple and catskin and learned jazz, big-band, pop and classical music while attending the North Carolina School for the Blind. A champion of guitar flat picking – a technique using a simple  flat pick rather than a thumb pick – Watson has an amazing repertoire ranging from Gershwin to Dylan, and has won tons of prizes.

Popular events where you can hear Watson, Pat Donohue and other wizard pickers and fiddlers include Asheville's Mountain Dance and Folk Festival in August or the annual Highland Games at Grandfather Mountain in July, off the Blue Ridge Parkway. Also look out for performances of dulcimers – a southern mountain lap instrument that produces a soft, almost melancholy sound.

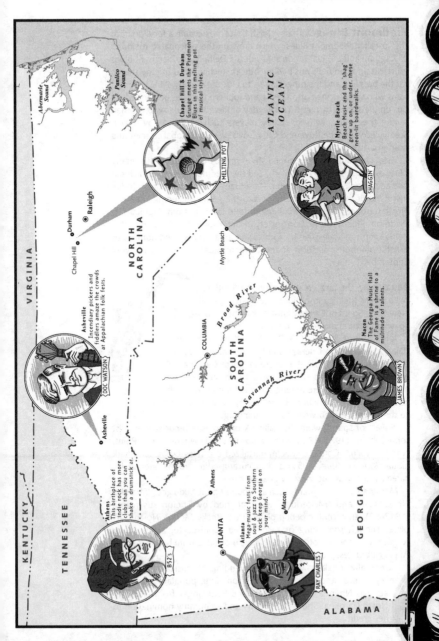

Piedmont Blues Durham, North Carolina, became a focal point of the so-called Piedmont Blues, which drew on the syncopated melodies of Ragtime and the plantation songs of the Delta Blues. Piedmont Blues guitarists and banjo players had an intricate technique, using the thumb for the bass line and the other fingers to pick the melody. African Americans who worked the cotton fields and tobacco factories performed for tips on the streets by night. The heyday of Piedmont Blues was reached during the 1930s, with legendary players such as 'Blind Boy' Fuller, Sonny Terry and the Reverend Gary Davis playing at tobacco sales and house parties in Durham.

After Durham's mayor banned street music during the 1940s, many blues artists moved to New York, and the Piedmont Blues – which did not adapt well to electric guitar – gradually fell into obscurity. Today just a handful of old-timers still record the genre, including Tar Heel, North Carolina, native Etta Baker and John Jackson, from Virginia. The Piedmont Blues Preservation Society in Greensboro (☎ 336-275-4944) helps keep the style alive by sponsoring area events. Piedmont Blues artists sometimes perform at the Durham Blues Festival, held every September.

Jazz Sadly, the jazz greats born in the Southeast have made their contributions elsewhere – usually New York. So it's not widely known that the Carolinas spawned several masters of modern jazz.

John Birks Gillespie (1917–93), better known as 'Dizzy,' was born in Cheraw, South Carolina. He attended the Laurinburg musical institute in North Carolina but moved to Philadelphia when he was 18. In the 1940s, he and Charlie Parker were among the great innovators of the frenetic language of bebop. There's a tiny museum dedicated to the bulge-cheeked virtuoso in Laurinburg.

'Sheets of sound' were the hallmark of exquisite tenor saxophonist John Coltrane (1926–67), who grew up in a small town near High Point, North Carolina. Coltrane was immortalized on Miles Davis' landmark album *Kind of Blue* (1959) and in cutting-edge groups later in his career, which was cut short by liver cancer.

Memorable jazz standards such as 'Round About Midnight', 'Straight, No Chaser' and 'Misterioso' were penned by Thelonious Monk (1917–82), an eccentric bebop pianist from Rocky Mount, North Carolina. Though something of a self-styled sophisticate, Monk never forgot his Southern roots: Collard greens protruded from his lapel at Big Apple club dates.

Generally speaking there's more blending of musical styles than ever before, and jazz is no exception. One popular 'crossover' artist is Nnenna Freelon, a jazz and R&B singer from Durham, North Carolina. She has an Emmy and a Grammy nomination to her credit.

Southern Rock Shades of the Confederacy can be heard in the Southern rock that emerged from mainstream rock in the early '70s. A blend of black R&B, jazz and country, Southern rock was oriented to concerts, with (for the era) unusually long tunes; some live recordings of a single song covered an entire album side. Its songs idolized individualism, Southern and rural life, and macho behavior – themes which were popular among white Southern working-class teenagers. In Atlanta during the '60s, producer and publisher Bill Lowery oversaw a small but talented corps of artists including Billy Joe Royal, Ray Stevens and Jerry Reed, but few hits produced a distinctive regional sound.

Enter the Allman Brothers, the first definitive Southern rock band. In 1969, Duane Allman and his brother Gregg, a vocalist and keyboard player, formed the original Allman Brothers Band, which included guitarist Dicky Betts and bassist Berry Oakley. They were among the first to sign with Capricorn Records, a fledgling Macon, Georgia company set up by Otis Redding's former manager, Phil Walden. The Allmans produced a rich fabric of hits, but the deaths of Duane Allman and Berry Oakley in motorcycle accidents in 1971 and 1972 – in Macon, within a block of each other – robbed the group of its creative verve. The Allmans' history features prominently in the Georgia Music Hall of Fame in Macon.

Lynyrd Skynyd penned the Southern rock anthem 'Sweet Home Alabama' and other hits for the Atlanta-based Sounds of the South label; its famous live recording of 'Free Bird' was made in Atlanta's Fox Theatre. Like the Allmans, Lynyrd Skynyrd suffered a tragic accident – an airplane crash that claimed the lives of four band members.

The heyday of the genre passed with the '70s, but quite a few old Southern rockers just keep on rockin'. The Marshall Tucker Band, from Spartanburg, South Carolina, still serves up an eclectic mix of jazz, western swing and unusual instrumentation. The fiery fiddle of Charlie Daniels, from Wilmington, North Carolina, is closer to country music. Other venerable names include .38 Special, Molly Hatchet, and the Outlaws, but the torch is being passed to younger bands such as Melt, also from Atlanta.

Pop & Alternative Chapel Hill has been on the cutting edge of

'alternative' music ever since the mid- '50s, when Danny Clark and the Hot Nuts made records filled with frat-house innuendo (which were stamped 'adults only' by zealous censors).

Largely self-taught, talented guitarist and vocalist James Taylor took all of four lessons in rudimentary blues and jazz from a blind guitar teacher in Chapel Hill where he grew up. He moved to the Northeast in the '70s, where he penned country and blues-flavored hits such as 'Carolina on My Mind' and 'Sweet Baby James.'

Chapel Hill bands excel in funky names – Superchunk, Mustard Plug, Sorry About Dresden, Southern Culture on the Skids, Citizen Fish and Mayflies USA are but a few examples. The sound isn't all grunge, of course. Among the more eclectic offerings, Taz Halloween sings fine jazz and blues to weird multimedia effects. Probably the most celebrated group at the moment is the Squirrel Nut Zippers, a retro-jazz band; kids dress up in a facsimile of their parents' (or grandparents') clothes to hear a pleasantly warped past.

The other small-town band incubator of the Southeast is Athens, where the likes of REM, Widespread Panic, the Indigo Girls and the B52s got their start in the late '70s and early '80s. The seeds of local New Wave were planted by art students of the University of Georgia, who would dress up in wigs and second-hand clothes to hit the town – and some of them picked up cheap guitars, farfisa organs and other equipment while they were at it. The first beehives of the B52s cost a song in a downtown thrift shop.

Although its salad days are over for now, Athens still has an incredibly active club scene; members of REM still play the legendary 40 Watt Club. Other prominent groups to look out for include Make Believe and Bokomolech.

As for South Carolina, its best-known alt-rockers remain the screamingly popular Hootie & the Blowfish, whose members went to college in Columbia.

Hip-Hop & Rap Atlanta's large black, urban community has proved a fertile ground for homemade hip-hop and rap. As a local studio head noted, the city has plenty of 'do-it-yourself rappers who cut a hot record, get it pressed, find love at local radio stations and clubs and sell copies out of car trunks at family reunions.'

The more original stars include hip-hoppers Outkast, who released a controversial song about Rosa Parks, the woman who refused to give up her bus seat to a white passenger in Montgomery back in 1955. Another popular single described bombs falling on Baghdad: '… thunder pounds when I stomp the ground, whoo, like a million elephants.'

Many groups manage to incorporate a range of musical forms while retaining their roots, which ain't necessarily in the city. The duo Field Mob from Albany, Georgia, blends country with rap and slang-sprinkled, drawly Southern lyrics.

Soul The unbridled energy of soul grew out of the R&B of the 1950s, thanks mainly to the pioneer efforts of Ray Charles.

James Brown, 'the Godfather of Soul,' was the only black R&B artist to make the transition to soul in the '60s, then to funk in the '70s. Born in 1933 to a poor family near Barnwell, South Carolina,

 Brown led the gospel band The Famous Flames in the mid- '40s and began working regularly in Macon. In 1956, the Flames cut their 'secularized' gospel song 'Please, Please, Please,' which became a top R&B hit. Brown's stage shows were stunningly professional with fast-paced dancing, knee drops and his trademark simulated collapse. He now lives in Beech Island 50 miles from his birthplace, and funds an annual turkey giveaway in nearby Augusta.

Apart from James Brown, Otis Redding (1941–67) embodied the soul sound in the '60s. Born in Dawson, Georgia, but raised in Macon, Redding's style was immediately recognizable for the catch in his voice. He first played locally with Johnny Jenkins and the Pinetoppers, and by 1957 he was managed by Phil Walden. Among other works, the hit 'Sittin' on the Dock of the Bay' shows Redding's mastery of rhythmic subtlety and timbral variation. He died in a plane crash in December 1967.

Richard Penniman – aka 'Little' Richard – was a rock and roll singer from Macon who incorporated soul and blues into classics such as 'Tutti Frutti' and 'Good Golly Miss Molly.' Other famous soul artists from Georgia include Gladys Knight (of The Pips fame), who signed with Motown.

Ray Charles This most famous son of Georgia has made an enormous impact on American music. Born into poverty in the backwoods of south Georgia during the Depression, Charles was four years old when he saw his brother drown in a bathtub; then he started to lose his sight, and went completely blind by the time he was seven.

'Soul is a way of life,' Charles once explained, 'but it's always the hard way.'

Self-taught on the piano, Charles was barely 18 when he cut his first single, 'Confession Blues.' By the summer of 1949 he'd released some 20 singles, mostly in the velvety style of crooner Nat 'King' Cole. In Atlanta he came into his own and recorded the 1955 hit 'I Got a Woman,' a gospel-blues tune with churchy piano; this and tunes like it would lay the foundation for a generation of soul vocalists in the '60s.

Charles charted a milestone in 1959 when, in a smoky dancehall near Pittsburgh, he cut 'What I'd Say,' a gospel call-and-response with a Latin beat. Sounding like a re-creation of a revival meeting, the song was condemned as blasphemy and banned by several radio stations – and became a million-seller. In 1962, he cut his greatest crossover ever, the album *Modern Sounds in Country and Western Music* – the first time a black jazz-blues artist had ventured into country, which was considered a white domain. Two of the traditional country songs Charles covered on this album reached the Top Ten in pop R & B charts.

Since then Charles has won just about every meaningful cultural and musical award, including the National Medal of Arts, 12 Grammies and a spot in the Rock and Roll Hall of Fame. He remains a beloved, almost saintly, figure swaying back and forth behind his grand piano, and performed his 'America the Beautiful' at Ronald Reagan's renomination and Bill Clinton's first inaugural ball.

Beach Music Beach music has been around for half a century in the Carolinas, although its origins lie in the post-WWII soul and R&B of urban black 'streetcorner' music. Purists maintain that beach music isn't surf music and has nothing to do with the Beach Boys. Songs generally are a relaxed 4/4 shuffle to which dancers can 'shag' – a sophisticated touch dance that's related to the jitterbug (but not to any Austin Powers movies). Fronted by Bill Pinkney, the Drifters were credited with popularizing beach music with their classic 'Under the Boardwalk' (1964), although the form seems to be as much about 1950s nostalgia as anything else. Performing groups tended to be African-American, and had curiously similar names (Coasters, Platters, Catalinas and so on).

Beach music thrived in the late '50s and early '60s but was somewhat forgotten during the Vietnam War years. Disco nearly killed it but in 1979, a group called SOS (Society of Stranders) organized a reunion of aging shaggers at Myrtle Beach. Resurgence followed. Considered lewd by parents of the '50s, the shag had become such a cultural icon that it was declared South Carolina's state dance in 1985. Today, beach music is usually performed by white groups such as The Embers, who are just as likely to play the governor's mansion as a beachside hall. SOS, meanwhile, still attracts thousands of fans to its zoo-like gathering in North Myrtle Beach.

Performing Arts

Generally, the performing arts receive reasonably good funding in the Southeast, particularly in the Piedmont cities. Risky, experimental productions are a bit thin in central venues – you'll need to plumb alternative quarters instead, sometimes well outside downtown.

Dancing in its various forms is a treasured pastime in all the geographies. Clogging, contra dancing (a folk dance performed to music of Celtic origin in which couples face each other in a line or in a square) and square dancing are popular in the mountains, but ballet and contemporary dance (including African American, Latino and Asian performances) can be found on many stages. Durham, North Carolina, has perhaps the nation's finest festival of modern steps, the American Dance Festival; see hip-hop united with Michael Jackson-inspired glides and floating waltz steps concentrated within a few minutes' viewing.

Big-ticket dramas and musical productions are staged in Atlanta, at venues such as the Alliance Theatre Company, or in Charlotte at the Blumenthal Performing Arts Center. Outdoor dramas are an unusual feature in summer in North Carolina, and stage programs in the mountains at Cherokee and Boone, as well as on the Outer Banks at Manteo are enduring attractions. Cabaret and comedy clubs can be found in some cities; see individual cities for listings.

SOCIETY & CONDUCT

Southern hospitality is legendary: most folks are friendly, accessible, hospitable and courteous, and would rather invite you in for lemonade than see you spend one more instant out on that hot sidewalk. However, they *can* be a bit xenophobic regarding outsiders, perhaps due in part to the stereotypical and generally negative image of Southerners broadcast by the mainstream media.

Female travelers from less chivalrous parts of the world may be somewhat surprised (or miffed) to find that many local

---

Southern Crackers

Poor white Southerners have long been subject to various nasty epithets including 'linthead,' 'hoosier,' 'peckerwood,' 'redneck' and 'cracker.' 'Cracker' is among the oldest labels and referred especially to poor whites from south Georgia and north Florida. Travelers in the 19th century wrote of poor white farmers who 'cracked' or pounded corn for food; another version spoke of whips cracking over the heads of animals. After the Civil War, Georgia and Florida sold off much of the public land that the crackers had used for grazing livestock, and their economic situation worsened yet again. In the 1970s, however, the term was used with ethnic pride by some Southern whites. The election of a white peanut farmer to the presidency in 1976 prompted media stories about Cracker Chic, and humorist Roy Blount Jr used *Crackers* as the title of a book on the Jimmy Carter era.

---

men continue to uphold traditional manners, like holding doors open for women. Male travelers, on the other hand, may risk offending local women by *not* holding doors open – *c'est la vie*.

Both men and women shake hands, while family and friends embrace and kiss with varying degrees of visible affection. Straight men don't usually hug or kiss each other, and Gallic-style cheek-pecking may be considered pretentious among women. Unless you're introduced to someone as a Mr, Ms, Miss, or Mrs, it's usually fine to use first names.

Many locals tend to use formal rules of address – no sir, yes ma'am – but they don't necessarily expect outsiders to be so polite. However, such small courtesies will certainly be noticed and appreciated; being extraordinarily polite and not coming on too strong will ease social interaction. Things tend to be less formal in larger cities and when dealing with certain social groups – youth or artists, for instance.

Be aware that being clean and tidy is important, and visitors who appear unkempt (wearing cut-offs, anything too revealing or – heaven forbid – being unshowered) will draw negative attention. People tend to dress a little more formally when attending the theater or a concert; you may find you're the only one in jeans at the *Nutcracker*. Conversely, a suit and tie will be out of place in most nightclubs. Ask first if you're not sure.

Dos & Don'ts

Locals may get edgy discussing racial dynamics. Be cautious about initiating such a discussion until you've established a good rapport with someone.

Further points to consider are American national pride, which is good to be aware of when discussing political and social issues. Critical comments, especially from a foreigner, might be construed as a slight to national honor and provoke a very negative reaction. Other iffy subjects include gun control, religion and the politics revolving around a woman's right (or lack thereof) to an abortion.

RELIGION

Religious life still plays a large role in the culture of the Southeast, although its influence has waned somewhat since WWII. Baptists predominate, but there are large numbers of churchgoers who adhere to other distinctive forms of ethnic Protestantism – an aspect which sets Georgia and the Carolinas somewhat apart from the rest of the South. Pockets of liberalism can surprise you; take Duke University in Durham, which allows same-sex marriage ceremonies in its Gothic chapel.

In the past, the Southeast has been nearly as divided over religion as it has been over race. Protestants did not tend to associate with Catholics or Jews, and intermarriage between faiths, even among different Protestant branches, was scandalous. The Ku Klux Klan persecuted Catholics and Jews along with blacks. Today it's still common for whites and blacks to attend their own churches.

Local residents are very up-front about their religious beliefs, and you might be asked about yours. A question like, 'Do you accept Jesus Christ into your life?' may be merely a conversation starter, not an evangelical query.

In Catholic churches, only baptized and indoctrinated Catholics are invited to participate in the Communion ritual of bread and wine. Protestant churches are more liberal in sharing their rituals.

Protestantism

Fire-and-brimstone sermons, creekside baptisms, vacation Bible school and strict blue laws are all part of a standard Bible Belt experience today. The fundamentalist Baptists who are a strong force in this region today resulted from a split in antebellum times known as the Great Revival. During the 1840s, debates occurred over the interpretation of religious doctrine concerning slavery, resulting in the establishment of the pro-slavery Southern Baptist Convention in 1845. Baptists and Methodists combined make up about half of the churchgoing population of the Southeast. The Piedmont region of the Carolinas is remarkably pluralistic, with groups including Friends, Lutherans, Moravians, Presbyterians, and the United Church of Christ.

Appalachian Religions The earliest contributors were the Cherokee, whose traditions of herbal healing survive to the present day. In the 18th century, however, English, Scotch-Irish and German immigrants brought dissenting Protestant beliefs to the New World. The English were primarily Non-Conformists or Puritans, and most Scotch-Irish were Presbyterians. German arrivals included members of the Reformed, Lutheran and Moravian churches, as well as more radical sects of Dunkers or Mennonites. By the 1850s a distinct religious body had emerged in Appalachia, stretching from Virginia to the northwestern tip of Alabama, and its followers were overwhelmingly poor.

These believers shared mountain attitudes of a love of nature, God beyond nature, and one another. At the same time, there was a Calvinist-inspired awe of God and a suspicion of the evils that lurked in the human heart. Presbyterians predominated in Appalachia early on, but from the early 1800s onward the Baptists also flourished, particularly after the Great Revival, and Methodists soon matched the Baptists in their missionary fervor. All denominations here, including Methodists, began to preach a modified Calvinism that became increasingly fundamentalist in the course of the 19th century.

As a result of poverty and geographical hurdles, the region remains underchurched today and many families fill the breach at home. It's unusual, for example, to find a mountain home without its own Bible, which even if it's not read often, is regularly opened for counsel.

African-American Christianity

During slavery, all expressions of African religious traditions were prohibited and repressed, and they had to be carried out in secrecy. Slaves were allowed (many were obligated) to attend Sunday services at their white slave-owner's church; some early black communities even founded their own churches during slavery. After emancipation, missionaries from Northern churches successfully set up congregations in black communities; the African-Methodist Episcopal church helped found many of the AME churches now prolific in the Southeast.

The church has always been a powerful unifying force in African-American communities. Early civil rights leaders, such as Dr Martin Luther King Jr, came from the preacher's ranks. Black churches have been the target of numerous racially motivated attacks, both historically (most well remembered from the Civil Rights era) and in a rash of arson across the South in 1995 that prompted a federal investigation.

Roman Catholicism

Catholicism has left a relatively small imprint on the Southeast, and the largest communities today are located in larger cities such as Atlanta, Raleigh and Char-

lotte. The Catholic Church played a leading cultural role in the 1960s, when desegregation in Catholic schools moved faster than in the public sector. In the last few decades, the influx of Spanish-speaking immigrants and a relocation of northern Catholics into the Southeast has increased the Church's influence.

Judaism

While Judaism is not often associated with the Southeast, a significant Jewish community took up early residence here. Intolerance of Jews in the region occurred at certain times and in certain places; the worst anti-Semitic incident was the 1915 lynching of Leo Frank in Georgia, for the alleged murder of a teenage girl. Over the centuries, however, the relative tolerance among the gentiles allowed Jews of diverse origins and cultural backgrounds to integrate more successfully into the landscape than is commonly supposed.

LANGUAGE

Southern variations on standard English are well known and a target of mimics – in fact, you're not likely to hear any standard English except in some Piedmont cities and Atlanta. In the Southeast, dialects vary widely in pronunciation, pace, delivery and, often, vocabulary. They vary not only by geography – accents in south Georgia can be markedly different from those in the Appalachians – but also by race and social class.

Mountain Language

The mountain language of Appalachia has, like that of the Ozarks, long been the object of much amusement; some speakers, for instance, tend to use pronouns 'hit' (it) and 'we'uns.' As is the case with other dialects, certain features enforce regional identity, such as the archaic use of 'done' as in 'He done made me goof.' Other familiar examples include the 'a-' prefix, to stress an action ('She was a-tellin' a lie'), or the use of singular verbs with plural subjects ('There was many boats on the river'). There is overlap between mountain and other

Southern usages, such as the third-person 'don't' ('She don't know'). Spend any time in the mountains and you'll find yourself talkin' similar-like.

Black English

Most African Americans in the US descend from two linguistic 'families': the Sudanic of the West African coast and the Bantu in East and Central Africa. Although there are many different languages within these two groups, there remains a structural similarity. Today, some of these syntactical features have been retained in the folk dialect called Black English. (In 1996, the term 'ebonics,' a fusion of 'ebony' and 'phonics,' was coined to describe this dialect.)

Black English emerged in the 17th century in Africa as a common trading language with English ships, and it was transported to North America via Jamaica. The common colonial policy of dispersing homogeneous groups caused Africans to rely on this *lingua franca* to communicate with each other. Primary characteristics include the absence of the phoneme 'th,' and a link between subject and object. (For example,

'He is black' in standard English becomes 'He black' in Black English.) There is also no obligatory marker for the plural (one cent, two cent) nor for the possessive ('teacher's book' collapses to 'teacher-book').

The most conservative form of Black English spoken in the US today is Gullah, which occurs in the coastal islands of South Carolina and Georgia. It distinguishes itself from the rest of American English through sound, word form and syntax. Special pronunciations include 'pit' for 'put,' 'enti' for 'ain't it' and 'nyoung' for 'young.' Sometimes the African influence is felt in endings, as in 'wikiti' for 'wicked.' The little word 'da' indicates action underway, such as 'We da go' for 'We are going.' The word 'una' is the plural of you, and is also found in languages of the Caribbean and parts of central America.

Incidentally, the famous Uncle Remus stories of Br'er Rabbit by Joel Chandler Harris are told in the language of Midlands Georgia, not Gullah. For more on Gullah, see the boxed text 'Gullah Culture' in the South Carolina chapter.

Facts for the Visitor

HIGHLIGHTS

For starters, here's a subjective list of some of the places, sights and experiences that make the Southeast a cool destination.

Antebellum Homes – Fancy you're a Southern belle or gent behind the grand pillars of these architectural jewels in, say, Charleston or Savannah.

Appalachian Trail – Backpack with the bears and say hey to hillbillies as you watch the fog rise over the peaks.

Beach Moments – Solitude isn't hard to find on the pristine, powdery sands of the Carolina coast; try Hilton Head or the Outer Banks.

Blue Ridge Mountains – If for nothing else, go for the stunning waterfalls, log cabins with wood-burning fireplaces, unique plant species and unforgettable views along the Blue Ridge Parkway.

Getting Down in Athens – Try to catch the next REM or B52s before they're famous – this musical breeding ground is without equal.

Nature Refuges – Paddle through swamps, count the birds, breathe the mountain air and regenerate.

Public Gardens – Aim your camera at the seas of blossoms at Charleston's Magnolia Gardens, Callaway Gardens in Georgia and Asheville's Biltmore Estate.

Lowcountry Cooking – Seek out a classic 'crab shack' and crack 'em with the locals, or savor some Lowcountry Boil, a spicy shrimp stew.

The Shag – Do this naughty-dance-gone-nice on Myrtle Beach, tho' Wilmington's not bad for shagging either.

Shooting the Rapids – Go for it! You haven't lived if your raft hasn't turned over on the Nantahala or Chattooga Rivers.

Southern Hospitality – Stand on a corner, open your travel map and before long you'll get invited over for iced tea on the porch.

SUGGESTED ITINERARIES

The Southeast is *big* – it takes two or more days to cross the region top to bottom, or roughly side to side – so short-term visitors should pick a corner and stick with it. Most people coming by air fly into Atlanta and rent a car, although if you wanted to explore the Carolinas you could also land in Charlotte or Raleigh-Durham.

Short Stays

A three-day trip would best be spent in or around one of the cities, probably Atlanta, to cut down on your time on the road. If you wanted to get out of the peachy capital you could rent a car, zip down to Stone Mountain Park, see the historic homes of Marietta and be back in time for dinner. Or you could go rafting on the Chattahoochee River and spend a day hiking in the national forest. Forget about 'zipping' over to the coast – Savannah is over five hours away.

If you can get a cheap connection, perhaps with a change in Atlanta, for a long weekend consider Savannah, Charleston, Asheville or Wilmington, which all have regional airports. If you're driving or taking the bus or train to the region, however, you might choose to bypass the cities altogether; for many travelers the rugged natural beauty of the region is the main draw.

You could split a week between Atlanta and Hilton Head, SC, or Atlanta and the Great Smoky Mountains (one of the country's most popular national parks), a 4½-hour drive to the north.

Two-Week Trips

In two weeks you could trace a circle starting at Atlanta and taking in the South Carolina coast, sticking to the interstate highways for the longer stretches. You'd take the I-75 through Macon to Savannah, work your way up the coast through Hilton Head, Beaufort and Charleston, drive northeast on the I-26 to Columbia and back to Atlanta on the I-20, visiting Augusta on this last leg. This would be a pretty full tour, allowing one to two days in each town; three or four weeks might suit your pace better and give you more flexibility.

A similar plan would work from, say, Raleigh-Durham; think in terms of circles. From Raleigh you could drive to Wilmington, up the coast to Manteo via the ferries and shoestring highway on the Outer Banks, and back to your starting point, for an intense one-week trip or a more relaxing two weeks.

Mountain Tour

The Appalachian Trail starts in north Georgia, but for long stretches of mountainous terrain you'll need to head north, into western North Carolina. You'd have to be close by to make a weekend really worthwhile; if you've a week or more you can spend a few days camping in the Great Smoky Mountains National Park, catch an outdoor drama in Cherokee, spend a day or two poking around Asheville and the Biltmore House before wending your way up the Blue Ridge Parkway. Numerous detours are worthwhile off the Parkway, of course, depending on your time – perhaps a music festival in Boone, skiing or hiking in the High Country, a few hours at Grandfather Mountain and a look at the artisans' wares of the Penland crafts school.

Two weeks would allow you to drive the entire length of the Parkway, into Virginia, taking in stops at waterfalls, state parks and other natural attractions right and left. Outdoors enthusiasts could spend longer in the Smokies and add a rafting trip on the Nantahala or other rivers in the region, llama treks, or day hikes in the Pisgah National Forest. Don't underestimate the time you'll need to get around the region; many mountain roads are well-maintained but slow, and while you can get off the Parkway onto faster highways, the latter don't always run parallel.

Plantation Homes Tour

The Southeast is sprinkled with lovely antebellum homes, including the grand whitewashed frame houses with Doric columns that everyone associates with *Gone with the Wind*. South Carolina is the place to see them in spades, especially around Charleston. A two- to three-day tour might start in Hilton Head and move on to Charleston, whose proud plantation homes include Boone Hall Plantation – which is

promoted as the inspiration for Tara. There's another good one close by, the Hampton Plantation Historic Sight, about halfway between Charleston and Myrtle Beach, and you can spend the night in some of them if you've got the spare cash. You could also simply base yourself in Charleston.

In a similar vein, the city of Athens has put together an Antebellum Trail with fine examples of antebellum architecture in the area – see www.antebellumtrail.org. Beaufort, SC, and Savannah are excellent for this purpose, too.

Georgia Music Tour

Obviously this will depend on your listening tastes, but the best choice for any kind of cohesive music-interest tour will be Georgia, for a dose of homespun blues, R&B, soul or Southern rock. You could start a triangular tour in Atlanta, timing your arrival with one of the big music events (such as the Music Midtown or Atlanta Jazz Festivals), moving southeast to Macon to visit the Georgia Music Hall of Fame and then northeast to Athens. Both Athens and Macon have recording studios and oodles of sizzling clubs, and you could easily spend a week doing nothing but attending concerts – check the Web sites of the local entertainment mags, such as www.atlanta.creativeloafing.com, before you go. Who knows – you might even run into a living legend, such as James Brown or a member of REM.

PLANNING

Most destinations in Georgia and the Carolinas can be visited without a whole lot of planning beyond looking for bargain airfare. During special events (and you may want to plan your trip to coincide with a festival), planning is more important, as the most desirable hotel rooms may be booked up well in advance. Popular festivals in smaller towns, such as bluegrass festivals in the Appalachians, can exhaust the limited local motel room supply quickly; here, too, reservations would be a good idea. Cities on busy interstate highways – such as Atlanta, Charlotte and Charleston – rarely get booked up.

When to Go

Spring and fall are the most temperate and scenic seasons in the Southeast, though many visitors are drawn like lemmings to beaches in the summer and the ski areas in winter. The tourist season runs roughly from early June to Labor Day, and many summer attractions close in the off-season. Lodging prices follow the crowds, meaning that beach hotels drop their rates while skiers are crowding the mountain resorts.

The shoulder seasons (ie, April, May, September and October) generally draw smaller crowds and lower hotel rates, and the temperatures are more pleasant than summer levels. In the plains, heat and humidity can reach insufferable extremes in July and August, although sea breezes help to cool things off along the coast. Hurricanes spin in off the Atlantic far too often; listen to the radio when you're near the beach, and see 'Big Blows' in the Facts about Georgia & the Carolinas chapter for more advice.

October is the 'leaf-peeping' season in the Appalachians, and hotels within a large radius tend to book up quickly. The southern and coastal plains generally enjoy mild winters, with median temperatures in the upper 40s°F (around 8°C); in the mountains, snow can fall in November, and the mercury routinely dips below freezing in January.

What Kind of Trip

Rural destinations can most readily be visited (and sometimes can *only* be visited) by private car. Travelers without a car are limited to large cities if they journey by plane or train, or large and small cities if they go by bus.

Outdoor adventuring – say, camping, backpacking or bike touring – is good most of the temperate months, though rain is frequent. Fall is the most predictably dry for long stretches.

Maps

As for most of the US, you can find good state and city maps for Georgia and the Carolinas. In smaller towns, chambers of commerce usually distribute county and city maps, though they may be of limited use. Outdoor stores are a good source for backwoods maps.

The American Automobile Association (AAA) issues the most comprehensive and dependable highway maps, which are free with AAA membership (see the Useful Organizations section, later in this chapter) and available for a price to nonmembers. These range from national, regional and state maps to very detailed maps of cities, counties and even relatively small towns.

You can purchase topographic maps from the US Geological Survey (USGS; ☎ 703-648-4090), Map & Book Sales, Denver, CO 80225. A federal agency, the USGS publishes very detailed topographic maps of the entire country, at different scales up to 1:250,000. Maps at 1:62,500, or approximately 1 inch=1 mile, are ideal for backcountry hiking and backpacking. Specialty bookstores and outdoor equipment specialists may carry topographic maps.

What to Bring

Casual clothing is fine, though it's good to pack a more formal outfit for certain social, business or church functions. Summer travelers should expect their feet to swell in the heat; pack only shoes with room to expand. Sunscreen, insect repellent and a hat are also wise additions to your luggage.

For outdoor adventuring, only light hiking boots are ever necessary; an old pair of sneakers will often suit river floats or exploring developed trails. In winter, a light overcoat and gloves are comfortable.

TOURIST OFFICES

The following tourist offices distribute statewide guides, maps, events calendars and often specialized guides such as B&B listings, African-American heritage sites or Civil War sites – all free of charge.

Each state also operates welcome centers at its borders, usually at major interstate highways. Some of them can arrange lodging or distribute a cheap-looking booklet with discount coupons for local motels. City welcome centers are often in the heart of tourist districts and are a good source of maps and brochures.

Georgia
Department of Industry, Trade & Tourism (☎ 800-847-4842, 404-656-3590), 285 Peachtree Center Ave NE, Marquis Two Tower, Suite 1000, Atlanta, GA 30303-1230
Web site: www.georgia.org

North Carolina
North Carolina Division of Tourism (☎ 800-847-4862, 919-733-8372), Film and Sports Development, PO Box 25249, 301 N Wilmington St, Raleigh, NC 27601
Web site: www.visitnc.com

South Carolina
South Carolina Department of Parks, Recreation and Tourism (☎ 803-734-1700), 1205 Pendleton St, Suite 106, Colombia, SC 29201
Web site: www.travelsc.com

Tourist Offices Abroad
The US does not have a well-developed overseas tourist-office system. However, each of the Southeastern states have a few representatives abroad.

Georgia
Belgium: Jim Blair, Managing Director, European Office, GDITT (☎ 011-32-2-647-7825, fax 011-32-2-640-6843, jblair@georgia.org), Avenue Louise 475, Box 11, 1050 Brussel, Belgium

Brazil: Margareth Castro Vieira, Travel South USA Brasil, M&P Intermarketing Brasil (☎ 55/31 491-8114, fax 55/31 443-4617, marviei@ibm.net), Caixa Postal 4040-31250-970, Belo Horizonte, MG Brasil

Germany: Claudia Biermann, TravelMarketing Romberg (☎ 49 2102 71 11 86, fax 49 2102 21 177, kleinevorholtc@t-online.de), Wallstr 56, D-40878 Ratingen/Duesseldorf, Germany

UK: John Furze, USA-1 Ltd (☎ 011-44-121-445-4554, john_furze@compuserve.com), 31 Blackwell Rd, Barnt Green, Worcestershire B45 8BT, England

North Carolina
Brazil: M&P Intermarketing Brasil (☎ 55/31 491-8114, fax 55/31 443-4617, marviei@ibm.net), Caixa Postal 4040-31250-970, Belo Horizonte, MG Brasil

Canada: NC Dept of Commerce (☎ 416-348-9567, ncco@on.aibn.com), 480 University Ave, Suite 106, Toronto, Ontario

France: Express Conseil (☎ 011-33-1-4477-8806, marina@ecltd.com), 5 bis, rue du Louvre, 75001 Paris, France

Germany: NC Tourism, Mangum Management (☎ 89 23 66 21 0, fax 89 23 66 21 92, think@mangum.de), Herzogspitalstrasse 5, 80331 Munich, Germany

Tokyo: Travel South USA (☎ 011-81-3-3814-3140, dewey@kennedy.gol.com), Koa Bldg 3F, 2-38-14, Hakusan, Bunkyo-Ku, Tokyo

UK: David Pearson, Cellet Travel Services Ltd (☎ 0156-479-4999, david@celet.co.uk), Brook House, 47 High Street, Henley-in-Arden, Warwickshire, B95 5AA, England

South Carolina
Germany: European Representative, South Carolina Tourism Office (☎ 61 02 722 752, fax 61 02 722 409), Herderstrasse 6-8, 63263 Neu-Isenburg, Germany

UK: Kieron Health, Travel & Tourism Marketing (☎ 01462-458-028, fax 011-44-1462-455-391, 10047.657@compuserve.com), 33 Market Place, Hitchin, Hertfordshire SG5 1DY, England

You can also contact your local US diplomatic office for information from the US Travel & Tourism Administration; see the Embassies & Consulates section later in this chapter for a listing.

VISAS & DOCUMENTS
In addition to required documents (see below), visitors should bring their driver's license and any health insurance or travel insurance cards. You'll need a picture ID to show that you're at least 21 to buy alcohol or to gain admission to many bars or clubs (make sure your driver's license has a photo, or else get some other form of photo ID).

Passports & Visas
With the exception of Canadians, who need only proper proof of Canadian citizenship, all foreign visitors to the US must have a valid passport, and most are also required to have a US visa. It's a good idea to keep photocopies of these documents; in case of theft, they'll be a lot easier to replace.

Your passport should be valid for at least six months longer than your intended stay in the US. Documents of financial stability and/or guarantees from a US resident are sometimes required, particularly for those from Third World countries.

Most foreign visitors need to obtain a visa from a US consulate or embassy. In most countries the process can be done by mail or through a travel agent. Canadians and those entering under the Visa Waiver Pilot Program may enter the country without a US visa for stays of 90 days or less. Currently these countries are: Andorra, Argentina, Australia, Austria, Belgium, Brunei, Denmark, Finland, France, Germany, Iceland, Ireland, Italy, Japan, Liechtenstein, Luxembourg, Monaco, the Netherlands, New Zealand, Norway, San Marino, Singapore, Slovenia, Spain, Sweden, Switzerland, the UK and Uruguay. Under this program you must have a round-trip ticket that is nonrefundable in the US, and you will not be allowed to extend your stay beyond 90 days. Check with the US embassy in your home country for any other requirements (see the US Embassies Abroad section, below).

Visa applicants may be required to 'demonstrate binding obligations' that will ensure their return back home. Because of this requirement, those planning to travel through other countries before arriving in the US are generally better off applying for their US visa while they are still in their home country – rather than while on the road.

The most common visa is a Non-Immigrant Visitor's Visa: B1 for business purposes, B2 for tourism or visiting friends and relatives. A visitor visa is good for one or five years with multiple entries, and it specifically prohibits the visitor from taking paid employment in the US. The validity period depends on what country you're from. The length of time you'll be allowed to stay in the US is ultimately determined by US immigration authorities at the port of entry. If you're coming to the US to work or study, you will probably need a different type of visa, and the company or institution you're connected with should make the arrangements. Allow six months in advance for processing the application.

For further information on work visas, see Work, later in this chapter.

Entering the US If you have a non-US passport, you must complete an Arrival/Departure Record (form I-94) before you go to the immigration desk. This rather badly designed form is usually handed out on the plane, along with the customs declaration. Many people take more than one attempt to get it right, and some airlines suggest you start at the last question and work upwards.

HIV & Entering the USA

Everyone entering the USA who isn't a US citizen is subject to the authority of the Immigration & Naturalization Service (INS), regardless of whether that person has legal immigration documents. The INS can keep someone from entering or staying in the USA by excluding or deporting them. This is especially relevant to travelers with the HIV virus. Though being HIV-positive is not a ground for deportation, it is a 'ground of exclusion' and the INS can invoke it to refuse admission.

Although the INS doesn't test people for HIV at customs, it may try to exclude anyone who answers yes to this question on the non-immigrant visa application form: 'Have you ever been afflicted with a communicable disease of public health significance?' INS officials may also stop people if they seem sick, are carrying AIDS/HIV medicine or, sadly, if the officer happens to think the person looks gay, though sexual orientation is not legally a ground of exclusion.

It's imperative that visitors know and assert their rights. Immigrants and visitors should avoid contact with the INS until they discuss their rights and options with a trained immigration advocate. For legal immigration information and referrals to immigration advocates, contact the National Immigration Project of the National Lawyers Guild (☎ 617-227-9727), 14 Beacon St, Suite 506, Boston, MA 02108; or Immigrant HIV Assistance Project, Bar Association of San Francisco (☎ 415-267-0795), 685 Market St, Suite 700, San Francisco, CA 94105.

For question 12, 'Address While in the United States,' give the address of the location where you will spend the first night.

The staff of the Immigration & Naturalization Service (INS) can be less than welcoming. Their main concern is to exclude those who are likely to work illegally or overstay, so visitors will be asked about their plans, and perhaps about whether they have sufficient funds for their stay. If they give you the thumbs-up, a three-month entry is usually approved.

It's a good idea to be able to list an itinerary that will account for the period for which you ask to be admitted, and to be able to show you have $300 or $400 for every week of your intended stay. These days, a couple of major credit cards will go a long way toward establishing 'sufficient funds.' Don't make too much of having friends, relatives or business contacts in the US – the INS official may decide that this will make you more likely to overstay.

Visa Extensions & Reentry If you want, need or hope to stay in the US longer than the date stamped on your passport, go to the local INS office, call ☎ 800-755-0777, or look in the local white pages telephone directory under US Government *before* the stamped date to apply for an extension. A visit any time after that will usually lead to an unamusing conversation with an INS official who will assume you want to work illegally. If you find yourself in that situation, it's a good idea to bring a US citizen with you to vouch for your character. It's also a good idea to have some verification that you have enough money to support yourself.

Alternatively, cross the border into Mexico or Canada and apply for another period of entry when you come back. US officials don't usually collect the Departure Record cards from your passport when you leave at a land border, so they may not notice if you've overstayed by a couple of days. Returning to the US, you go through the same procedure as when you entered the US for the first time, so be ready with your proposed itinerary and evidence of sufficient funds. If you try this border hopping more than once, to get a third six-month period of entry, you may find the INS very strict. Generally it seems that they are reluctant to let you stay more than a year.

Travel Insurance

A travel insurance policy to cover theft, lost tickets and medical problems is a good idea, especially in the US, where some hospitals will refuse care without evidence of insurance. There is a wide variety of policies, and your travel agent will have recommendations. International student travel policies handled by STA Travel and other student travel organizations are usually a good value. Some policies offer lower and higher medical expenses options, and the higher one is chiefly for countries such as the US with extremely high medical costs. Within the US, Access America (☎ 800-729-6021, www.accessamerica.com) and Travel Guard (☎ 877-216-4885, www.travel-guard.com) are both quite reasonable and reliable insurers.

Some policies specifically exclude 'dangerous activities' such as scuba diving, motorcycling and even trekking. If these activities are on your agenda, avoid this sort of policy. Check the fine print.

You may prefer a policy that pays doctors or hospitals directly, rather than one where you pay first and make a claim later. If you have to claim later, keep *all* documentation. Some policies ask you to call back (reverse charges) to a center in your home country for an immediate assessment of your problem.

Check whether the policy covers ambulance fees or an emergency flight home. If you need two seats, somebody has to pay for it!

International Driving Permit

An International Driving Permit is a useful accessory for foreign visitors in the US. Local traffic police are more likely to accept it as valid identification than an unfamiliar document from another country. Your national automobile association can provide one for a small fee. In the US, you can obtain one for a $10 fee from travel agencies such as STA Travel or the AAA; bring along two passport photos and your home license. They're usually valid for one year.

Copies
Before you leave home, you should photocopy all important documents (passport data page and visa page, credit cards, travel insurance policy, air/bus/train tickets, driving license etc). Leave one copy with someone at home and keep another with you, separate from the originals.

It's also a good idea to store details of your vital travel documents in Lonely Planet's free online Travel Vault in case you lose the photocopies or can't be bothered with them. Your password-protected Travel Vault is accessible online anywhere in the world – create it at www.ekno.lonelyplanet.com.

EMBASSIES & CONSULATES
US Embassies Abroad
US diplomatic offices abroad include the following:

Australia
(☎ 2-6214-5600), 21 Moonah Place, Yarralumla ACT 2600
(☎ 2-9373-9200), Level 59 MLC Center 19-29 Martin Place, Sydney NSW 2000
(☎ 3-9526-5900), 553 St Kilda Rd, Melbourne, Victoria

Austria
(☎ 1-313-39), Boltzmanngasse 16, A-1090, Vienna

Belgium
(☎ 2-508-2111), Blvd du Regent 27, B-1000, Brussels

Canada
(☎ 613-238-5335), 490 Sussex Dr, Ottawa, Ontario K1N 1G8
(☎ 604-685-4311), 1095 W Pender St, Vancouver, BC V6E 2M6
(☎ 514-398-9695), 1155 rue St-Alexandre, Montreal, Quebec H2Z 1Z2

Denmark
(☎ 35-55-31-44), Dag Hammarskjölds Allé 24, 2100 Copenhagen

Finland
(☎ 9-171-931), Itäinen Puistotie 14B, 00140 Helsinki

France
(☎ 01 43 12 2222), 2 ave Gabriel, 75008 Paris

Germany
(☎ 30-8305-0), Neustädtische Kirchstr 4-5, 10117 Berlin
Clayallee 170, 14195 Berlin

Ireland
(☎ 1-668-8777), 42 Elgin Rd, Ballsbridge, Dublin 4

Israel
(☎ 3-519-7575), 71 Hayarkon St, Tel Aviv 63903

Italy
(☎ 6-46-741), Via Vittorio Veneto 119a-121, Rome 00187

Japan
(☎ 3-3224-5000), 1-10-5 Akasaka 1-Chome, Minato-ku, Tokyo 107-8420

Mexico
(☎ 5-209-9100), Paseo de la Reforma 305, Colonia Cuauhtemoc, 06500 Mexico City

Netherlands
(☎ 70-310-9209), Lange Voorhout 102, 2514 EJ The Hague
(☎ 20-575-5309), Museumplein 19, 1071 DJ Amsterdam

New Zealand
(☎ 644-472-2068), 29 Fitzherbert Terrace, Thorndon, Wellington

Norway
(☎ 22-44-85-50), Drammensveien 18, 0244 Oslo

Russia
(☎ 095-728-5000), Novinskiy Bulivar 19/23, Moscow 121099

South Africa
(☎ 12-342-1048), 877 Pretorius St, Box 9536, Pretoria 0001

Spain
(☎ 91-587-2200), Calle Serrano 75, 28006 Madrid

Sweden
(☎ 8-783-5300), Dag Hammarskjölds Väg 31, SE-115 89 Stockholm

Switzerland
(☎ 31-357-70 11), Jubiläumsstrasse 93, 3001 Berne

UK
(☎ 20-7499-9000), 24 Grosvenor Square, London W1A 1AE
(☎ 131-556-8315), 3 Regent Terrace, Edinburgh EH7 5BW
(☎ 28-9032-8239), Queens House, 14 Queen St, Belfast BT1 6EQ

Other US Embassies and Consulates can be found on the government's Web site http://usembassy.state.gov/.

Consulates in the USA

Embassies are in Washington, DC, though it's possible that your country maintains a diplomatic mission in Atlanta. See the list below, or check the yellow pages telephone directory under 'Consulates.'

Australia
(☎ 404-760-3400), Buckhead Plaza NW

Austria
(☎ 404-264-9858), 4200 Northside Pkwy NW

Belgium
(☎ 404-521-1079), 235 Peachtree St SW

Canada
(☎ 404-532-2000), 100 Colony Sq, 1175 Peachtree St NE

France
(☎ 404-522-4226), 285 Peachtree Center Ave NE

Germany
(☎ 404-659-4760), 285 Peachtree Center Ave NE

Italy
(☎ 404-303-0503), 755 Mount Vernon Hwy NE

Japan
(☎ 404-892-2700), 100 Colony Sq, 1175 Peachtree St NE

Mexico
(☎ 404-266-0777), 3220 Peachtree Dr NE

Netherlands
(☎ 770-937-7123), 2015 S Park Place SE

New Zealand
(☎ 404-888-5196), 75 14th St NE

Norway
(☎ 404-239-0885), 3715 Northside Pkwy NW

UK
(☎ 404-524-5856), 245 Peachtree Center Ave NE

The Web site www.polisci.com/web/embassies.htm provides a fairly up-to-date listing of links to foreign embassies in the US.

Your Own Embassy

It's important to realize what your own embassy – the embassy of the country of which you are a citizen – can and can't do to help you if you get into trouble. Generally speaking, it won't be much help in emergencies if the trouble you're in is remotely your own fault. Remember that you are bound by the laws of the country you are in. Your embassy will not be sympathetic if you

end up in jail after committing a crime locally, even if such actions are legal in your own country.

In genuine emergencies, you might get some assistance, but only if other channels have been exhausted. If you need to get home urgently, a free ticket home is exceedingly unlikely – the embassy would expect you to have insurance. If all your money and documents are stolen, it might assist you with getting a new passport, but a loan for onward travel is out of the question.

Some embassies used to keep letters for travelers or have a small reading room with home newspapers, but these days most of the mail-holding services have been stopped and even newspapers tend to be out of date.

CUSTOMS

US Customs allows each person older than the age of 21 to bring one liter of liquor and 200 cigarettes duty free into the US. US citizens are allowed to import, duty free, $400 worth of gifts from abroad, while non-US citizens are allowed to bring in $100 worth. Forget bringing fresh meats, fruits, vegetables or plants – most of them can (and will) be confiscated.

US law permits you to bring in, or take out, as much as US$10,000 in US or foreign currency, traveler's checks or letters of credit without formality. Larger amounts of any or all of the above – there are no limits – must be declared to customs.

MONEY

The US dollar is divided into 100 cents (¢). Coins come in denominations of 1¢ (penny), 5¢ (nickel), 10¢ (dime), 25¢ (quarter) and 50¢ (the rare half-dollar). There are also $1 coins that the government has tried to bring into circulation, the silver-colored Susan B Anthony coin and the new gold-colored Sacajawea coin, which look irritatingly similar to quarters. Keep a stash of quarters handy for vending machines and parking meters. Notes, commonly called bills, come in $1, $2, $5, $10, $20, $50 and $100 denominations – $2 bills are rare, but perfectly legal.

Exchanging Money

At press time, exchange rates were:

country	unit		US dollars
Australia	A$1	=	$0.51
Canada	C$1	=	$0.65
Euro	€1	=	$0.85
Hong Kong	HK$10	=	$1.28
Japan	¥100	=	$0.80
New Zealand	NZ$1	=	$0.41
United Kingdom	UK£1	=	$1.40

Most banks in major cities will exchange cash or traveler's checks in major foreign currencies, though banks in smaller cities and outlying areas don't do so very often, and it may take them some time. Although you'll get a better rate at a bank, Thomas Cook, American Express and exchange windows in airports also offer exchange.

Cash & Traveler's Checks

Though carrying cash is more risky, it's still a good idea to travel with some for the convenience; it's useful to help pay for tips, and some smaller, more remote places might not accept credit cards or traveler's checks.

Traveler's checks offer greater protection from theft or loss and in many places can be used as cash. American Express and Thomas Cook are widely accepted and have efficient replacement policies.

Keeping a record of the check numbers and the checks you have used is vital when it comes to replacing lost checks. Save this record separate from the checks themselves.

You'll save yourself trouble and expense if you buy traveler's checks in US dollars. The savings you *might* make on exchange rates by carrying traveler's checks in a foreign currency don't make up for the hassle of exchanging them at banks and other facilities. Restaurants, hotels and most stores accept US-dollar traveler's checks as if they were cash, so if you're carrying traveler's checks in US dollars, the odds are you'll rarely have to use a bank or pay an exchange fee.

Take most of the checks in large denominations. It's only toward the end of a stay that you may want to change a small denomination check to make sure you aren't left with too much local currency.

ATMs

Automated teller machines (ATMs) are a convenient way of obtaining cash from a bank account within the US or abroad. Most banks charge a $1 to $4 fee for using their ATM with a card not issued by them – it's federal law that you must be warned in advance of how much your account will be charged.

However, their convenience can't be beat: Small-town banks in the middle of nowhere and shopping centers have ATMs, and they often operate 24 hours a day. There are various ATM networks (Exchange, Accel, Plus and Cirrus are widespread throughout the US), and most banks are affiliated with several.

Using a credit, debit or charge card, you can withdraw money from an ATM normally with a 2% fee ($2 minimum) plus the non-issuing bank service charge. Check with your bank or credit card company for exact information.

Credit & Debit Cards

Major credit cards are accepted at hotels, restaurants, gas stations, shops and car-rental agencies throughout the US. In fact, without one you'll find it hard to perform certain transactions, such as renting a car or purchasing tickets to performances.

Even if you prefer to rely on traveler's checks and ATMs, it's a good idea to carry a credit card for emergencies. If you're planning to rely primarily upon credit cards, it would be wise to have a Visa or MasterCard in your deck, since other cards aren't as widely accepted.

Carry copies of your credit card numbers separately from the cards. If you lose your credit cards or they get stolen, contact the company immediately. Following are toll-free numbers for the main credit card companies.

Visa	☎ 800-336-8472
MasterCard	☎ 800-826-2181
	☎ 800-307-7309
American Express	☎ 800-528-4800
Discover	☎ 800-347-2683
Diners Club	☎ 800-234-6377

International Transfers You can instruct your bank back home to send you a draft. Specify the city, bank and branch to which you want your money directed, or ask your home bank to tell you where a suitable one is, and make sure you get the details right. The procedure is easier if you've authorized someone back home to access your account.

Money sent by telegraphic transfer should reach you within a week; by mail allow at least two weeks. When it arrives it will most likely be converted into local currency – you can take it as cash or buy traveler's checks.

You can also transfer money by American Express, Thomas Cook or Western Union, though the latter has fewer international offices.

Security

Carry your money (and only the money you'll need for that day) somewhere inside your clothing (in a money belt, a bra or socks) rather than in a handbag or an outside pocket. Put the money in several places. Most hotels and hostels provide safekeeping, so you can leave your money and other valuables with them. Hide or don't wear any valuable jewelry. A safety pin or key ring to hold the zipper tags of a daypack together can help deter theft.

Costs

Costs for accommodations vary widely, depending on the season, what city or town you are staying in, whether or not festivals are happening and the type of accommodations you choose. Generally, rates are highest in the larger cities, with Atlanta, Savannah, Charleston and Charlotte at the top end of the spectrum. The cheapest motel rates will usually be in the $30 to $40 range, but prices tend to skyrocket during festivals and other special events. For B&Bs, unique cabins and luxury hotels, expect to pay $75 to $130 or even more. Rustic camping is inexpensive – about $8 or so per night – but only costlier sites have amenities such as hot showers.

Food, especially Southern-style cuisine, is fairly reasonable. The occasional splurge at a first-rate restaurant will cost anywhere between $25 and $50 per person depending on where you are, but good restaurant meals can be found for $10 – or even half that for lunch. Self-catering at markets may get you by even more cheaply.

Bargaining isn't a generally accepted practice, but you can arouse competitive instincts to finagle a deal. For example, at hotels in the off-season, casually mentioning a rival's rate may prompt a manager to lower the quoted rate. Discount coupons are widely available – check for circulars in Sunday papers and at supermarkets, tourist offices, chambers of commerce and welcome centers.

Urban public transportation is relatively cheap, and buses or streetcars cost from 80¢ to $1.50, depending on distance and the system. Owning or renting a car is much cheaper than in other parts of the world, and in some areas a car is the only way of getting around. Rentals can be inexpensive in large cities, and gasoline costs a fraction of what it does in Europe and most of the rest of the world. Promotional deals are published every Sunday in the travel sections of US papers, and some deals are available only on rental agency Web sites. Shop carefully. For more information on buying and renting a car, see the Getting Around chapter.

Taxes & Refunds

Almost everything you pay for in the US is taxed. Occasionally, the tax is included in the advertised price (eg, plane tickets, gas, drinks in a bar and entrance tickets for museums or theaters). Restaurant meals and drinks, accommodations and most other purchases are taxed, and this is added on top of the advertised cost. Unless otherwise stated, the prices given in this book don't reflect local taxes. International visitors can apply for a sales tax refund on forms available at airports or stores displaying a tax-free sign. When inquiring about hotel or motel rates, be sure to ask about tax amounts, which can exceed 10%.

POST & COMMUNICATIONS
Postal Rates
Postage rates increase every few years. At press time, rates for 1st-class mail within the USA were 34¢ for letters up to 1oz (23¢ for each additional ounce) and 23¢ for postcards.

International airmail rates (except to Canada and Mexico) are 80¢ for a 1oz letter and 70¢ for postcards. Airmail to Canada and Mexico costs 60¢ for a 1oz letter, 85¢ for a 2oz letter, and 50¢ for a postcard. Aerogrammes are 70¢.

The cost for parcels airmailed anywhere within the USA is $3.50 for up to 1lb and $3.95 for up to 2lb; the cost increases per pound up to $7.55 for 5lb. For heavier items, rates differ according to the distance mailed. Books, periodicals, and computer disks can be sent by a cheaper 4th-class rate.

For 24-hour postal information, call ☎ 800-275-8777 or check www.usps.com. These services give zip (postal) codes for any given address, the rules about parcel sizes and the location and phone number of any post office.

Sending Mail
If you have the correct postage, you can drop your mail into any blue mailbox. However, to send a package 16oz (1lb) or larger, you must bring it to a post office. The address of each town's main post office is given in the regional chapters. In addition, larger towns have branch post offices and post office centers in some supermarkets and drug stores.

Usually, post offices open 8 am to 5 pm weekdays and 8 am to 3 pm on Saturday, but it all depends on the branch.

Receiving Mail
You can have mail sent to you care of General Delivery at any post office that has its own zip (postal) code. These addresses are provided in the text. Mail is usually held for 10 days before it's returned to sender; you might request your correspondents to write 'hold for arrival' on their letters. Mail should be addressed like this:

Name
c/o General Delivery
3900 Crown Rd
Atlanta, GA 30321
USA

You can also rent a post office box at US post offices or at businesses such as Mail Boxes Etc if you're staying a month or more. Alternatively, have mail sent to the local representative of American Express or Thomas Cook, which provide mail service for their customers.

Telephone
All phone numbers within the US consist of a three-digit area code followed by a seven-digit local number. If you are calling locally, just dial the seven-digit number. If you are calling long distance, dial 1 + the three-digit area code + the seven-digit number. If you're calling from abroad, note that the international country code for the US is 1.

For local directory assistance, dial ☎ 411. For directory assistance outside your area code, dial 1 + the three-digit area code of the place you want to call + 555-1212. For example, to obtain directory assistance for Atlanta, dial ☎ 1-404-555-1212.

A local and national area code map is in the telephone directory. Be aware that metropolitan areas are being divided into multiple new area codes. These changes are not reflected in older phone books. When in doubt, ask the operator.

The 800, 888, and 877 area codes are designated for toll-free numbers within the US and sometimes Canada. Calling areas can be restricted to outside the local area or within the US. For toll-free directory assistance, call ☎ 800-555-1212.

The 900 prefix is designated for calls for which the caller pays a premium rate – chat lines, horoscopes, jokes etc.

Local calls usually cost 35¢ at pay phones. Long-distance rates vary depending on the destination and which telephone company you use – call the operator for rate information. Don't ask the operator to put your call through, however, because operator-assisted calls are much more expensive than direct-dial calls. Generally, nights (11 pm to 8 am), all day Saturday and from 8 am to 5 pm Sunday are the cheapest times to call. Daytime calls (8 am to 5 pm, Monday to Friday) are full-price within the USA.

In an attempt to make their phone numbers snappy and memorable, many businesses use words, which translate to numbers on the phone keypad. To translate: 1 is unassigned, 2 – ABC, 3 – DEF, 4 – GHI, 5 – JKL, 6 – MNO, 7 – PRS, 8 – TUV, 9 – WXY. (Sorry, no Qs or Zs.)

International Calls To make a direct international call, dial 011, then the country code (found in the front of most phone directories), followed by the area code and the phone number. You may need to wait as long as 45 seconds for the ringing to start. International rates vary depending on the time of day and the destination. Call the operator (☎ 0) for rates. The first minute is always more expensive than extra minutes.

Hotel & Pay Phones Many hotels (especially the more expensive ones) add a service charge of 50¢ to $1 for each local call made from a room phone, and they also have hefty surcharges for long-distance calls. (Motel 6 doesn't even allow long-distance calls unless you have an AT&T account.) Public pay phones, which can be found in most lobbies, are always cheaper. You can pump change into, use a credit or phone card with, or make collect calls from pay phones.

eKno Communication Services There's a wide range of local and international phonecards. Lonely Planet's eKno Communication Card is aimed specifically at independent travelers and provides budget international calls, a range of messaging services, free email and travel information – but for local calls, you're usually better off with a local card. You can join online at www.ekno.lonelyplanet.com or by phone from the US by dialing ☎ 800-707-0031. To use eKno from the US once you have joined, dial ☎ 800-706-1333.

Check the eKno Web site for joining and access numbers from other countries and updates on super budget local access numbers and new features.

Other phonecards are widely available in airports, US post offices, Western Union and other sources.

Fax
You can typically find fax machines at shipping companies such as Mail Boxes Etc, photocopy services and hotel business service centers, but be prepared to pay high prices (more than $1 a page).

Email & Internet Access
In recent years, it's become very easy to get online. Campus or public libraries may provide connections for free; other options are an Internet cafe, a copy center or a hotel that caters to business travelers. Through Yahoo!, Hotmail or other web-based accounts you can set up a free email address that you can log into from any Web-connected computer anywhere in the world.

INTERNET RESOURCES
The World Wide Web is a rich resource for travelers. You can research your trip, hunt down bargain airfares, book hotels, check on weather conditions and chat with locals and other travelers about the best places to visit (or avoid!).

There's no better place to start your Web explorations than the Lonely Planet Web site (www.lonelyplanet.com). Here you'll find succinct summaries on traveling to most places on earth, postcards from other travelers, and the Thorn Tree bulletin board, where you can ask questions before you go or dispense advice when you get back. You can also find travel news and updates for many of our most popular guidebooks, and the subWWWay section links you to the most useful travel resources elsewhere on the Web.

BOOKS
Beyond the wealth of evocative literature that you might wish to read before a trip to the Southeast (see the Literature section in

the Facts about Georgia & the Carolinas chapter), nonfiction books can also enhance your visit tremendously. Visitors should note, however, that outside of major cities and university towns there are few high-quality bookstores. Big chains such as Barnes & Noble and Borders are found in major cities throughout the region.

Most books are published in different editions by different publishers in different countries. As a result, a book might be a hardcover rarity in one country but readily available in paperback in another. Fortunately, bookstores and libraries can search by title or author, so your local bookstore or library is the best placed to advise you on the availability of the following recommendations.

Lonely Planet

Lonely Planet's *Louisiana & the Deep South* is ideal for visitors planning to explore the region; in addition to Louisiana, the guide covers Mississippi, Alabama and Tennessee. If you're going north, check out *Virginia & the Capital Region*. The *New Orleans* city guide is essential for visitors planning on spending a lot of time in the Crescent City, and if sightseeing is just something you do to kill time between meals, then check out Lonely Planet's *World Food: New Orleans*. *Hiking in the USA* covers hiking trails and gateway cities in North Carolina's Great Smoky Mountains and southern Appalachia.

Guidebooks

The *Smithsonian Guide to Historic America* for the Carolinas and Georgia includes an exhaustive review of regional historic sites and lush color photographs.

The *Jazz & Blues Lover's Guide to the US,* by Christiane Bird, covers music sights and hundreds of clubs in the entire country. (Its 1994 listing is in need of an update, but its chapters dealing with the Southeast are very informative.)

The Sierra Club's *Adventuring Along the Southeast Coast* is a useful guide to the Lowcountry, beaches and barrier islands of the region. It describes hikes, backpacking and canoe/kayak trips, and includes bike paths up and down the coast.

Members of the American Automobile Association may want to carry AAA's free regional *TourBook* of the Carolinas and Georgia, which contains listings for sights and most chain motels/hotels in the region.

History & Culture

Charles Hudson's *The Southeastern Indians* is considered the seminal work on the area's archaeological and Native American history. The heritage of western North Carolina's Cherokee Indians is explored in a wide range of adult and children's books on history, folklore and spirituality distributed by the Eastern Band of the Cherokee; write for their catalog (PO Box 256, Cherokee, NC 28719). *Trail of Tears: The Rise & Fall of the Cherokee Nation,* by John Ehle, is a popular history of the tragedy that reads like a novel.

Of the tomes written on the Civil War, one considered a major sourcebook is the three-volume *The Civil War: A Narrative,* written over a 20-year period by Mississippi historian Shelby Foote (whose wry and poignant observations appeared throughout the PBS *Civil War* TV series). The *Civil War Almanac,* edited by John S Bowman and introduced by noted historian Henry Steele Commager, is an authoritative single-volume book with a detailed chronology and biographies of key players.

Stetson Kennedy's 1959 *Jim Crow Guide: The Way It Was* is an eye-opening survey of the Jim Crow South. The civil rights era from 1954 to 1965 is chronicled in Juan William's *Eyes on the Prize* (also a PBS documentary series by the same name). *Free at Last,* by Margaret Edds, covers the behind-the-scenes struggles for civil rights in several Southern cities. *Baptized in Blood,* by Charles Reagan Wilson, helps the visitor understand why, for many Southerners, the War between the States isn't over.

Tony Horowitz' *Confederates in the Attic: Dispatches from the Unfinished Civil War* is a quirky travelogue that explores the Civil War reenactment phenomenon. The author covers rituals such as 'bloating' – waving the

Confederate flag as a symbol of heritage, or of hate and racial division.

The gargantuan *Encyclopedia of Southern Culture,* edited by Charles Reagan Wilson and William Ferris, covers everything from agriculture to 'women's life,' with excellent sections on literature and music.

A Walk in the Woods is a witty account of adventures on the Appalachian Trail by acclaimed travel writer Bill Bryson.

Cookbooks

Readers who want to delve into the region's culinary delights might pick up Kathryn Tucker's *Southern Cooking to Remember,* which includes Lowcountry seafood, Appalachian stack cakes and wild duck from Georgia marshlands. The *Southeastern Wildlife Cookbook* from University of South Carolina Press is a collection of recipes for fish and game, as well as savory oddities from the wild. A literary taste of the mountains is revealed in *The Foxfire Book of Appalachian Cookery,* published by UNC in Chapel Hill. *The Backcountry Housewife: A Study of 18th-Century Foods* by Kay Moss and Kathryn Hoffman has historical anecdotes and recipes from unpublished archives. For the key to local comfort foods, try the *Charleston Junior League Cookbook.*

FILMS

The Southeast's enormously varied landscape – mountains, plantation homes, beaches, swamps – makes for excellent film locations. With a little tweaking, a Carolina harbor can be made to look like New England, if you're careful with the shrubbery.

Many films have been made from books listed in the Literature section of the Facts about Georgia & the Carolinas chapter. Apart from this, the PBS-produced *Civil War* series, available on home video, sheds a drawn-out light on the region's history. *Eyes on the Prize* is another good PBS documentary that details civil rights history; part II focuses on the final years of Martin Luther King's life.

Deliverance, based on the James Dickey novel, tells how four Atlanta businessmen get more than they bargained for on the Chattooga River in SC – not the best thing to watch before shooting the rapids. The popular 1991 movie *Fried Green Tomatoes,* a nostalgic tragi-comedy starring Kathy Bates, was filmed in Juliette, a small town north of Macon, Georgia (although the film was set in Alabama). Tourists troop to the Whistle Stop Café where the unripe veggies are still served (usually as a small garnish, not a main course). Perhaps the greatest epic film of all time was *Gone With the Wind,* effectively a Civil War soap opera that made Rhett Butler and Scarlett O'Hara the epitome of feisty Southern romance.

North Carolina has a thriving film industry, although some of the action has shifted to cheaper Canadian sets in recent years. *Bull Durham* is a smart flick about minor-league baseball, with veteran Kevin Costner and Susan Sarandon helping out an undisciplined but talented pitcher (Tim Robbins). *The Last of the Mohicans* is a kinetic update of the James Fenimoore Cooper classic, filmed partly around Chimney Rock, with Daniel Day-Lewis as a wiry Hawkeye. An oft-rented backdrop is the Biltmore House near Asheville, where actor Peter Sellers played an unwittingly brilliant Chauncy Gardener in *Being There.* Hundreds of movies have been made in and around Wilmington since Hollywood mogul Dino de Laurentis filmed *Firestarter* from the Stephen King novel in 1984. Much of David Lynch's cult thriller *Blue Velvet,* with Isabella Rosellini in tears and Dennis Hopper in an oxygen mask, was shot in downtown Wilmington.

Shot in South Carolina, *The Patriot* features a pacifistic Mel Gibson in the story of Revolutionary War heroes Francis 'Swamp Fox' Marion and Andrew Pickens; the sumptuous footage of swamps, oceans and forests is pure eye candy. Idyllic Beaufort, SC, is another popular location for movies; *The Big Chill, The Great Santini, Forrest Gump* and *Forces of Nature* are just a few of the titles filmed in the town. Almost all of Pat Conroy's novels have been made into movies. The most worthwhile is *Conrack,* with a young Jon Voight trying to bring commonsense education to a black school on the South Carolina coast.

NEWSPAPERS & MAGAZINES

The *Atlanta Constitution* and the *Charlotte Observer* are the closest you'll come to pan-regional newspapers. Dailies in Savannah, Raleigh, Charleston and smaller towns are best on state and local news. Newspapers with an international focus such as the *New York Times*, the *Financial Times* and the *Wall Street Journal,* or the weekly *Economist,* can be found in major cities only, and often not readily.

RADIO & TV

Travelers can tune into hundreds of radio stations. Most have a range of less than 100 miles, and around major cities scores of stations crowd the airwaves with a wide variety of music and entertainment. You can hear wonderful music programs – blue-grass, country, jazz and gritty, homegrown R&B – on radio stations throughout the region, though Top 40 pop tunes tend to predominate. In parts of the 'Bible belt' you'll pick up the local Christian broad-casting stations featuring 'Christian music,' news and commentary. Local public broad-casting system (PBS) radio stations usually air nationally syndicated news and feature programs, such as the daily news program 'All Things Considered' or the weekly variety program 'A Prairie Home Companion' by Garrison Keillor.

Almost all hotel rooms have TVs (most with cable), although many B&Bs do not. Television sets in all but the smallest towns will usually receive the major American TV networks (ABC, CBS, NBC and FOX) and PBS. Cable TV guarantees clear reception and will include CNN and TBS – two cable channels originating out of Atlanta.

PHOTOGRAPHY & VIDEO

Photographers will want to have cameras and bags hand-checked when passing through airport security – waving a trans-parent plastic bag containing your film rolls usually helps. Most X-ray scanners don't

harm film these days, but you never know. Summertime travelers need to be aware that extreme heat can damage film.

For purchasing film, only stores in major cities will offer a wide selection of specialty film (black & white, professional slide etc); check expiration dates on film. Inexpensive, quick film processing is widely available, but visitors from Europe will find it's cheaper to buy film at home before coming. Tips for the best photography and videography: Avoid shooting midday, when light and shadows are too contrasting and the sun's glare causes washed-out images. The 'golden hours' around dawn and dusk offer the most dramatic lighting. Always protect camera lenses with a haze or ultraviolet (UV) filter.

Overseas visitors considering buying videotapes should note that the US uses the national television system committee (NTSC) color TV standard, which is incom-patible with other standards, such as phase alternative line (PAL).

TIME

The region covered in this guide falls under Eastern Standard Time, five hours behind Greenwich Mean Time (ie, when it's noon in Atlanta, it's 5 pm in London). All South-eastern states observe daylight saving time (comparable to British Summer Time).

ELECTRICITY

Electric current is 110-120 volts, 60-cycle. Appliances built to take 220-240 volt, 50-cycle current (as in Europe and Asia) will need a converter (transformer) and a US-style plug adapter with two flat pins. Some gadgets such as hair dryers will run more slowly.

WEIGHTS & MEASURES

The US uses a modified version of the tra-ditional imperial measuring system of feet, yards, miles, ounces, pounds and gallons. Three feet equal 1 yard (0.914 meters); 1760 yards or 5280 feet equal 1 mile. Dry weights are in ounces (oz), pounds (lbs) and tons (16 oz equal 1 lb; 2000 lbs equal 1 ton), but liquid measures differ from dry measures.

One pint equals 16 fluid ounces; 2 pints equal 1 quart, a common measure for liquids such as milk, which is also sold in half gallons (2 quarts) and gallons (4 quarts). Gasoline is dispensed by the US gallon, which is about 20% less than the imperial gallon. See the inside back cover of this book for a conversion chart.

LAUNDRY

Pricier hotels and motels usually provide laundry service, and many budget motels provide coin-operated washers and dryers. You can also find either self-service laundries (called 'washaterias' or 'washerettes') or wash-and-fold service in most towns. Laundries usually have machines to dispense change and to sell single-serving supplies of detergent. A wash typically costs around $1, a dry another $1. You can find laundry and dry-cleaning services under 'Laundries' or 'Cleaners' in the yellow pages telephone directory.

TOILETS

You will find relatively clean public toilets (usually marked 'restrooms') in airports, attractions, shopping malls and visitor information centers. Restrooms in small restaurants and bars, bus and train stations, highway rest areas or fuel stations may or may not be as well maintained, but are generally usable (they commonly run low on toilet tissue, soap and towels). The quality of public facilities in parks and off the street, if available, may vary considerably.

HEALTH

For most foreign visitors no immunizations are required for entry, though cholera and yellow fever vaccinations may be required of travelers from areas with a history of those diseases. There are no unexpected health dangers, and excellent medical attention is readily available. The only real health concern is that a collision with the medical system can cause severe injuries to your financial state.

Hospitals and medical centers, walk-in clinics and referral services are easily found throughout the region.

In a serious emergency, call ☎ 911 for an ambulance to take you to the nearest hospital's emergency room. But note that charges for this service in the US are incredibly high.

Predeparture Preparations

Make sure you're healthy before you start traveling. If you are embarking on a long trip, make sure your teeth are in good shape. If you wear glasses, take a spare pair and your prescription. You can get new spectacles made up quickly and competently for well under $100, depending on the prescription and frame you choose. If you require a particular medication, take an adequate supply and bring a prescription in case you lose it.

Health Insurance Make sure that you have adequate health insurance coverage. See Travel Insurance under Visas & Documents earlier in this chapter for details.

Travel & Climate-Related Problems

Motion Sickness Eating lightly before and during a trip will reduce the chances of motion sickness. If you are prone to motion sickness, try to find a place that minimizes disturbance – for example, near the wing on aircraft or near the center on buses. Fresh air usually helps. Commercial anti-motion sickness preparations, which can cause drowsiness, have to be taken before the trip commences; once you feel sick, it's too late. Ginger, a natural preventative, is available in capsule form from health food stores.

Jet Lag Jet lag is experienced when a person travels by air across more than three time zones (each time zone represents a one-hour time difference). It occurs because many of the functions of the human body are regulated by internal 24-hour cycles called circadian rhythms. When we travel long distances rapidly, our bodies take time to adjust to the 'new time' of our destination, and we may experience fatigue, disorientation, insomnia, anxiety, impaired concentration and loss of appetite. These effects will usually be gone within three days of arrival, but there are ways of minimizing the impact of jet lag:

- Rest for a couple of days prior to departure; try to avoid late nights and last-minute dashes for traveler's checks or passports.
- Try to select flight schedules that minimize sleep deprivation; arriving in the early evening means you can go to sleep soon after you arrive. For very long flights, try to organize a stopover.
- Avoid excessive eating (which bloats the stomach) and alcohol (which causes dehydration) during the flight. Instead, drink plenty of noncarbonated, nonalcoholic drinks such as fruit juice or water.
- Make yourself comfortable during the flight by wearing loose-fitting clothes and perhaps bringing an eye mask and earplugs to help you sleep.

Heat Exhaustion Without heeding certain precautions, visitors not acclimated to a subtropical climate may experience discomfort from extreme summertime heat, humidity and overexposure to the sun. Avoid exposure to the midday sun and heat – have a plan to be indoors – and confine strenuous activity to early morning and late afternoon. Wear sunscreen and a hat, and even carry an umbrella to shield more sensitive types from the sun. Rent a car with air-conditioning and light-colored interiors. Drinking lots of water is also good.

Note also that many establishments overcompensate for the heat by overchilling their interiors – brace yourself for the bodily shock of alternating between the 100°F exterior and 70°F interiors. Carry a cover-up.

Heatstroke This serious, occasionally fatal, condition can occur if the body's heat-regulating mechanism breaks down and the body temperature rises to dangerous levels. Long, continuous periods of exposure to high temperatures and insufficient fluids can leave you vulnerable to heatstroke.

The symptoms are feeling unwell, not sweating very much (or at all) and a high body temperature (102°F to 106°F or 39°C to 41°C). Where sweating has ceased the

Medical Kit Check List

The following is a list of items you should consider including in your medical kit – consult your pharmacist for brands available in your country.

- ☐ **Aspirin or paracetamol** (acetaminophen in the USA) – for pain or fever

- ☐ **Antihistamine** – for allergies, (eg, hay fever); to ease the itch from insect bites or stings; and to prevent motion sickness

- ☐ **Cold and flu tablets, throat lozenges and nasal decongestant**

- ☐ **Multivitamins** – consider for long trips, when dietary vitamin intake may not be adequate

- ☐ **Antibiotics** – consider including these if you're traveling well off the beaten track; see your doctor, as they must be prescribed, and carry the prescription with you

- ☐ **Loperamide or diphenoxylate** –'blockers' for diarrhea

- ☐ **Prochlorperazine or metaclopramide** – for nausea and vomiting

- ☐ **Rehydration mixture** – to prevent dehydration, which may occur, for example, during bouts of diarrhea; particularly important when traveling with children

- ☐ **Insect repellent, sunscreen, lip balm and eye drops**

- ☐ **Calamine lotion, sting relief spray or aloe vera** – to ease irritation from sunburn and insect bites or stings

- ☐ **Antifungal cream or powder** – for fungal skin infections and thrush

- ☐ **Antiseptic (such as povidone-iodine)** – for cuts and grazes

- ☐ **Bandages, Band-Aids (plasters) and other wound dressings**

- ☐ **Water purification tablets or iodine**

- ☐ **Scissors, tweezers and a thermometer** – note that mercury thermometers are prohibited by airlines skin becomes flushed and red. Severe, throbbing headaches and lack of coordination will also occur, and the sufferer may be confused or aggressive. Eventually the victim will become delirious or convulse. Hospitalization is essential, but in the interim get victims out of the sun, remove their clothing, cover them with a wet sheet or towel and then fan continually. Give fluids if they are conscious.

Fungal Infections Occurring with greater frequency in hot weather, fungal infections are most likely to occur on the scalp, between the toes or fingers (athlete's foot), in the groin (jock itch or crotch rot) and on the body (ringworm). You get ringworm (which is a fungal infection, not a worm) from infected animals or by walking on damp areas, such as shower floors.

To prevent fungal infections, wear loose, comfortable clothes, avoid artificial fibers, wash frequently and dry carefully. If you do get an infection, wash the infected area daily with a disinfectant or medicated soap and water, and rinse and dry well. Apply an antifungal powder and try to expose the infected area to air or sunlight as much as possible. Change underwear and towels frequently and wash them often in hot water.

Infectious Diseases

Diarrhea A change of water, food or climate can all cause 'the runs.' Diarrhea caused by contaminated food or water is more serious, but it's unlikely in the US. Despite all your precautions, you may still have a mild bout of traveler's diarrhea from exotic food or drink. Dehydration is the main danger with any diarrhea, particularly for children, who can become dehydrated quite quickly. Fluid replacement remains the mainstay of management. Weak black tea with a little sugar, soda water or soft drinks diluted 50% with water are all good. With severe diarrhea, a rehydrating solution is necessary to replace minerals and salts. These solutions, such as Pedialyte, are available at pharmacies.

Hepatitis Hepatitis is a general term for inflammation of the liver. There are many causes of this condition: Poor sanitation, contact with infected blood products, drugs, alcohol and contact with an infected person are but a few. The symptoms are fever, chills, headache, fatigue and a feeling of weakness and aches and pains, followed by loss of appetite, nausea, vomiting, abdominal pain, dark urine, light-colored feces and jaundiced skin. The whites of the eyes may also turn yellow.

You should seek medical advice, but there is not much you can do apart from resting, drinking lots of fluids, eating lightly and avoiding fatty foods. People who have had hepatitis should avoid alcohol for some time after the illness, as the liver needs time to recover. Viral hepatitis is an infection of the liver, which can have several unpleasant symptoms, or no symptoms at all, with the infected person not knowing that they have the disease.

Tetanus Tetanus is difficult to treat but is preventable with immunization. Tetanus occurs when a wound becomes infected by a germ that lives in the feces of animals or people, so clean all cuts, punctures or animal bites.

HIV/AIDS Exposure to blood, blood products or bodily fluids may put an individual at risk for getting HIV, the human immunodeficiency virus which may develop into AIDS. Infection can come from unprotected sex or sharing contaminated needles, among other things. Apart from sexual abstinence, the most effective preventative is always to practice safer sex using condoms. It is impossible to detect a person's HIV status without a blood test.

HIV/AIDS can also be spread through infected blood transfusions, though the blood supply in the US is now well screened. It can also be spread if needles are reused for acupuncture, tattooing or body piercing.

A good resource for help and information is the Centers for Disease Control and Prevention (check the local phone book).

The US AIDS hotline (☎ 800-342-2437, in Spanish ☎ 800-344-7432) offers advice and support.

Cuts, Bites & Stings
Cuts & Scratches Skin punctures can easily become infected in hot climates and heal slowly. Treat any cut with an antiseptic such as Betadine. Where possible avoid bandages and Band-Aids, which can keep wounds wet.

Bites & Stings Bee and wasp stings and nonpoisonous spider bites are usually more painful than dangerous. Calamine lotion will give relief, and ice packs will reduce the pain and swelling. More common are mosquito bites. Mosquitoes usually appear at dusk, and can be found around stagnant water. Use insect repellent: *Consumer Reports* magazine rates a product called 'Ultra Muskol' the highest, though Avon's Skin So Soft hand lotion is fine for everyday repelling. You might want to carry an insect bite cream, such as Benadryl. Clothing that covers your limbs is a good deterrent to insects.

Ticks Ticks are parasitic arachnids that may be present in brush, forest and grasslands, where hikers may get them on their legs or in their boots. The adults suck blood from hosts by burying their head into skin, but they are often found unattached and can simply be brushed off. Always check your body for ticks after walking through a high-grass or thickly forested area.

To remove an attached tick, use a pair of tweezers, grab it behind the head and gently pull it straight out – do not twist it. (If no tweezers are available, use your fingers, but protect them from contamination with a piece of tissue or paper.) Do not touch the tick with a hot object like a match or a cigarette – this can cause it to regurgitate noxious gut substances or saliva into the wound. And do not rub oil, alcohol, or petroleum jelly on it.

If you feel ill in the next couple of weeks, consult a doctor, as ticks can carry Lyme disease.

BLACK TRAVELERS
African Americans are as much a part of the Southeast as iced tea, plantations and barbecue. Their heritage is a major reason why visitors from around the globe come to the region.

The stereotype of redneck Southern whites lynching blacks comes from a bygone era and does not truly reflect today's Southeast. In all but a few isolated pockets – and certainly at all tourist attractions – black visitors will feel welcome. Atlanta, for instance, has a large black community and is acknowledged as one of the most desirable homes for African Americans. In those rare areas where blacks may find themselves uncomfortable, outsiders of any color or culture are generally spurned as well.

Although most blacks and whites comfortably coexist in the Southeast, centuries of discrimination and segregation have resulted in many communities, churches and institutions – at almost every socioeconomic level – that remain predominantly black or white. Churches may have a sprinkling of other races in their congregations, but, in general, they are attended by one race. To a lesser extent, this also applies to the region's nightlife – dance clubs, bars, theaters and performance centers. Black visitors can enjoy nightlife in traditionally African-American neighborhoods as well as other parts of town. However, outsiders of any color should avoid bars with parking lots full of pickup trucks bearing bumper stickers reading, 'The South Will Rise Again,' 'Keep the Confederate Flag Flying' or related slogans.

At golf courses, tennis courts, stables, parks, pools, beaches and sporting events blacks are welcome. With that said, keep in mind that there are still private clubs with white-only membership policies.

Resources & Organizations
If you find your rights jeopardized, call the police or one of the following agencies. The National Association for the Advancement of Colored People (NAACP; ☎ 202-638-2269, www.naacp.org) is the largest civil

rights organization in the US and has branches throughout the country. Its Legal Affairs Department (☎ 410-358-8900) can refer you to a local branch where you can get guidance.

If you need an attorney, contact the National Legal Aid & Defender's Association (☎ 202-452-0620, www.nlada.org), which provides low-cost legal assistance and has offices in major cities around the country. Call the main number or check with local directory information under 'Legal Aid Society' or 'Legal Services' for an office near you.

WOMEN TRAVELERS

If you're a woman traveler, especially a woman traveling alone, it's a good idea to keep aware of your surroundings. In general, exercise more vigilance in large cities than in rural areas. Try to avoid the 'bad' or unsafe neighborhoods or districts; if you must go into or through these areas, it's best to go in a car or taxi. Nighttime is more dangerous, but in the worst areas crime can occur even in the daytime. If you are unsure which areas are considered unsafe, ask at your hotel or telephone the tourist office for advice.

While there's less to watch out for in rural areas, women may still be subject to unwelcome attention by men unaccustomed to seeing women traveling independently. Try to avoid hiking or camping alone, especially in unfamiliar places. Hikers all over the world use the 'buddy system,' not only for protection from other humans, but also for aid in case of unexpected falls or other injuries.

In an emergency, call the police (☎ 911). In rural areas where ☎ 911 isn't active, just dial '0' for the operator and ask for the police. Cities and larger towns have crisis centers and women's shelters that provide help and support; they are listed in the telephone directory, or the police can refer you to them.

Don't hitchhike alone, and don't pick up hitchhikers when you're driving alone. If you get stuck on a road and need help, it's a good idea to have a premade sign to signal for help. At night, avoid straying from your car to flag down help; turn on the hazard lights and wait for the police to arrive. Be extra careful at night on public transit, and remember to check the times of the last bus or train before you go out at night.

To deal with potential dangers, many women protect themselves with a whistle, mace, cayenne pepper spray or some self-defense training. Laws regarding sprays vary, so be informed based on your destination. On board an airplane, it is a federal felony to carry pepper spray, owing to its combustible design.

Resources & Organizations

Women's bookstores are good places to find out about gatherings, readings and meetings, and they often have bulletin boards where you can find or place travel and short-term housing notices.

National resources with regional affiliates include:

National Organization for Women
An advocacy organization, NOW is a good resource for political and women's rights issues. The national center can refer you to state and local chapters. (☎ 202-331-0066, now@now.org), 733 15th St NW, 2nd floor, Washington, DC 20005 Web site: www.now.org

Planned Parenthood
This organization operates clinics throughout the country and offers advice on medical issues such as women's health, birth control and sexually transmitted diseases. (☎ 212-541-7800), 810 Seventh Ave, New York, NY 10019

GAY & LESBIAN TRAVELERS

There are gay people everywhere in the US, but by far the most visible communities are in the major cities. In the cities and on both coasts it's easier for gay men and women to live their lives with a certain amount of openness. As you travel into the middle of the country, though, this gets harder to do.

Atlanta has a reasonably large and active gay community, with more than 30 gay nightclubs, a local Pride festival, gay-friendly lodgings, specialist bookshops and resource centers (see 'Gay Atlanta' in the Atlanta chapter). The Atlanta Gay/Lesbian Center (☎ 404-523-7500, 159 Ralph McGill

Blvd, 6th floor) is the local clearinghouse for organizations and information. The atmosphere isn't as relaxed as San Francisco – few gay couples hold hands on the street, and 'PDA' (public displays of affection) can raise eyebrows – but still, things have come a long way.

In rural towns the local attitudes can turn intolerant or hostile, so be careful. But it's hard to predict; the Blue Ridge Mountains town of Asheville has an energetic gay population, and low-key scenes can be found in Charleston, Wilmington and some of the Piedmont towns in North Carolina.

Resources & Organizations

The largest gay listings publication in the Southeast is the *Front Page*, a biweekly that covers both the Carolinas. Georgia's gay community focuses on the Atlanta-based guide *Out & Active*.

The Women's Traveller, which lists lesbian resources, and *Damron's Address Book* for men are both published by Damron Company (☎ 415-255-0404, 800-462-6654), PO Box 422458, San Francisco, CA 94142-2458. Also helpful are *Men's Travel In Your Pocket* and *Women's Travel In Your Pocket*, which are both published by Ferrari Publications (☎ 602-863-2408, fax 602-439-3952, www.ferrariguides.com), PO Box 37887, Phoenix, AZ 85069. Neil Miller's *In Search of Gay America*, a book about gay and lesbian life across America in the 1980s, is a bit dated but gives a good view of life outside major cities.

The Gay Yellow Pages (☎ 212-674-0120), PO Box 533, Village Station, NY 10014-0533, has good national and regional editions.

Useful national resources include: National Gay/Lesbian Task Force (☎ 202-332-6483 in Washington, DC) and Lambda Legal Defense Fund (☎ 212-809-8585 in New York City, ☎ 213-937-2728 in Los Angeles).

DISABLED TRAVELERS

Travel within the US is becoming easier for people with disabilities. Public buildings are now required by law to be wheelchair accessible and have accommodating rest-rooms, and transportation must be made accessible to all. Telephone companies are required to provide relay operators for the hearing impaired. The most compliance is found in federal facilities and in modern and newly renovated properties in larger cities. Look to chain motels for the most modern accessible rooms and fully equipped suites. Many banks now provide ATM instructions in Braille. Major carrental agencies in larger cities offer hand-controlled models at no extra charge.

All major airlines, Greyhound buses and Amtrak trains allow service animals to accompany passengers and frequently sell two-for-one packages when attendants of seriously disabled passengers are required. Airlines will also provide assistance for connecting, boarding and deplaning the flight – just ask for assistance when making your reservation. (Note: Airlines must accept wheelchairs as checked baggage and have an onboard chair available, though some advance notice may be required on smaller aircraft.)

Of course, the more populous the area, the greater the likelihood of facilities for the disabled. Outside of big, modern cities, it's important to call ahead to see what is available. Some of the best attractions in the region are historic buildings, including house museums and B&B lodgings, and these are not generally wheelchair accessible, or may have only select accessible rooms.

Resources & Organizations

A number of organizations and tour providers specialize in the needs of disabled travelers.

Access-Able Travel Source
This travel resource has an excellent Web site with links to international disability sites, travel newsletters, guidebooks and travel tips for US destinations, including lists of attractions that can be enjoyed by people with hearing, vision and/or mobility impairment. (☎ 303-232-2979, fax 303-239-8486), PO Box 1796, Wheat Ridge, CO 80034
Web site: www.access-able.com

Mobility International USA
This organization advises disabled travelers on

mobility issues. It primarily runs an educational exchange program. (☎ 541-343-1284, fax 541-343-6812), PO Box 10767, Eugene, OR 97440
Web site: www.miusa.org

Moss Rehabilitation Hospital's Travel Information Service
This rehabilitation center can provide hospital and doctor referrals for disabled travelers. (☎ 215-456-9600, TTY 215-456-9602), 1200 W Tabor Rd, Philadelphia, PA 19141-3099

Society for the Advancement of Travel for the Handicapped (SATH)
This society provides information for disabled travelers and publishes a quarterly magazine. (☎ 212-447-7284, sathtravel@aol.com), 347 Fifth Ave, No 610, New York, NY 10016

Twin Peaks Press
This press offers a quarterly newsletter and several useful handbooks for disabled travelers, including *Travel for the Disabled* and the *Directory of Travel Agencies for the Disabled*. (☎ 800-637-2256, 360-694-2462), PO Box 129, Vancouver, WA 98666

SENIOR TRAVELERS

The Southeast is particularly gracious towards seniors. What's more, the mild climate, low prices, golf courses and extensive camping facilities for RVs also appeal to many older travelers. Senior travelers can often find discounts at hotels, campgrounds, restaurants, parks, museums and other attractions. The age at which senior discounts apply starts at 50, though it more commonly applies to those 65 or older. Be sure to inquire about discount rates when you make your reservation.

Visitors to national parks and campgrounds can cut costs greatly by using the Golden Age Passport (for information, see the Useful Organizations section later in this chapter).

Resources & Organizations

National advocacy groups that can you help in the planning of your travels include the following:

American Association of Retired Persons

AARP is an advocacy group for Americans 50 years of age and older and is a good resource for travel bargains. US residents can get one-year/three-year memberships for $8/20. Citizens of other countries can get the same memberships for $10/24. (☎ 800-424-3410), 601 E St NW, Washington, DC 20049
Web site: www.aarp.org

Elderhostel

This organization is a nonprofit that encourages travel through scholarship. The programs, which are conducted throughout the Southeast, last one to three weeks and include meals and accommodations; they're open to people 55 years of age and older and their companions. The cost is extremely reasonable. The organization also has service programs in association with Habitat for Humanity. (☎ 617-426-8056), 75 Federal St, Boston, MA 02110-1941
Web site: www.elderhostel.org

Grand Circle Travel

This group offers escorted tours and travel information in a variety of formats and has a free, useful booklet, 'Going Abroad: 101 Tips for Mature Travelers.' (℅ 800-597-3544, 617-350-7500), 347 Congress St, Boston, MA 02210
Web site: www.gct.com

National Council of Senior Citizens

Membership in this group (you needn't be a US citizen) gives access to added Medicare insurance, a mail-order prescription service and a variety of discount information and travel-related advice. Fees are $13/30/150 for one year/three years/lifetime. (☎ 202-347-8800), 1331 F St NW, Washington DC, 20004

TRAVEL WITH CHILDREN

The Southeast is a very family-friendly destination with many discounts, services, facilities and attractions designed to entertain kids, including such considerate touches as high chairs on wheels at cafeterias.

The definition of 'child' varies widely – some places count anyone under 18 eligible for children's discounts, while other places only include children under six.

Many hotels and motels allow children to share a room with their parents for free or for a modest fee, though B&Bs rarely do and some don't allow children at all. More expensive hotels can arrange baby-sitting services or organize 'kids' clubs' for younger children. Restaurants offer inexpensive children's menus with a limited selection of kid-friendly foods at cheap prices for patrons under 12 or 10 years of age.

Airlines offer discount children's tickets, but these are often more expensive than the cheapest economy adult tickets. Most buses and tours have discounted children's prices, though the discounts aren't substantial. Car rental companies provide infant seats for their cars on request.

For ideas on how to keep the little ones entertained, turn to *The Unofficial Guide to the Southeast With Kids* by Bob Sehlinger. Lonely Planet's *Travel With Children,* by Maureen Wheeler, offers advice and reassurance.

USEFUL ORGANIZATIONS
American Automobile Association

For its members, AAA ('triple-A') provides great travel information, distributes free road maps and guidebooks and sells American Express traveler's checks without commission. The AAA membership card will often get you discounts for accommodations, car rental and admission charges. If you plan to do a lot of driving – even in a rental car – it is usually worth joining AAA. It cost $59 the first year and $39 for subsequent years.

Unfortunately, unless you're a resident of the US, you can't become a AAA member. However, members of other auto clubs, such as the Automobile Association in the UK, are entitled to the same services if they bring their membership cards and/or a letter of introduction.

AAA also provides emergency roadside service to members in the event of an accident or breakdown or if you lock your keys in the car. Service is free within a given radius of the nearest service center, and service providers will tow your car to a mechanic if they can't fix it. The nationwide toll-free roadside assistance number is ☎ 800-222-4357 (800-AAA-HELP). All major cities and many smaller towns have a AAA office where you can start membership or get affiliate benefits.
Web site: www.aaa.com

National Park Service & US Forest Service

The federal government controls public lands through at least two groups. The National Park Service (NPS) administers the use of designated national parks. The US Forest Service (USFS), a division of the US Department of Agriculture, administers the use of designated national forests. National forests are less protected than parks, allowing commercial use (including logging and mining) of some areas.

For more information, write to NPS Southeast Region, 100 Alabama St SW, 1924 Bldg, Atlanta, GA 30303, or USFS Southern Region, 1720 Peachtree Rd NW, Atlanta, GA 30309. Also, check out the NPS Web site at www.nps.gov. The Internet site of GORP (Great Outdoor Recreation Pages) is another handy resource, at www.gorp.com.

For camping information, see the Accommodations section, later in this chapter. General information about other publicly owned land is available from each state's Fish and Wildlife Service or from the Web site www.recreation.gov.

National Parks Passports The NPS has several discount passes available. You can apply in person for any of the following 'passports' at any national park or regional office of the USFS or NPS.

National Parks Passes (formerly Golden Eagle Passports) cost $52 annually and offer one-year entry into national parks for the holder and accompanying guests; only entrance fees are covered and there is no age restriction.

Golden Age Passports cost $10 and allow US residents 62 years and older unlimited entry to all sites in the national park system, with 50% discounts on camping and other use fees.

Golden Access Passports offer the same to US residents who are medically blind or permanently disabled.

DANGERS & ANNOYANCES
Although street crime is a serious issue in large urban areas, most notably Atlanta, visitors need not be obsessed with security.

Always lock cars and put valuables out of sight, whether leaving the car for a few minutes or longer, and whether you are in a town or in the remote backcountry. Rent a car with a lockable trunk. If your car is bumped from behind in a remote area, it's best to keep going to a well-lit area or service station.

Be aware of your surroundings and who may be watching you. Avoid walking on dimly lit streets at night, particularly when alone. Walk purposefully. Avoid unnecessary displays of money or jewelry. Try to use ATMs in well-trafficked areas.

In hotels, don't leave valuables lying around your room. Use safety-deposit boxes or at least place valuables in a locked bag. Don't open your door to strangers – check the peephole or call the front desk if unexpected guests try to enter.

The US has a widespread reputation, partly true but also propagated and exaggerated by the media, as a dangerous place because of the availability of firearms. Guns do play a significant role in a hunting and self-protecting rural culture such as the Southeast. Many people own guns, and some people may carry guns.

When walking in the woods during hunting seasons (generally fall and winter; inquire locally), rangers recommend hikers wear 'blaze' orange vests.

A major summer annoyance in the coastal and marshy areas (especially the Okefenokee Swamp and along the Outer Banks) are the swarms of mosquitoes and no-see-ums. Make sure you bring plenty of insect repellent with the active ingredient DEET (some locals swear by an Avon product with repellent qualities called Skin So Soft, readily available locally).

EMERGENCIES

Throughout most of the US, dial ☎ 911 for emergency service of any sort. This is a free call from any phone. Rural phones might not have this service, in which case dial ☎ 0 for the operator and ask for emergency assistance – it's still free. Each state also maintains toll-free numbers for traffic information and emergencies.

Lost or Stolen Documents

Carry a photocopy of your passport separately from your passport. Copy the pages with your photo and personal details, passport number and US visa. If it is lost or stolen, this will make replacing it easier. In this event, you should call your embassy. Similarly, carry copies of your traveler's check numbers and credit card numbers.

LEGAL MATTERS

If you are stopped by the police for any reason, bear in mind that there is no system of paying fines on the spot. For traffic offenses, the police officer will explain your options to you. Attempting to pay the fine to the officer is frowned upon at best and may compound your troubles by resulting in a charge of bribery. Should the officer decide that you should pay up front, the officer can exercise his or her authority and take you directly to the magistrate instead of allowing you the usual 30-day period to pay the fine.

If you are arrested for more serious offenses, you have the right to remain silent. There is no legal reason to speak to a police officer if you don't wish, but never walk away from an officer until given permission. All persons who are arrested are legally allowed (and given) the right to make one phone call. If you don't have a lawyer or family member to help you, call your embassy. The police will give you the number upon request.

The minimum age for gambling is 21.

Drinking & Driving Laws

The drinking age is 21, and you need an ID (identification with your photograph on it) to prove your age. Drinking and driving is a serious offense; you could incur stiff fines, jail time and penalties if caught driving under the influence of alcohol (called 'DUI' or 'DWI'). It is illegal even to carry an open container of alcohol in a car. During some holidays and special events, roadblocks are sometimes set up to deter drunk drivers.

In North Carolina, establishments that reap more than half their revenues from alcohol sales have to call themselves private clubs, which charge a membership fee. Visitors can usually get in places by asking an amenable member to 'invite' them along as guests (who pay their own admission).

Each state has its own driving laws, and what's legal in one state may be illegal in others. Some general rules are that you must be at least 16 years of age to drive (younger with certain restrictions in some states). Seat belts and motorcycle helmets must be worn, and motorbikes must be driven with their lights on.

Speed limits are 65 mph on interstates and freeways unless otherwise posted. Speed limits on other highways are 55 mph or less. In cities, limits vary from 25 to 45 mph. In small towns, motorists may run into speed traps, a handy source of municipal revenue. Watch for school zones, which can be as low as 15 mph during school hours – these limits are strictly enforced and result in very costly tickets should you be pulled over for exceeding them.

BUSINESS HOURS

Standard US business hours prevail in the larger towns, but watch out for seasonal opening times in tourist communities. Public and private office hours are normally 9 am to 5 pm weekdays (Monday through Friday). Most stores are open Monday through Saturday, from 9 or 10 am to around 6 pm, or later in big cities or shopping malls. Some convenience stores or fuel stations may be open 24 hours, usually in the larger cities or at interstate freeway exits. Post offices open 8 am to 4 pm or 5:30 pm on weekdays, and some are open 8 am to 3 pm Saturday.

In the Southeast, most businesses are closed Sunday. Even tourist-oriented businesses and attractions are usually closed Sunday morning. Many tourist-oriented restaurants and shops may stay open weekends but then close Monday or Tuesday.

Businesses, especially banks and federal and state offices, typically close on major holidays; in some instances, they might close on the nearest Monday instead, creating a three-day weekend.

PUBLIC HOLIDAYS

On major holidays expect celebrations, parades or observances, and be prepared for the closure of local businesses. See the destination chapters for more events and complete information on those mentioned below.

January

New Year's Day
January 1 is a federal holiday.

Martin Luther King Jr Day
Observed on the third Monday, this holiday celebrates this civil rights leader's birthday (January 15, 1929).

Robert E Lee's Birthday
On January 19, more than a few Southerners remember the Confederate general.

February

Presidents' Day
Held on the third Monday, this day commemorates the birthdays of Abraham Lincoln (February 12, 1809) and George Washington (February 22, 1732).

April

Confederate Memorial Day
Fallen Southern heroes, and to a certain extent the fallen South, are remembered on April 26.

May

Memorial Day
On the last Monday in May, Americans honor the war dead.

July

Independence Day
July 4 is a national holiday.

September

Labor Day
Observed on the first Monday, this holiday honors working people.

October

Columbus Day
The Italian-born explorer is remembered on the second Monday of the month.

November

Veterans Day
On November 11, Americans honor their war veterans.

Thanksgiving
On the fourth Thursday, Americans give thanks before stuffing themselves with turkey and pumpkin pie.

December
Christmas
This major holiday falls on December 25. The night before (Christmas Eve) people attend church services, go caroling, and cruise neighborhoods looking for the best light displays.

ACTIVITIES
The most common outdoor activities in the Southeast have something of a Hemingway-esque quality: salt and freshwater fishing, hunting, hiking, horseback riding, boating and camping are all popular. Sea kayaking and beach swimming are big along the coast, along with kite-flying and hang-gliding. River running, mountain biking and backpacking are a real kick in the mountains. Golf is huge in resorts such as Hilton Head, Augusta and Pinehurst.

Bicyclists, as well as pedestrians, will find this region is largely car-dependent and inaccessible. Off-road biking trails can be found in the region's national forests, but forest service roads themselves are also well suited for mountain or dirt biking. North Carolina has the most bicycle paths (3,000 miles). Contact the USFS (see the Useful Organizations section earlier in this chapter) or see the national forest listings in the regional chapters.

Backpacking opportunities are numerous and varied, with hiking trails snaking through the Appalachians but also along bogs and beachheads. National forests, along with state parks, feature some of the most developed trails in each state. National wildlife refuges offer the best chance to see local wildlife in a variety of peaceful settings. Visit www.recreation.gov and enter the state name for an overview.

Appalachian Trail
After walking a section of the Appalachian Trail, travel author Bill Bryson wrote that he had 'discovered an America that millions of people scarcely know exists.' Many people wrongly assume that the trail is ancient, but it was really the brainchild of a Massachusetts regional planner, Benton MacKaye. After its inception in 1921, the trail was designed, constructed and marked by volunteer hiking clubs assembled by the Appalachian Trail Conference in the 1920s and '30s. In 1968, Congress made the AT a linear national park and authorized funds to buy up the remaining lands along its course.

The trail starts (or finishes) at Mt Katahdin in Maine and runs 2160 miles to **Springer Mountain,** in the Chattahoochee National Forest of northern Georgia. At the southern end, it meanders along the North Carolina-Tennessee border for 68 miles, passing some of the highest ridges in the Great Smoky Mountains National Park. The North Carolina section accounts for 300 miles, and Georgia for 75 miles.

The most popular stretch within the park begins at **Newfound Gap,** where a relatively gentle climb leads 7 miles to the highest point along the trail, **Clingman's Dome** (6643 feet) in North Carolina. About 4 miles beyond the dome stands **Charlie's Bunion,** an open cliff with a sheer 1000-foot drop-off.

In Georgia, **Springer Mountain** is reachable via an 8-mile trace in Amicalola Falls State Park. North toward the border lies the 238-acre **Vogel State Park,** one of Georgia's most popular.

Backpackers who attempt to hike the length of the trail are a breed apart. Called 'thru-hikers,' these hearty souls adopt trail names by which they're known for the extent of their journey (Indian names are popular). About 150 make it of the 1500 people who set out every year. Earl Shaffer became the first person to hike the length of the trail in 1948, and repeated the feat at age 77.

Information For general trail information, contact the Appalachian Trail Conference (ATC; ☎ 304-535-6331, www.atconf.org), PO Box 807, Harpers Ferry, West Virginia 25425, or the Appalachian Scenic Trail (☎ 304-535-6331), Harpers Ferry Center, PO Box 50, Harpers Ferry, West Virginia 25425-0897. The ATC distributes and publishes guidebooks and maps on every section of the trail, as well as *The Appalachian Trailway News.*

Camping Appalachian Trail campers can use the 260 **primitive shelters** along the trail – they're generally spaced 8 to 12 miles apart (about one day's walk). These three-sided shelters are reserved for hikers with three or more nights in different locations ($1 per night), and are not for casual campers (there's no road access nearby, so you can't just drive up and spend the night; you really have to hike there). There's wire fencing on the front of the shelters, which you shut to keep out the bears.

WORK

The USFS puts volunteers to work as campground hosts and forest hands. Each state has its own USFS headquarters; the regional Southern USFS Information Center is in Atlanta (☎ 404-347-2384), 1720 Peachtree Rd NW, Atlanta, GA 30367. The beach resorts along the Outer Banks, North Carolina as well as Myrtle Beach, South Carolina, hire lots of young people to work in hotels, restaurants and beach attractions.

If you're not a US citizen, you'll need to apply for a work visa from the US embassy in your home country before you leave. The type of visa varies depending on how long you're staying and the kind of work you plan to do. Generally, you'll need either a J-1 visa, which you can obtain by joining a visitor-exchange program, or an H-2B visa, which you get when being sponsored by a US employer. The latter is not easy to obtain (since the employer has to prove that no US citizen or permanent resident can do the job); the former is issued mostly to students for work in summer camps.

ACCOMMODATIONS

Of the many types of overnight accommodations available in the Southeast – from a state park cabin in the woods to a luxurious suite overlooking downtown Atlanta – perhaps the most distinctive lodging the region has to offer is in historic homes transformed into B&Bs and inns. They tend to be expensive but good for the occasional splurge.

Budget travelers can find plenty of roadside chain motels for comfortable, if unexciting, accommodations. It's a general rule of thumb that visiting cities on the week-ends and the country during the week helps keep costs down, but many other factors (festivals and seasonal appeal are two) can come into play.

During peak seasons or festivals, it's wise to reserve well in advance to get your first choice; simply showing up might mean you'll have to spend the night outside town. Also, since hotels in these towns depend on having full occupancy during festivals, it isn't uncommon that you be asked to pay a deposit (sometimes a personal check) when reserving the room. Prices in this guide can only be an approximate guideline at best. Also, be prepared to add room tax – 2% to 6% in most cities, but with sales and other local taxes, your bill can swell by up to 15%. Children often stay free with their parents, but rules for this vary; inquire if traveling with a family.

You can often find discounts from the so-called rack rate quoted to guests who arrive without a reservation. Discounts of 10% or more are commonly granted to members of the American Automobile Association (AAA), as well as senior citizens, students, military personnel, government employees and those with some corporate affiliations. Even people walking in off the street without a reservation can often negotiate a discount if they're armed with the knowledge that occupancy is down. Conversely, don't expect a discount at a hotel that is booked for a convention.

Another note: The 800 telephone numbers of the chains are not your best bet for getting a good deal or checking on room availability. These hotlines also can't guarantee a particular room (say, one with a balcony or a view or one that's been remodeled). Lower rates are often quoted at the local numbers.

Camping

Camping is the cheapest, and can be the most enjoyable, approach to a vacation. Visitors can take advantage of hundreds of private and public campgrounds at prices of $10 per night or even less.

National wilderness areas offer the most natural and rugged camping adventures in

A Note on Camping

When camping in an undeveloped area, choose a campsite at least 200 feet (approximately 70 adult steps) from water and wash up at camp, not in the stream, using biodegradable soap. Dig a 6-inch-deep hole to use as a latrine and cover and camouflage it well when leaving the site. Burn toilet paper, unless fires are prohibited. Carry out all trash. Use a portable charcoal grill or camping stove; don't build new fires. If there already is a fire ring, use only dead and downed wood (if allowed) or wood you have carried in yourself. Make sure to leave the campsite as you found it.

Even though developed areas usually have toilets and drinking water, it's always a good idea to have a few gallons of water when venturing out to the boonies.

the Southeast. With a rented boat or sea kayak, you can camp on wild, stunningly beautiful islands along the coast, such as Skidaway Island in Georgia or the Cape Lookout National Seashore in North Carolina. In the off-seasons you'll have miles of beach to yourself.

National parks maintain impressive campgrounds, often in beautiful areas. For reservations or information for national park campgrounds, call ☎ 800-365-2267 or reserve via the National Park Service Web site (www.nps.gov). By snail mail, write National Park Service Public Inquiry, Dept of Interior, PO Box 37127, Washington, DC 20013-7127. The Web site www.reserveusa.com is another handy resource for reserving camping sites ahead of time.

National forests in all Southeast states provide primitive campsites – tables, grills, drinking water, vault toilets, some cold showers – for $6 to $8 a night. These are first-come, first-served, and the maximum stay is 14 nights. You may also camp anywhere in a national forest unless posted otherwise; no fee or permit is required. Current information about national forests can be

obtained from ranger stations, which are listed in the text. National forest campground and reservation information can be obtained by calling ☎ 800-280-2267.

State park campgrounds are more developed, often with flush toilets and hot showers. Most are first-come, first-served. County parks or recreational areas may also offer camping; facilities vary considerably but are likely not plush.

Private campgrounds may run the gamut, but are most often on the 'camping resort' side of things and include developed sites, RV hookups and other amenities, such as a swimming pool, stocked trout pond or even hayrides. These can climb to around $20. Kampgrounds of America (KOA) is a national network of private campgrounds with sites usually ranging from $12 to $15. You can get the annual directory of KOA sites by calling or writing: KOA (☎ 406-248-7444, www.koa.com), PO Box 30558, Billings, MT 59114-0558.

To make reservations at national, state and local parks, you must pay with Visa, MasterCard or Discover. If you know what state park or national forest campground you'd like to stay at, call ☎ 800-280-2267 for reservations. For sites in national parks, call Destinet at ☎ 800-365-2267.

Cabins

Renting a cabin for a week or two is popular for families in the Southeast, but not particularly easy for those who do not live in the region, except at state park cabins. Most state parks offer cabin rentals that can take eight to 12 people; prices are extremely reasonable. These are not shacks – they usually have central heating and air-conditioning, and they supply all the necessary dishware, cookware and linens. Some were built by the Civilian Conservation Corps (CCC) in the 1930s, and today these stone-and-wood cabins are the most desirable picks. But because of their popularity and low rates, cabins may be booked up months, if not a full year, in advance.

For private cabins, local chambers of commerce generally maintain listings of properties available for short-term rental. Note that since many cabins are outfitted to accommodate families, some bedrooms are likely outfitted with twin beds and may not be optimal for several couples traveling together.

Hostels

The 'official' youth hostels in the US are affiliated with Hostelling International (HI), which is a member of the International Youth Hostel Federation. Sadly, hostels are scarce in the region covered in this book. In Georgia there are HI hostels in Atlanta and Savannah, and independent hostels in Athens, Brunswick and Dawsonville; North Carolina has HI hostels in Kitty Hawk on the Outer Banks and in Pembroke (about 10 miles east of Lumberton). Rates vary from $10 to $20 a night. A party atmosphere often prevails, which means you're likely to meet people but may have a hard time getting a good night's rest. Most hostels have a few private rooms for $30 to $45 a night.

Web sites: www.hiayh.org/, www.hostels.com

Motels

Invented in the 1920s, the all-American motel is usually a roadside lodging with parking and rooms that can be accessed from the parking lot. Security isn't as tight as at a hotel (where one must pass the front desk before going to the rooms), but rates are generally cheaper. In the Southeast, motels with rates of $30 to $40 can be found, especially in small towns on major highways and in the motel strips of larger towns. At this price the beds may sag, heat or air-con may be noisy or uneven, and the odor of disinfectant or incense may be powerful, but rooms come with private bath and the sheets and towels should be clean. Housecleaning tends to improve as the rates increase. Also, rooms are often priced according to the number of beds they have. Rooms with two double beds may be ideal for families.

The cheapest budget hotels and motels may not accept reservations, but at least phone from the road to see what's available; even if they don't take reservations, they'll often hold a room for an hour or two.

Some of even the cheapest motels may advertise kitchenettes. These may cost a few dollars more but give you the chance to cook a simple meal for yourself. Kitchenettes vary from a two-ring burner to a spiffy little mini-kitchen and may or may not have utensils.

Chain Motels While chains are not too exciting, they are reliably clean and come with dependable air-conditioning units. (The downside to this is that often there's no way to open the windows – you have no choice but to crank the air-con.) The consistently cheapest national chain is Motel 6. Rooms start below $40 for a single in smaller towns, in the $50s in larger towns. They usually charge a flat $6 for each extra person. Super 8, Days Inn and Econo Lodge are a little more expensive. These provide basic clean rooms with TVs, phone and private bath; most have pools.

Stepping up to chains with rates in the $45 to $80 range (depending on location), you'll find nicer rooms; cafes, restaurants or bars may be on the premises, and the swimming pool may be indoors with a spa or exercise room also available. Best Western, La Quinta, Comfort Inn and Sleep Inn are in this category.

Normally, you have to give a credit card number to make a room reservation. If you don't show and don't call to cancel, you will be charged the first night's rental. Cancellation policies vary, so find out when you book. Make sure to let the place know if you plan on a late arrival – many will give your room away if you haven't arrived or called by 6 pm.

Reservation operators at toll-free numbers might not be aware of special local discounts and availability. The reservation numbers of some of the best-known chains are:

Best Western	☎ 800-528-1234
Comfort Inn, Sleep Inn	☎ 800-221-2222
Days Inn	☎ 800-329-7466
Econo Lodge, Rodeway Inn	☎ 800-424-4777
E-Z 8 Motels	☎ 800-326-6835

Howard Johnson	☎ 800-446-4656
Motel 6	☎ 800-466-8356
Super 8 Motel	☎ 800-800-8000
Travelodge	☎ 800-578-7878

Hotels

City hotels in the region are often geared to business travelers, and their rates sometimes drop on weekends. Chains such as Marriott and Sheraton provide rooms from $80 a night; in larger cities prices are higher. These may include health clubs with sauna and hot tub, room service and restaurants and taverns on the premises.

Inns & B&Bs

European visitors should note that North American inns and B&Bs are not the cheap and cheerful accommodations found on the continent or in Britain. In the Southeast, many such places are kept in wonderfully preserved historic homes, offering visitors a personal up close look at the architectural and cultural heritage of the region. These accommodations can vary widely, from a hotel-like inn with many guests and little personal contact to a home-like experience where your hosts live in the property and treat you as their personal guests.

The nature of the rooms may also vary widely – some inns have all the modern conveniences (private baths, TV, phones, heat and air-conditioning), others maintain a historic authenticity (shared baths, no TV or phone, ceiling fans, quirky plumbing and the like). They may be furnished with period reproductions or antiques. Rates range widely, from $50 for a weeknight stay at a small place to $200 for an all-out historic plantation house.

Be aware that B&B regulations may vary considerably. Some welcome small children, while others have an age minimum, usually around 12 years. Most B&Bs prohibit smoking, if not entirely, at least in rooms. A continental or full hot breakfast is almost always included, but other meals may be provided as well. Check whether a certain room (view, private bath) can be reserved, or if room choice is on a first-come, first-served basis. Finally, find out whether credit cards, personal checks or traveler's checks are accepted, or if payment is by cash only.

FOOD

Throughout the region, cuisine ranges from plentiful and cheap fast-food choices (as little as $2 for a meal, but not necessarily a very nutritious or tasty one) to elaborate steak houses where a three-course meal and wine cost more than $50 per person. The more distinctive cuisine of the region is served along the coast, where seafood and fish specialties predominate.

Southern American cuisine is inexpensive and typically served up in heaps. Southerners take their time preparing and serving meals, and the local preference seems to be for food served less than piping hot.

When you eat at a restaurant, expect the final bill to be inflated by about 25% above prices quoted in the menu because of the addition of 8% or so sales tax and a 15% or

Tipping

Tipping is expected in restaurants and better hotels, and by taxi drivers, bartenders, hairdressers and baggage carriers. In restaurants, waitstaff are paid minimal wages and rely upon tips for their livelihoods – it's incentive-creation, US style. Leave 15% on the table unless the service is terrible (in which case a complaint to the manager is warranted), or up to 20% if the service is great. Never tip in fast-food or take-out restaurants. At cafeterias or buffet-style restaurants with drink waiters, it's customary to leave $1 or $2, depending on the size of your party or your requests.

Taxi drivers expect 10% and hairdressers get 15% if their service is satisfactory. Baggage carriers (skycaps in airports, bellhops in hotels) generally get $1 for the first bag and 50¢ for each additional bag. Ushers and gas station attendants no longer get tips nowadays.

so tip. (Tipping is not expected in fast-food take-out restaurants.)

The style of service may differ from other regions. All-you-can-eat luncheon and dinner buffets are common (cafeterias are very popular), and some restaurants serve 'family-style,' seating unrelated groups at the same table to pass plates around and serve yourself. Note that some families say a prayer before eating; restaurant patrons would not necessarily be expected to join in (guests at a family's home *would* be expected to do so), but it would be respectful to wait silently until they're done before serving or eating. Server tips are slightly lower at buffet and family-style restaurants (around 10%); at cafeterias, it's kind to leave a tip for the table-clearer ($1 or $2).

Budget travelers will want to seek out farmers markets, such as those in Raleigh, Charleston and Atlanta, for the freshest produce at the lowest prices. Grocery stores and deli counters commonly offer prepared foods for take-out bargains. Restaurants offer discounts on meals for children and seniors, sometimes also for military and clergy in uniform.

Regional chain restaurants offer a healthier and more regionally distinctive alternative to standard American fast food; cafeterias in particular are often just as cheap and quick as McDonald's, and you can see what looks good before ordering. Two that are good and reliable are Morrison's Cafeterias and Piccadilly Cafeterias; you can generally find them near shopping malls off freeway exits.

Most restaurants offer the choice of nonsmoking and smoking areas; some prohibit smoking. Many restaurants are air-conditioned to the point of refrigeration; even if it's 100°F out, you might want to have a sweater handy for lunch.

Breakfast

Restaurants serve breakfast from around 6 to 11 am; some budget motels put out a simple complimentary breakfast bar (juice, pastries, cold cereals) from around 7 to 9 am, which can be a good way to save time as well as money. Otherwise, standard breakfast choices range from a Danish and coffee for under $2 to a full Southern breakfast of eggs, breakfast meat (bacon, ham or sausage), 'grits' (a hot cereal of ground hominy seasoned with butter and salt) and biscuits-and-gravy, all for around $6 with juice and coffee. A meal that size isn't necessarily conducive to an active day, but may be just the thing after an action-filled night. Some coffee shop chains offer breakfast around the clock. In coffee shops, free coffee refills are offered by attentive waitresses ('Top that off for ya, hon?').

Lunch

Lunch is served from around 11:30 am to 2 or 3 pm; sandwiches, salads, hamburgers and other short orders for around $4 to $5 are common choices. At better restaurants, many lunch entrees are identical to their dinner choices but cost only about half as much (a $12 dinner plate might go for $7 at lunch).

Dinner

Dinner is the largest meal of the day, starting around 6 pm (posher or Latin-style restaurants may see a rush later, at around 8 pm). Traditional Sunday dinner is eaten earlier, as early as noon, and throughout the region many restaurants close early that day, around 2, 3 or 4 pm; visitors whose timing is off may be stranded. Some city hotels and restaurants offer elaborate Sunday brunch buffets, but many restaurants are closed until midday. Farther south, you might still hear dinner occasionally called 'supper.'

Southeastern Cuisine

Classic Southern country cooking is often described as 'hearty' – no doubt because it tastes wonderful, is satisfying, makes you feel relaxed and, if enjoyed in great quantities, eventually produces a nice, cushy coat of fat around your arteries. You'll find plenty of that in Georgia and the Carolinas, but often jazzed up with, say, a spicy sauce or herbal crust.

A 'meat-and-three' plate means you pick an entree and three well-cooked vegetables, typically okra, corn, black-eyed peas, collard greens, mustard greens or turnip greens. Other side items might include macaroni and cheese, Jell-O salad, mashed potatoes or your choice of a flaky biscuit, cornbread or hush puppies – small fried rounds of dough, named from what was said to the whining dogs looking for scraps at fish fries.

'Chitlins' are boiled pig intestines typically eaten with cabbage and served alongside pork, coleslaw and sweet potato pie. A dying South Carolina tradition called the 'chitlin strut' entailed a feast after the first pigs were slaughtered in the fall. When the intestines are fried, they're called fried chitterlings.

You might be more inclined to try one of the region's other specialties – peaches. Peaches are one of Georgia's signature crops (brought by the Spanish in the mid-16th century), and can be found fresh or in pies, cobblers and ice cream. South Carolina is actually billed as the 'Peach Capital of the USA,' though most would think, from all the peachy propaganda, that Georgia could claim that title. Watermelons are another common fruit grown locally. The sweet Vidalia onion is grown only in the Georgia town of the same name.

Of course, there are plenty of recipes, not just ingredients, that are particular to the Southeast. Frogmore stew consists of sausage, corn, shrimp, celery and seasonings, and was born when a tired fisherman took all of the ingredients out of his cupboard and dumped them into a pot. It's named after Frogmore, SC, an early African-American settlement on St Helena island.

Hoppin' John, a hearty stew with ham and black-eyed peas, is traditionally eaten on New Year's Day to bring good luck; collards usually accompany the meal to represent money.

Pimento cheese is like peanut butter to some folks in the region, and is often eaten as a spread on white bread or like mayonnaise on a hamburger.

Peanuts – also known as groundpeas, pinders and goobers – were introduced to non-Southerners during the Civil War, which started an industry for this little-known, high-protein snack. You'll see them sold throughout the region, especially on chilly winter days. The peanuts are boiled, shells and all, in a big pot of salty water until the shells are soft but not mushy.

Barbecue A particularly revered Southern cuisine is barbecue, which can be made with smoked or marinated meat, grilled and then eaten with 'dip' (BBQ sauce). Pork is the meat of choice (offered chopped, sliced, 'pulled,' or in ribs), but barbecued chicken and beef are also available.

In Georgia, barbecue is *always* made from pork, pulled or shredded, with a wide range of sauces. In the Southeast, most BBQ sauces are either vinegar- or tomato-based, though you'll also find mustard-based BBQ, a Carolina specialty. Sauce recipes are often closely guarded family secrets.

A plate of barbecued meat (just called 'barbecue') is usually served with a slice of white bread and a side of coleslaw, baked beans or macaroni salad. The classic venue is a no-frills roadside stand with a hickory-smoking chimney out back.

Seafood Specialties In the Southeastern plains – broadly termed the Lowcountry – seafood tends to be boiled rather than fried, spicy and served with a variety of cooked vegetables. A big favorite is she-crab soup, which was invented in Charleston by an African-American cook who used the female crab with roe for extra flavor. 'Lowcountry Boil' is a spicy mélange of boiled shrimp, sausage, potatoes and corn.

At your typical crab shack, plates of un-cracked shellfish – oysters, crabs, clams, mussels and shrimp – are brought to tables

covered with brown paper or newsprint. You'll be offered cracking tools and plastic bibs, and when you're done, the server will collect the whole mess in the paper and toss it away in one quick swipe.

A newer tradition is the 'raw bar,' typically with a trendy atmosphere, where you can sample local shellfish at a per-item cost.

DRINKS
Nonalcoholic Drinks

Most Americans start the day with a cup of coffee. On the whole, the roasts tend to be weaker than European varieties, but stiffer brews can be had at coffee-shop chains (eg, Starbucks) that are sweeping America. Brewed decaffeinated coffee is widely available, too. Iced tea, sweetened or unsweetened with a slice of lemon, is considered the 'house wine' of the Southeast. This is what they'll bring if you ask for 'tea' (if you want hot tea, you'll have to be specific). Coca-Cola or Pepsi, 7-Up, root beer and the like are also common choices; lemonade is a popular summer drink. Restaurants serve iced tap water at no charge with a meal.

Alcoholic Drinks

Wine tends to be served in finer restaurants, where the food is less regional. Micro-brewed beer is increasingly popular, and you'll find cozy brewpubs in most cities. Hard liquor is widely available, and bourbon and coke remains a Southern favorite. A mint julep is a tall frosted drink made with bourbon, sugar and ice and garnished with sprigs of mint; although it's as familiar as Tara, you'll see few Southerners actually order one.

Beverage laws vary from state to state, and liquor sales in stores and restaurants may be restricted on Sunday. 'Dry counties,' counties in which the sale of alcohol is illegal, are scattered throughout the region. It's illegal to drive with open containers of alcohol in the car; drunk driving is a serious felony offense. Drinking alcohol outdoors is generally prohibited, but it's tolerated at open-air music festivals.

The minimum drinking age is 21 throughout the region, and photo identification is often requested at stores and restaurants as proof of age (this ritual is called being 'carded'). Persons under 21 (minors) are not allowed in bars and pubs, even to order nonalcoholic beverages. Unfortunately, this means that most dance clubs are also off-limits to minors. Minors are, however, welcome in the dining areas of restaurants where alcohol may be served.

ENTERTAINMENT
Music & Clubs

From the infectious bluegrass of the Appalachians to the 'shag' beach tunes of the Carolina coast, you'll find wonderful live music performed in a variety of inviting venues throughout the region – it's a primary draw for visitors. Georgia is a great fountainhead of talent, and arguably no state other than Louisiana offers as potent a mix of jazz, blues and Southern rock (see the special section Music in the Facts About the Region chapter). Comedy and cabaret can be found, too – see the individual towns for listings of the 'hot' clubs to seek out.

Discos and nightclubs without live music often feature DJs (disc jockeys) playing records. Bars and pubs sometimes feature jukeboxes and often set up pool tables or dartboards. However, take every opportunity to hear live music – it's widely available, diverse, regionally distinctive and usually pretty inexpensive.

Performing Arts

Atlanta is the region's hub for performing arts, with a symphony orchestra, opera and ballet companies of national repute. The drama scene is particularly lively, and you might catch Shakespeare, murder mysteries or a musical coproduced by pop icon Elton John (who keeps a penthouse downtown). Even smaller cities such as Charleston have their own orchestras, and urban areas throughout the Piedmont offer a plethora of musical, dance and drama events. Open-air theater is a joy in the warmer months; *The Lost Colony*, performed in Manteo all summer long, is the country's longest-running outdoor drama (since 1937).

Colleges and universities also host performing arts events that are open to the public.

SPECTATOR SPORTS

Folks in the Southeast take their sports *very* seriously, and sports arenas are regarded with the same reverence accorded church or city hall. Virtually any team – major or minor leagues, college or high school – command a clannish loyalty that seems strange in other walks of life. Big-ticket games are good, but there's nothing quite like jostling with cheering fans at a local sporting event.

The region's sole major league baseball team is mega-successful: the Atlanta Braves, who chalked up eight division titles, five National League Championships and a World Series win during the 1990s. Otherwise, there are plenty of minor franchises that serve as 'farm clubs' for the big teams. The Durham Bulls (of *Bull Durham* movie fame) are nearly as famous as their first-class affiliate, the Braves. Call early for tickets, as Bulls games sell out months in advance.

Atlanta shines in pro football as well: The Falcons have made the NFL playoffs eight times, and in 1999 they played in, but lost, the Superbowl. The creation of a NFL South division in 2002 will routinely pit the Falcons against a newish Charlotte-based team, the Carolina Panthers. Just as often, it's the college athletes who really get the blood racing. In South Carolina, the gridiron is ruled by the formidable Clemson Tigers, whose gritty rivalry with Georgia Tech's Yellow Jackets is the stuff of legend. Indoor arena football – played on a padded 50-yard field by teams of eight – is a quirky but fast-growing league sport.

The Atlanta Hawks pro basketball team is struggling after the departure of its former coach, Lenny Wilkens, who in 1996 became the first NBA coach to win 1,000 games. Always a threat, the Charlotte Hornets have managed to reach the playoffs just once. College basketball generates a scary devotion in North Carolina, which hosts four of the nine teams in the Atlantic Coast Conference (which also includes Clemson and Georgia Tech). The championships usually include one or two of the following: UNC in Chapel Hill, Duke University in Durham, NCSU in Raleigh, and Wake Forest in Winston-Salem. Women's collegiate basketball is also hot, with UNC Chapel Hill consistently near the top of the rankings.

Played in refrigerated halls, ice hockey has become quite popular, and several cities have pro teams (viz the brand-new Atlanta Thrashers, who like the Braves and the Hawks are owned by Ted Turner). In a class all its own, NASCAR stock car racing draws hundreds of thousands of fans to Lowe's Speedway in Charlotte each year.

SHOPPING

From rickety roadside stands to fancy museum shops, traditional crafts are available throughout the Southeast, and you'd be crazy not to take advantage of the huge selection: Handwoven blankets, tooled leather, pottery and baskets made from native materials are but a few examples. Checking out small cabin shops and meeting artisans are among the best pleasures of traveling in the Appalachians.

Historic house museums often have gift shops with a collection of souvenirs such as hickory-wood bird-callers or Christmas ornaments with hand-painted motifs. Packages of gift-wrapped Southern food specialties make inexpensive souvenirs – it's easy to find fancy kitchen herbs in small canvas sacks, jars of local jellies and honeys daintily topped with calico-print fabric, and colorful pickled relishes made of corn, cucumber and red pepper.

Nicely made bead jewelry, dolls, etchings and other Native American items are sold on the reservation in Cherokee, but can also be found in private galleries and shops.

African crafts – masks, bright prints and wooden figurines, as well as a variety of fine and folk arts – are produced by local African-American artists and often exhibited in dedicated galleries.

Shopping malls are ubiquitous in cities (there are more than 50 in Atlanta alone) and here you can find all the necessities – clothing, travel supplies, recreational and sporting equipment, you name it. Furniture is a huge industry in North Carolina and towns such as High Point, Hickory and Lexington are synonymous with factory outlets.

Antique shops also abound. Visitors bureaus usually have a guide to the local antique district, but beware: That wind-up gramophone, Civil War sword or Victorian shoe-cleaning kit might be cheaper at places that aren't on the map. There's a fine line between treasure and junk, and the more chaotic shops and flea markets tend to offer the best bargain-hunting. Prices may be negotiable; it can't hurt to try.

Music recordings of bands you've heard are great souvenirs; tapes and CDs can be cheaper if bought at the venue, and aren't always available in stores.

Getting There & Away

The two most common ways to reach the Southeastern states covered in this book are by air and by car, but you can also get there by train and by bus. Travelers coming from the Midwest, Northeast and Great Plains states don't have far to go if they want to drive, and in general, excellent highways connect the region to every part of the US.

Travelers from farther afield usually fly in, then rent a car. The region's main gateways, Atlanta (ATL), Charlotte (CHS) and Raleigh-Durham (RDU), are international airports with good connections abroad. International travelers who wish to fly to secondary airports such as Piedmont-Triad or Charleston will probably change planes in another US gateway.

AIR

US domestic airfares vary tremendously depending on the season you travel, the day of the week you fly, the length of your stay and the flexibility the ticket allows for flight changes and refunds. Fares also vary depending on which airport you are flying into – at a given time, your cheapest option could be flying into Atlanta, Charlotte or Raleigh-Durham, while smaller airports in Charleston, Winston-Salem or Savannah might offer even cheaper fares at other times. No single airport in the region has a lock on the best deals.

Nothing determines fares more than demand, and when things are slow, regardless of the season, airlines will lower their fares to fill empty seats. There's a lot of competition, and at any given time any one of the airlines could have the cheapest fare. In general, high season for nationwide airline travel rates in the US is mid-June to mid-September (summer) and the weeks before and after Christmas. See Buying Tickets, later in this section, for advice on getting the best deals.

> ## Warning
>
> The information in this chapter is particularly vulnerable to change: Prices for international travel are volatile, routes are introduced and canceled, schedules change, special deals come and go, and rules and visa requirements are amended. Airlines and governments seem to take a perverse pleasure in making price structures and regulations as complicated as possible. You should check directly with the airline or a travel agent to make sure you understand how a fare (and any ticket you may buy) works. In addition, the travel industry is highly competitive, and there are many lurks and perks.
>
> The upshot of this is that you should get opinions, quotes and advice from as many airlines and travel agents as possible before you part with your hard-earned cash. The details given in this chapter should be regarded as pointers and are not a substitute for your own careful, up-to-date research.

Airports

There are oodles of international flights to Atlanta (at Hartsfield Atlanta International Airport, ☎ 404-530-6834), and to a lesser extent Charlotte and Raleigh-Durham. Otherwise, international travelers often arrive on connecting flights from such traditional ports of entry as New York, Los Angeles and Miami.

Atlanta recently overtook Chicago O'Hare as the country's busiest airport. It has services of 32 airlines to 180 destinations, with Delta being its largest customer. Other majors include Northwest Airlines, a close affiliate of KLM Royal Dutch Airlines, which provides direct flights from Amsterdam with connections from other European countries.

Charlotte Douglas International Airport (☎ 704-359-4000) is served by 11 carriers, including American, British Airways, Delta, United and US Airways, with reasonably good links to London.

Raleigh-Durham International Airport (☎ 919-840-2123) is served by 14 major airlines such as Continental, Delta, Northwest, TWA and United, but tends to be more expensive to fly into than Charlotte or Atlanta. The Piedmont Triad International Airport (☎ 336-665-5666), between Greensboro and Winston-Salem, has strong regional links.

Airlines

The following are the major international airlines that serve the region:

Air Canada	☎ 888-247-2262
Air France	☎ 800-237-2747
Air New Zealand	☎ 800-262-1234
American Airlines	☎ 800-433-7300
British Airways	☎ 800-247-9297
Canadian Airlines	☎ 800-426-7000
Continental Airlines	☎ 800-231-0856
Japan Air Lines	☎ 800-525-3663
KLM	☎ 800-374-7747
Northwest Airlines	☎ 800-447-4747
Qantas Airways	☎ 800-227-4500
TWA	☎ 800-221-2000
United Airlines	☎ 800-538-2929
US Airways	☎ 800-428-4322
Virgin Atlantic	☎ 800-862-8621

The following are the major domestic airlines that serve the region:

AirTran Airways	☎ 800-247-8726
Alaska Airlines	☎ 800-426-0333
America West	☎ 800-235-9292
American Airlines	☎ 800-433-7300
Continental Airlines	☎ 800-525-0280
Delta	☎ 800-221-1212
Northwest Airlines	☎ 800-225-2525
Southwest	☎ 800-435-9792
TWA	☎ 800-892-4141
United Airlines	☎ 800-241-6522

Buying Tickets

The plane ticket will probably be the single most expensive item in your budget, and buying it can be intimidating. So rather than just walking into the nearest travel agent or airline office, you should do a bit of research and shop around first. It's always worth putting aside a few hours to check into the current state of the market. Start shopping for a ticket early. Low advertised fares are often available on a limited basis and sell out quickly. Some of the cheapest tickets must be bought months in advance, and popular flights often sell out early. Talk to recent travelers – they may offer more specific cost-saving advice. Look at the ads in newspapers and magazines and consult the Internet.

If you are buying tickets within the US, the *New York Times, Los Angeles Times, Chicago Tribune, San Francisco Examiner* and other major newspapers all produce weekly travel sections with numerous travel agents' ads. Discount agencies Council Travel (☎ 800-226-8624, www.ciee.org) and STA (☎ 800-777-0112, www.statravel.com) have offices in major cities nationwide. The magazine *Travel Unlimited,* PO Box 1058, Allston, MA 02134, publishes details of the cheapest airfares and courier possibilities.

Those coming from outside the US might start by perusing travel sections of magazines such as *Time Out* and *TNT* in the UK, or the Saturday editions of newspapers such as the *Sydney Morning Herald* and *The Age* in Australia. Ads in these publications offer cheap fares, but don't be surprised if they happen to be sold out when you contact the agents: They're usually low-season fares on obscure airlines with conditions attached.

Airlines themselves can supply information on routes and timetables, but many times they do not supply the cheapest tickets. Airlines do, however, often have competitive low-season, student and senior citizens' fares. Find out the fare, the route, the duration of the journey and any restrictions on the ticket.

Once you have your ticket, write down its number, together with the flight number and other details, and keep the information separate from the ticket. If the ticket is lost or stolen this will help you get a replacement.

Standby tickets can be cheap, but tend to be scarce on today's overbooked US flights.

Air Travel Glossary

Cancellation Penalties If you have to cancel or change a discounted ticket, there are often heavy penalties involved; insurance can sometimes be taken out against these penalties. Some airlines impose penalties on regular tickets as well, particularly against 'no-show' passengers.

Courier Fares Businesses often need to send urgent documents or freight securely and quickly. Courier companies hire people to accompany the package through customs and, in return, offer a discount ticket which is sometimes a phenomenal bargain. However, you may have to surrender all your baggage allowance and take only carry-on luggage.

Full Fares Airlines traditionally offer 1st class (coded F), business class (coded J) and economy class (coded Y) tickets. These days, so many promotional and discounted fares are available that few passengers pay full economy fare.

Lost Tickets If you lose your airline ticket, an airline will usually treat it like a traveler's check and, after inquiries, issue you with another one. Legally, however, an airline is entitled to treat it like cash: If you lose it, it's gone forever. Take good care of your tickets.

Onward Tickets An entry requirement for many countries is a ticket out of the country. If you're unsure of your next move, the easiest solution is to buy the cheapest onward ticket to a neighboring country or a ticket from a reliable airline that can later be refunded if you do not use it.

Open-Jaw Tickets These are return tickets that permit you to fly into one place but return from another. If available, these tickets can save you backtracking to your arrival point.

Overbooking Because almost every flight has some passengers that fail to show up, airlines often book more passengers than they have seats. Usually excess passengers make up for the no-shows, but occasionally somebody gets 'bumped' onto the next available flight. Guess who it is most likely to be? The passengers who check in late.

Promotional Fares These are officially discounted fares, available from travel agencies or direct from the airline.

Reconfirmation If you don't reconfirm your flight at least 72 hours prior to departure, the airline may delete your name from the passenger list. Call to find out if your airline requires reconfirmation.

Restrictions Discounted tickets often have various restrictions – for example, they may need to be paid for in advance, or altering them may incur a penalty. Other restrictions include minimum and maximum periods you must be away.

Round-the-World Tickets RTW tickets give you a limited period (usually a year) in which to circumnavigate the globe. You can go anywhere the carrying airlines go as long as you don't backtrack. The number of stopovers or total number of separate flights is decided before you set off, and these tickets usually cost a bit more than a basic return flight.

Transferred Tickets Airline tickets cannot be transferred from one person to another. Travelers sometimes try to sell the return half of a ticket, but officials can ask you to prove that you are the person named on the ticket. On an international flight, tickets are compared with passports.

Travel Periods Ticket prices vary with the time of year. There is a low (off-peak) season and a high (peak) season, and often a low-shoulder season and a high-shoulder season as well. Usually the fare depends on your outward flight – if you depart in the high season and return in the low season, you pay the high-season fare.

When flying standby, call the airline a day or two before the flight and make a 'standby reservation.' This way you get priority over all the others who just appear and hope to get on the flight the same day. Remember to buy travel insurance as early as possible (see Travel Insurance under Visas & Documents in the Facts for the Visitor chapter).

Use the fares quoted in this book as a guide only. They are approximate and based on the rates advertised by travel agents and airlines at press time. Quoted airfares do not necessarily constitute a recommendation for the carrier.

Online Purchase Most airlines have their own Web sites with online ticket sales, often discounted for online customers. Sometimes contacting an airline directly is the best way to find cheap deals. Although the Web is certainly one way to get good deals, it doesn't always produce the lowest fares. Shopping carefully, using a variety of information sources, continues to make the most sense.

To buy a ticket via the Web, you'll need to use a credit card – this transaction is straightforward and secure, as card details are encrypted. Commercial reservation networks offer airline ticketing as well as information and bookings for hotels, car rental, and other services. Networks include the following:

American Express Travel	http://travel.american express.com/travel/personal
Atevo Travel	www.atevo.com
Biztravel.com	www.biztravel.com
Excite Travel	www.travel.excite.com
Microsoft Expedia	www.expedia.com
Priceline	www.priceline.com
Travelocity	www.travelocity.com

Some Web sites specialize in cheap fares:

1-800-Airfare	www.1800airfare.com
Cheap Tickets	www.cheaptickets.com
LowestFare.com	www.lowestfare.com
Yahoo Travel Specials	http://travel.yahoo.com/

Discount Tickets Airline deals can be learned about in a variety of ways. You can find out about advance purchase fares simply by calling the airline a week or two ahead of time, or in some cases even earlier. Other airline specials might require a certain number of days between arrival and return, or staying in your destination on Saturday night, or flying on specific days. Some special fares are released through selected travel agents.

The cheapest tickets are often nonrefundable and require an extra fee for changing your flight. Many travel insurance policies will cover this loss if you have to change your flight for an emergency. Return (roundtrip) tickets usually work out cheaper – often *much* cheaper – than two one-way fares. However, the recent emergence of smaller airlines specializing in one-way fares is making it easy to avoid buying roundtrip tickets. America West and Southwest, from the western US, and AirTran Airways, from the eastern US, sell one-way fares that are half the cost of a regular roundtrip fare. These airlines also connect major airports with smaller, regional airports.

If traveling from the UK, you will probably find that the cheapest flights are advertised by obscure bucket shops whose names haven't yet reached the telephone directory. Many such firms are honest and solvent, but there are a few rogues who will take your money and disappear, to reopen elsewhere a month or two later under a new name. If you feel suspicious about a firm, don't give them all the money at once – leave a deposit of 20% or so and pay the balance on receiving the ticket. If they insist on cash in advance, go elsewhere. And once you have the ticket, call the airline to confirm that you are booked on the flight.

You may decide to pay more than the rock-bottom fare and opt for the safety of a better-known travel agent. Established firms like STA Travel, which has offices worldwide, Council Travel in the US and Travel CUTS in Canada are valid alternatives, and they offer good prices to most destinations.

Visit USA Passes Almost all domestic carriers offer Visit USA passes to non-US citizens. The passes are actually a book of coupons that you buy – each coupon equals a flight. They must be booked outside the US, and you must be a non-US resident and have a return ticket to a destination outside the US (but not Canada or Mexico). Some airlines make a distinction between coupons for direct flights to/from the US, and for coupons for flights within the US. In any case, it's a good idea to ask your travel agent about the various deals on offer.

Generally, you must have your trip planned out in order to purchase the coupons. If you decide to change destinations once in the US, you will usually be fined $75. Prices for the coupons can vary enormously depending on the airline and time of year; in summer, Continental Airlines charges roughly US$479 for three flight coupons (minimum purchase) and $760 for eight (maximum purchase). However, Delta and a few others allow you to buy up to 10 coupons, which can work out cheaper. Northwest, American, and United tend to offer the most comprehensive networks for passes, while US Airways is consistently among the cheapest. Children's coupons always cost less.

Round-the-World Tickets Round-the-World (RTW) tickets can be a great deal if you want to visit other regions as well as the US. Often they work out to be no more expensive or even cheaper than an ordinary roundtrip ticket.

The official RTW tickets are usually put together by a combination of two airlines, and permit you to fly anywhere you want on their route systems as long as you do not backtrack. Other restrictions are that you must usually book the first sector in advance and cancellation penalties apply. There may be restrictions on the number of stops permitted, and tickets are usually valid for between 90 days and a year. An alternative type of RTW ticket is one put together by a travel agent using a combination of discounted tickets.

Most airlines restrict the number of sectors that can be flown within the US and Canada to three or four, and some airlines black out a few heavily traveled routes (like Honolulu to Tokyo). In most cases a 14-day advance purchase is required. After the ticket is purchased, dates can be changed without penalty and tickets can be rewritten to add or delete stops for $50 each.

Travelers with Special Needs

If you have special needs of any sort – a broken leg, dietary restrictions, reliance on a wheelchair, responsibility for a baby, fear of flying – you should let the airline know as soon as possible so that they can make arrangements accordingly. You should remind them when you reconfirm your booking (at least 72 hours before departure) and again when you check in at the airport. It may also be worth calling a number of airlines before you make your booking to find out how they can handle your particular needs.

Airports and airlines can be surprisingly helpful, but they do need advance warning. Deaf travelers can ask for airport and in-flight announcements to be written down for them. Most international airports can provide escorts, when needed, from check-in desk to plane, and there should be ramps, elevators, wheelchair accessible toilets and reachable or TTY phones. Aircraft toilets, on the other hand, are likely to present a problem for people who need to transfer; travelers should discuss this with the airline at an early stage and, if necessary, with their doctor.

Guide dogs will likely have to travel in a specially pressurized baggage compartment with other animals, away from their owner, though smaller guide dogs may be admitted to the cabin. Guide dogs are not subject to quarantine as long as they have proof of being vaccinated against rabies.

Children under two travel for as little as 10% of the standard fare (or free, on some airlines), as long as they don't occupy a seat. (They don't get a baggage allowance either, however.) 'Skycots' should be provided by the airline for children who have a paid seat if requested in advance; these will hold a child weighing up to about 22lb. Children between two and 12 can usually occupy a seat for half to two-thirds of the full fare, and do get a baggage allowance. Strollers can often be taken on as carry-on.

Baggage & Other Restrictions

On most domestic and international flights you are limited to two checked bags. There could be a charge if you bring more or if the size and/or weight of the bags exceeds the airline's limits.

If your luggage is delayed upon arrival (which is rare), some airlines will give a cash advance to purchase necessities. If sporting equipment is misplaced, the airline may pay for rentals. Should the luggage be lost, it is important to submit a claim. The airline doesn't have to pay the full amount of the claim; rather they can estimate the value of your lost items. It may take them anywhere from six weeks to three months to process the claim and pay you.

Smoking is prohibited on all domestic flights within the US. Many international flights are following suit, so be sure to call and find out. Incidentally, the restriction applies to the passenger cabin and the lavatories but not the cockpit. Many airports in the US also restrict smoking, but they compensate by having 'smoking rooms.'

Items that are illegal to take on a plane, either checked or as carry-on, include aerosols of polishes, waxes, etc; tear gas and pepper spray; camp stoves with fuel; and divers' tanks that are full. Matches should also not be checked.

Arriving in the US

Even if you are continuing immediately to another city, the first airport that you land in is where you must carry out immigration and customs formalities. Even if your luggage is checked from, say, London to Denver, you will still have to take it through customs if you first land in New York.

If you have a non-US passport, with a visa, you must complete an Arrival/Departure Record (form I-94) before going to the immigration desk. See Visas & Documents in the Facts for the Visitor chapter for advice on filling out this form and for information on what to expect from immigration officials.

Departure Tax

Airport departure taxes are normally included in the cost of tickets bought in the US, while tickets purchased abroad may or may not have this included. There's also a $6 airport departure tax charged to all passengers bound for a foreign destination. However, this fee, as well as a $6.50 North American Free Trade Agreement (NAFTA) tax charged to passengers entering the US from a foreign country, are hidden taxes added to the purchase price of your airline ticket.

The US

During the months before press time, roundtrip airfares from New York to Charlotte, Charleston or Atlanta ranged from $99 to $189.

From Boston, the fares to the three regional hubs ranged from $120 to $225. From Washington, DC, fares were $109 to $205.

From Chicago, fares varied wildly, from $150 to $350.

From San Francisco, airfares hovered between $250 and $400, with Atlanta fares consistently dipping to the lower end of this range.

From Southern California, sometimes the best fares are for flights out of Orange County or Ontario, but check Los Angeles (LAX) first. Rates fluctuate from around $260 to $390.

Canada

Travel CUTS has offices in all major cities. The Toronto *Globe & Mail* and *Vancouver*

Sun carry travel agents' ads. Typically, to reach the Southeast apart from Atlanta, you'll have to fly into another US gateway and change planes. US/Canadian airline partnerships do offer 'through ticketing;' this is when you check in at one airport with one airline, and later change airlines at another airport but don't have to check in again because the first airline gave you boarding passes for all connections, even though you are actually flying on another airline on a subsequent leg. Low-season roundtrip airfares from Vancouver are C$520. Fares from Toronto are C$250 to C$370, while from Montreal it'll cost from C$350 to C$410.

The UK

Most British travel agents are registered with the ABTA (Association of British Travel Agents). Some agents are bonded under agreements such as the Air Transport Operators License (ATOL); if you buy a ticket from such an agent and it then goes out of business, ATOL guarantees a refund or an alternative. Unregistered or unbonded bucket shops are riskier but sometimes cheaper.

London is arguably the world's headquarters for bucket shops, which are well advertised and can usually beat published airline fares. Three good, reliable agents for cheap tickets in the UK are Trailfinders (☎ 020-7628-7628, www.trailfinder.com), 1 Threadneedle St, London, EC2R 8JX; Council Travel (☎ 020-7437-7767, www.counciltravel.com), 28A Poland St, London, W1; and STA Travel (☎ 020-7581-4132, www.statravel.com), 86 Old Brompton Rd, London SW7 3LQ.

Direct flights from London to New York connect with flights to Southeast cities for around £290. Nonstop flights to Atlanta are sometimes the cheapest way to the region, as low as £200.

Continental Europe

In Amsterdam, NBBS (☎ 020-624-09-89, www.nbbs.nl) is a popular travel agent with several branches. Fares range from f600 to f1050. There's a f70 additional tax on all return flights.

In Paris, Council Travel (☎ 01-44-55-55-44) is at 22, rue des Pyramides, 75001 Paris. Or try FUAJ (Fédération unie des auberges de jeunesse; ☎ 01-44-89-87-27, www.fuaj.org), 27 rue Pajol, 75018 Paris. For great student fares, contact Usit CONNECT (☎ 01-42-34-56-90), 6 rue de Vaugirard, 75006 Paris or (☎ 01-44-41-89-80), 1 place de Odéon. Paris flight fares are 2500FF to 3100FF.

Council Travel has two offices in Germany: in Düsseldorf at Franz-Adolf Strasse 18 (☎ 0211-36-30-30) and in Munich at Adalbertsrasse 32 (☎ 089-39-50-22). STA Travel has several offices in Germany, including one in Frankfurt at Bergerstrasse 118 (☎ 069-43-01-91) and two in Berlin, at Dorotheenstrasse 300 (☎ 030-20-16-50-63) and at Goethestrasse 73 (☎ 030-311-09-50). Frankfurt flight fares are about DM790 to DM920.

Australia & New Zealand

In Australia and New Zealand, STA Travel and Flight Centres International are major dealers in cheap airfares; check the travel agents' ads in the yellow pages and call around. Qantas flies to Los Angeles from Sydney, Melbourne (via Sydney or Auckland) and Cairns. United flies to San Francisco from Sydney and Melbourne (via Sydney), and to Los Angeles. From these cities connections can be made to US domestic flights.

The cheapest tickets have a 21-day advance-purchase requirement, with a minimum stay of seven days and a maximum stay of 60 days. In low season, fares to Atlanta from Sydney cost about A$1500, and from Auckland about NZ$2100; high season fares can be several hundred dollars more.

Flying with Air New Zealand is usually slightly cheaper than with Qantas, and both airlines offer tickets with longer stays or stopovers, but you pay more.

Asia

Hong Kong is the discount plane ticket capital of the region, but its bucket shops can be unreliable. Ask the advice of other travelers before buying a ticket. STA Travel (www.statravel.com), which is dependable, has branches in Guangzhou, Tokyo, Osaka, Singapore, Bangkok and Kuala Lumpur. Many if not most flights to the continental US go via Honolulu, Hawaii.

United Airlines has three flights a day to Honolulu from Tokyo with connections to West Coast cities. Northwest and Japan Air Lines also have daily flights to the West Coast from Tokyo; Japan Air Lines also flies to Honolulu from Osaka, Nagoya, Fukuoka and Sapporo.

Central & South America

Most flights from Central and South America go via Miami, Houston or Los Angeles, though some fly via New York. Most countries' international flag carriers (like Aerolíneas Argentinas and Lan-Chile), as well as US airlines like United and American, serve these destinations, with onward connections. Continental has flights from about 20 cities in Mexico and Central America, including San José, Guatemala City, Cancun and Merida.

LAND

Bus

Greyhound (☎ 800-231-2222, www.greyhound .com) is the only nationwide bus company with good coverage in Southeastern cities and towns. Buses are air-conditioned, and most are decently maintained. However, dealing with Greyhound on the telephone is often a major investment of time and patience.

Fares are not necessarily cheap, and depend on the distance, day of the week and how far in advance the ticket is bought. The best deals are 'plan-ahead' specials that require ticket purchase two weeks prior to your departure date. Services can be infrequent, sometimes just once a day and at weird times. Some Greyhound specials are not so special, particularly if you are not traveling alone. For instance, the North American Discovery Pass (formerly called Ameripass) is not such a bargain at $185/209 international travelers/North American residents for unlimited stops within a seven-day period. For that price, you can rent a car (which allows you to double or triple your savings if two or more people travel together and split the costs). Admittedly, though, Ameripass offers a unique way to travel the US, particularly if you opt for the 60-day package ($509/599).

Some sample routes are as follows:

from	to	duration (approx hrs)	fare
New York	Atlanta	18	$98
Chattanooga	Atlanta	2	$18
Miami	Atlanta	16	$94
Dallas	Atlanta	17½	$83
Washington, DC	Raleigh	7½	$66
New York	Myrtle Beach	11	$55
Chicago	Winston Salem	17	$108

Buses to/from the West Coast take two to three days and cost upwards of $140.

Train

Amtrak (☎ 800-872-7245, www.amtrak.com) is the only railroad in the US that provides cross-country passenger service, with several lines running from New York down the east coast towards New Orleans or Florida. As with Greyhound buses, trains tend to be infrequent, and the daily service may actually depart in the middle of the night.

The *Crescent* runs between New York City and New Orleans, with stops including Washington, DC; Greensboro and Charlotte, North Carolina; Greenville, South Carolina; Atlanta, Georgia; Birmingham, Alabama; and Meridian, Mississippi.

Other services parallel the East Coast going to/from Florida. They all follow a common route between New York and Richmond, Virginia, but at Rocky Mount, North Carolina (near Raleigh), the services separate:

Silver Palm and *Silver Meteor* go closer to the coast, with stops at Fayetteville, North Carolina; Charleston, South Carolina; Savannah, Georgia; and Jacksonville, Florida.

Silver Star veers inland, with stops including Raleigh, North Carolina; Columbia, South Carolina; then Savannah and Jacksonville.

Carolinian and *Piedmont* go farther inland, to/ from Charlotte, North Carolina, via Raleigh, Durham and Winston-Salem.

Links to the Midwest and West Coast require changes somewhere, most commonly in New Orleans or Washington, DC.

Rail travel in the US isn't cheap, but you can cut costs by purchasing special fares in advance. Fares vary according to type of seating; you can travel in coach seats or in various types of sleeping compartments. The child fare is half the adult fare (children must be traveling with an adult paying full fare). A 15% student discount pass is available for $20 per year. Anyone over age 62 qualifies for a 15% discount. Special fares are also available for disabled travelers.

The USA Rail Pass is available from travel agents outside of North America, but foreign-passport holders can purchase it from Amtrak once inside the USA. The pass offers unlimited coach-class travel within a specific region for either 15 or 30 days, with the price depending on region, number of days, and season traveled. At press time, the 30-day East Coast pass was $275 in high season, $225 in low season.

Present your pass at an Amtrak office to get a ticket for each trip. Reservations should be made as well, as far in advance as possible. You can get on and off as often as you like, but each segment of the journey must be booked. At some rural stations, trains will only stop if there's a reservation. Tickets are not for specific seats, but a conductor on board may allocate you a seat. Sleeper or 1st-class accommodations cost extra and must be reserved separately.

In conjunction with Canada's VIA Rail, Amtrak offers the North America Rail Pass that gets you unlimited travel on US and Canadian railways for 30 consecutive days for US$471 in the off-peak season, or US$674 in the peak season (from June 1 to October 15).

Some sample individual fares are as follows (all one-way):

from	to	duration (approx hrs)	fare
New York	Atlanta	19	$107
New Orleans	Atlanta	11	$50
New York	Charleston	14	$167
Richmond	Columbia	5	$96
Washington, DC	Raleigh	6	$69

Car & Motorcycle

Foreign drivers of cars and riders of motorcycles will need their vehicle's registration papers, liability insurance and an international driver's permit, in addition to their domestic driver's license. Canadian and Mexican driver's licenses are accepted.

See the Getting Around chapter for more information on driving in the region, including car rental.

Drive-Aways Drive-aways are cars that belong to owners who can't drive them to a specific destination but are willing to allow someone else to drive for them. For example, if somebody moves from Atlanta to Washington, DC, they may elect to fly and leave the car with a drive-away agency. The agency will find a driver and take care of all necessary insurance and permits. If you happen to want to drive from Atlanta to DC, and have a valid driver's license and a clean driving record, you can apply to drive the car.

Normally, you have to pay a small refundable deposit. You pay for the gas (though sometimes a gas allowance is given). You are allowed a set number of days to deliver the car – usually based on driving eight hours a day. You are also allowed a limited number of miles, based on the best route and allowing for reasonable side trips, so you can't just zigzag all over the country. However, this is a cheap way to get around if you like long-distance driving and meet eligibility requirements.

Drive-away companies often advertise in the classified sections of newspapers under 'Travel.' They are also listed in the yellow pages under 'Automobile Transporters & Drive-Away Companies.' You need to be flexible about dates and destinations when you call. If you are going to a popular area, you may be able to leave within two days or less, or you may have to wait over a week before a car becomes available. The routes most easily available are coast to coast, although intermediate trips are certainly possible.

ORGANIZED TOURS

In getting to and from the Southeast, package tours can be an efficient and relatively inexpensive way to go, especially for those interested in seeing the whole country. However, many tours do not focus on the Southeast and instead give travelers only one or two days in, say, Atlanta or Charleston.

TrekAmerica (☎ 800-221-0596, 201-983-1144, fax 201-983-8551), PO Box 189, Rockaway, NJ 07866, offers roundtrip camping, hiking and lodging tours to different areas of the country. In England, they are at (☎ 01295-256777, fax 01295-257399), 4 Water Perry Court, Banbury, Oxon OX16 8QG, and in Australia contact Adventure World (☎ 9956-7766, 800-221-931, fax 4956-

7707), 75 Walker St, North Sydney, NSW 2060. These tours are designed for small, young international groups. Tour prices vary with season, with July to September being the most expensive, and don't include airfare. Some side trips and cultural events are included in the price, and participants help with cooking and camping chores. Web site: www.trekamerica.com

AmeriCan Adventures (☎ 800-873-5872, fax 310-324-3562, amadlax@aol.com), PO Box 1155, Gardena, CA 90249, offers seven-to 21-day camping trips to different parts of the US. They also have an office in the UK (☎ 01892-512700, fax 01892-522066, email amadsales@twins.co.uk), 64 Mount Pleasant Ave, Tunbridge Wells, Kent TN1 1QY. Web site: www.americanadventures.com

Road Runner USA/Canada (☎ 800-873-5872), a big Massachusetts-based company, leads small group tours in conjunction with Hostelling International to regions of the US and across the country. The Confederate Trail tour begins in New York and ends in Florida, but spends a fair amount of time in the Southeast; prices start at around $720.

For tours within, rather than to, the region, see the Getting Around chapter.

Getting Around

There's no question about it: if you want to see the scattered rural attractions that lie between the cities of the Southeast, the best way is by car. The highways are good, and public transportation isn't as frequent or as widespread as in many other countries. Of course, a focused trip or tour can work nicely with air, train or bus transit between major destinations.

AIR

Very few tourists fly between small regional airports in this region, as it's expensive and service is primarily geared toward business passengers. However, one can travel between the major hubs of Atlanta, Charlotte and Raleigh in order to get quickly from one end of the region to the other.

Contact these airlines for regional flight information:

AirTran Airways	☎ 800-247-8726
American Eagle	☎ 800-433-7300
Atlantic Southeast/ Delta Connection	☎ 800-282-3424
ComAir	☎ 800-221-1212
Continental Express	☎ 800-525-0280
Midway	☎ 800-446-4392
Midwest Express	☎ 800-452-2022
Spirit	☎ 800-772-7117
TWExpress	☎ 800-221-2000
US Airways Express	☎ 800-428-4322

BUS

In the US, long-haul bus transit is the domain of Greyhound (☎ 800-231-2222 for reservations, www.greyhound.com), which links the dispersed smaller towns of the Southeast. The quality of the neighborhoods in which bus stations are located, and the facilities offered there, may vary widely, but stations are generally well-maintained and staffed.

North-south routes cover the Southeast pretty well but east-west links can be sparse, especially in western South Carolina or

northeastern Georgia. Some Appalachian towns don't have any bus service at all, so forget about bussing your way through the mountains. Many stations still bear the logo of Continental Trailways, a one-time rival that Greyhound swallowed some years ago. Along the Atlantic coast some routes are covered by Carolina Trailways, a Greyhound affiliate.

The major city-to-city corridors within the Southeast have services that are quite swift and frequent, such as Atlanta-Charlotte ($62, six hours) en route to New York. However, links between some tourist destinations are surprisingly bad – your choice might be a single bus, leaving in the wee hours, with transfers and layovers along the way (not to mention crunchy passengers). Prices, duration and frequencies can vary sharply depending on the day; call ahead or risk disappointment.

Some sample routes: Raleigh-Wilmington ($29, a long 6¼ hours with transfers, once daily), Atlanta-Macon ($14, 1½ hours, 13 daily), Charlotte-Columbia ($16, 1¾ hours, four daily) and Savannah-Charleston ($24, 3¼ hours, twice daily). See destination chapters for bus routes and fares.

Buying Tickets

Tickets can be bought by phone or Internet with a credit card (MasterCard, Visa or Discover) and then received by mail if purchased 10 days in advance or picked up at the terminal with proper identification. Greyhound terminals also accept American Express, traveler's checks and cash. Note that all buses are non-smoking, and reservations are made with ticket purchases only.

Greyhound occasionally runs a mileage-based discount-fare program that can be a bargain, especially for very long distances, but it's a good idea to check the regular fare anyway. As with regular fares, promotional fares are subject to change. There are also Discovery Passes that may save you money; see the Getting There & Away chapter for information. To contact Greyhound about local offices, fares, schedules or routes, call ☎ 800-231-2222 or ☎ 402-330-8552 from outside the US.

Web site: www.greyhound.com

TRAIN

Amtrak (☎ 800-872-7255) can be an efficient way to travel through popular corridors, such as the New York-Atlanta-New Orleans route. Routes covered in the Getting There & Away chapter serve destinations within the region.

As with bus transit, the quality of the neighborhoods in which train stations are located, and the facilities offered there, may vary widely. See destination chapters for details of fares, and the Getting There & Away chapter for information on buying tickets.

CAR & MOTORCYCLE

Driving offers visitors the most flexibility at a reasonable cost. For visitors traveling alone, cars are convenient but isolating, and possibly expensive; bus and train fares become more competitive with car-rental costs for single travelers. However, since distances are great and both buses and trains can be infrequent, it's worth considering a car.

Visitors can legally drive in the USA for up to 12 months with their home driver's license. An International Driving Permit (IDP) is a useful adjunct (see Visas & Documents in the Facts for the Visitor chapter).

If you do drive, read the Road Rules section of this chapter carefully. To avert theft, do not leave items such as cell phones, purses, compact discs, cameras, baggage or even sunglasses visible inside the car. Tuck items under the seat, or even better, put them in the trunk and make sure your car does not have trunk entry through the back seat; if it does, make sure this is locked. Don't leave anything in the car overnight.

Rental

Major international rental agencies like Hertz, Avis, Budget and A-1 have offices throughout the region, but there are also local agencies. Most rental companies require that you have a major credit card, that you be at least 25 years old, and that you have a valid driver's license. Alamo, Thrifty, Budget and Rent-A-Wreck may rent to drivers between the ages of 21 and 24 for an additional charge (usually around $20 per day).

Here are some major car-rental agencies:

Alamo	☎ 800-327-9633
Avis	☎ 800-831-2847
Budget	☎ 800-527-0700
Dollar	☎ 800-800-4000
Enterprise	☎ 800-325-8007
Hertz	☎ 800-654-3131
Thrifty	☎ 800-367-2277

Many rental agencies have bargain rates for weekend or weeklong rentals, especially outside the peak summer season or in conjunction with airline tickets. Prices vary greatly according to region, season and type or size of car. You might pay as little as $20 per day or as much as $50, with unlimited mileage included at the top end.

If you're arranging a rental before you reach the USA, check all the options with your travel agent first. Watch out for hidden charges: For fly-drive packages, local taxes may be incurred when you collect the car, and there may be an extra charge for an additional driver. Note that some major rental agencies don't offer unlimited mileage in less competitive markets – be sure to calculate the cost of your estimated mileage before you rent.

Once you're in a city, shop around. Use toll-free numbers to check the big companies, but try the local ones too. Many airports have a courtesy phone and a board with advertisements for car rental agencies. You can spend 30 minutes calling a dozen of them toll-free, select the most suitable, and they'll pick you up and take you to their lot. Be sure to ask for the best rate – discounts may be offered for renting on weekends, for three days, by the week or month, or even for renting a car in one place and returning it to another if the company needs to move cars in that direction. In any case, a 'one-way' rental can be useful. The extra drop-off charge ranges from nothing to $200.

Compare the total cost, including insurance and mileage; one company may charge a little less for the car but a little more for the insurance. Also estimate the distance you'll be driving. An 'unlimited mileage' plan works out more economically than a 'cost-per-mile' plan if you'll be driving long distances.

Take time to mull over the insurance angles. Liability coverage is required by law in most states, but isn't always included in rental contracts – because many Americans are covered for rental cars under their regular car liability insurance policy. You need liability coverage, but don't pay extra if sufficient coverage is already included with the rental. Insurance against damage to the car, called collision damage waiver (CDW) or loss damage waiver (LDW), is usually optional ($8 to $12 per day) but you may have to pay the first $100 or $500 of any repairs. This cost ('deductible') may be avoided by paying additional premiums. Credit cards such as MasterCard Gold and American Express will cover your CDW if you rent for at least 15 days and charge the rental to your card. Check with your credit card company before you leave home to see what insurance coverage they include.

Some companies won't rent a car for more than about four weeks at a stretch, or will require you to bring the vehicle in for a mileage check and oil change every four weeks. Fly-drive packages are more likely to permit long-term rentals.

Purchase

If you're spending several months in the US, buying a car is worth considering; a car is more flexible than public transportation and buying one is likely to be cheaper than renting one. However, it can also be complicated and requires research. A good source of information is the American Automobile Association (AAA); see the Useful Organizations section of the Facts for the Visitor chapter for details on contacting them.

Driving Distances (in miles)

	Asheville	Athens	Atlanta	Augusta	Charleston	Charlotte	Columbia	Greenville	Macon	Myrtle Beach	Raleigh	Savannah
Athens	162											
Atlanta	207	65										
Augusta	177	98	145									
Charleston	285	297	344	199								
Charlotte	113	202	248	173	214							
Columbia	165	202	224	79	120	94						
Greenville	64	98	144	113	224	104	104					
Macon	314	91	84	137	276	293	216	189				
Myrtle Beach	295	316	363	218	98	182	139	243	355			
Raleigh	241	377	427	282	245	143	203	279	419	198		
Savannah	316	230	249	142	108	269	215	255	168	206	379	
Wilmington	310	387	434	289	169	197	208	301	426	71	127	277

It's possible to purchase a viable car for about $2000, but you can't expect to go too far before you'll need some repair work that could cost several hundred dollars or more. It doesn't hurt to spend more to get a quality vehicle. It's also worth spending $75 or so to have a mechanic check it for defects before you buy it. You can check out the official valuation of a used car by looking it up in the *Blue Book,* a listing of cars by make, model and year issued and the average resale price. Local public libraries have copies, as well as back issues of *Consumer Reports* that tally the repair records of common makes.

If you want to purchase a car, contact the Department of Motor Vehicles (DMV) to find out about registration fees and insurance – a vexing procedure. As an example, say you are a 30-year-old non-US citizen and you want to buy a 1984 Honda. If this is the first time you have registered a car in the US, you may have to fork over a $300 fee first and then $100 to $200 more for the actual registration.

Inspect the title carefully before purchasing the car; the name of the owner on the title must match the ID of the person selling you the car. If you're a foreigner, it may be useful to get a notarized document authorizing your use of the car. This will avoid nasty red tape at the motor vehicle bureau when you want to change the title.

While insurance is not obligatory in every state, all states have financial responsibility laws. Without liability insurance, a serious accident could easily dry up your funds, so watch out. To get insurance, some states require you to hold a US driver's license for at least 18 months. After that, you may still have to pay anywhere from $300 to $1200 a year for insurance, depending on where the car is registered. Collision coverage has become very expensive, with high deductibles; unless the car is valuable, you may want to consider passing on it.

Road Rules

The speed limit is generally 55mph or 65mph on highways, 25mph in cities and towns, and as low as 15mph in school zones

(strictly enforced during school hours). It's forbidden to pass a school bus when its taillights are flashing. On the interstate highways in designated rural areas, the speed limit can get as high as 75mph. Always watch for posted speed limits. Some towns have started hiding surveillance cameras *inside* traffic lights, which will take a photo of your license plate if you run a red light – these devils are often signposted.

Most states have laws against littering – if you are seen throwing anything from a vehicle, you can be fined $1000 and forced to pick up your litter.

In winter, it's a good idea to carry snow chains, but in the Southeast you'll only ever need them in the mountains.

Penalties are severe for DUI – driving under the influence of alcohol and/or drugs. Police can give roadside sobriety checks (making you touch your nose, walk in a straight line, etc) to see if you've been drinking or using drugs. If you fail, they'll require you to take a breath test, urine test, or blood test. If you refuse to be tested, you'll be treated as if you'd taken the test and failed. The maximum legal blood alcohol concentration is 0.08%.

During festive holidays and special events, road blocks are sometimes set up to catch drunk drivers, but some radio stations get wind of them and broadcast the locations. It's illegal to carry open containers of alcohol in a vehicle, even if they're empty or if only the passengers are imbibing. Containers that are full and sealed may be carried, but if they have been opened, they must be carried in the trunk.

Also see Legal Matters in the Facts for the Visitor chapter for more information.

BICYCLE

Notwithstanding the odd hurricane, flood or snow flurry, the Southeast is amenable to bike touring. The topography – mountains, beaches, and plains in between – offers something for all groups, and motorists are generally courteous. Some cities require helmets, others don't, but as a safety precaution helmets should always be worn. Also, as a safety measure cyclists should carry at least two full water bottles, a pump and patch kit. The availability of spare parts and repair shops varies, from plentiful along the coast (eg, the Outer Banks, Myrtle Beach and Savannah) to middling in the Piedmont and unheard-of in the back of beyond. In parts of the Appalachians, however, mountain biking (in the original sense) is becoming popular, although developed bike trails are still relatively rare.

The Outer Banks, flat as a pancake and piping hot in summer, have several good official bike paths and lots of unofficial ones. You'll find brilliant trails all along this part of the Atlantic coast, from the removed peace of Georgia's St Simon's Island to the neon glare of Myrtle Beach. The steady breeze down here takes the edge off the heat, and your mind off the sun – be sure to wear sunscreen. Historic districts are great for a spin, too (try Savannah).

The harsh summer temperatures should generally be avoided, and frequent rains may dampen bicyclists. Fall is the most consistently dry season, and many outfitters schedule group tours during that time. See Organized Tours, later in this chapter, for more bike-touring information.

For independent bicyclists, rentals are extremely limited in the region, so you may want to bring your bike with you. Bicycles can be transported by air. You can put them in a bike box, available from the airlines, but check with the airline for details well in advance, preferably before you pay for your ticket. Be aware that some airlines welcome bicycles, while others treat them as an undesirable nuisance and do everything possible to discourage them.

HITCHHIKING
Hitchhiking is never entirely safe in any country in the world, and we don't recommend it. Travelers who decide to hitch should understand that they are taking a small but potentially life-threatening risk. People who nevertheless choose to hitch will be safer if they travel in pairs, let someone know where they are planning to go, keep their luggage light and with them at all times, and sit by a door.

WALKING
You can cross the region on foot along the Appalachian Trail, part of the 2159-mile route along the spine of the mountain range (to get in the mood, read Bill Bryson's exhilarating tales of the trail in A Walk in the Woods). Another challenge is the recently completed 908-mile Mountains-to-Sea Trail from the Great Smoky Mountains all the way to Jockey's Ridge in the Outer Banks. Hiking trails abound in the national parks and many protected areas. For less strenuous activity, go for urban strolls in Columbus, Charleston, or Asheville, in neighborhoods filled with monuments and notable architecture.

LOCAL TRANSPORTATION
Cities and metropolitan areas operate local bus transit, and coverage ranges from extensive in Atlanta or Charlotte to pitiful or non-existent in the small towns. Historically, public transit has been largely the domain of poorer and generally underserved residents, and it's not uncommon for municipal transit systems in the Southeast to exist largely to transport domestic workers from poor neighborhoods to places of employment in rich neighborhoods – routes incompatible with the needs of travelers.

In historic towns or resort areas (such as Wilmington, Macon or Savannah), mock trolleys (they have buses underneath) may provide local transportation to major sites, along with commentary.

Taxis are common in bigger cities, and can easily be flagged for a fare. In small towns you generally must phone for a cab, and since distances are longer, taxis will be more expensive. Taxi fares will be between $1.25 and $1.75 for the first mile, $1 to $1.50 for each additional mile, with an added 10% tip (possibly more in cities). There are flat-rate cab fares for certain zones in Atlanta, Charlotte and other places.

Hotels often provide free shuttles to/from the airport.

ORGANIZED TOURS
For adventure excursions or specialized tours – such as mountain culture, natural

wonders or historic districts – an organized tour might be your best bet.

Carolina Culture Tours (☎ 888-286-6272), 20 Battery Park Ave Suite 617, Asheville, NC 22801, conducts well-respected trips on Lowcountry cooking, Piedmont crafts, bluegrass and much more, lasting a couple of days to a week. Prices start around $90 per day for the cheapest tours, rising to $1200 per week including room and board.
Web site: www.culturetours.com

For outdoor activities, operators provide all equipment and provisions, and guides know the territory best. Most of these are localized (see the destination chapters), but a few will traverse the region.

Backroads (☎ 510-527-1555, 800-462-2848), 801 Cedar St, Berkeley, CA 94710, has bicycling and hiking tours of the region that have multiple starting dates in the spring and a couple in the fall. Accommodations are included in the trip prices. The trips are varied; for example, one lets you bike, walk and sea kayak from Charleston to Savannah.
Web site: www.backroads.com

Lancaster Tours (☎ 803-285-5185, 800-621-4580, www.lancaster-tours.com), 2321 Airport Rd, Lancaster, SC 29270, conducts coach tours, particularly for students, throughout the Southeast. They offer trips as short as three days/two night to areas including Myrtle Beach, Atlanta, Charleston and the Outer Banks.

Georgia

Facts about Georgia

The largest state east of the Mississippi River, Georgia is much more diverse than stereotypes suggest – in its landscape, cultures, people and recreational possibilities. The state is a rambling land of pines, magnolias and moss-draped oak trees. Its farm and timber heritage survive, and it's a leading producer of pecans, peaches, peanuts, tobacco and forest products.

The North Georgia mountains offer wonderful hiking, mountain biking, canoeing and rafting. The center of the state presents a vast landscape of gently rolling farms and forests, populated by three mid-sized cities. The southern part of Georgia is a flat, coastal plain that still retains much of the rural culture that once characterized the entire state. Home to alligators and other marvelous wildlife, the Okefenokee Swamp, in the state's southeastern corner, is a great place to canoe. Not far away are Georgia's barrier islands, with secluded beaches, wild horses, disappearing cultures and serene marshlands.

Atlanta, the state's capital, is a bustling international center of business and a nexus of art, cultural activities and lively nightlife. On the coast, Savannah is a finely preserved paean to antebellum architecture; it's one of the best walking cities in the nation.

In the 1970s, the state became one of the fastest-growing areas of the country – a distinction that it retains today. Between 1990 and 2000, the state's population grew by 26.4%. The state's residents are also diverse – 65% white and 29% African American. Strong economic opportunities, whether in semi-rural textile mills or Atlanta's booming business climate, have attracted other nationalities; 5% of the population is Hispanic and 2% is of Asian heritage.

HISTORY

The Spanish were the first Europeans to visit what is now Georgia. Juan Ponce de León may have come to the state's coast in

Facts at a Glance

Nickname – Empire State of the South, Peach State

Population – 8.2 million (10th largest)

Area – 59,441 sq miles (24th largest)

Admitted to Union – 1778 (4th state to ratify the Constitution), seceded in 1861 (5th), readmitted in 1865, expelled in 1869, readmitted yet again in 1870

Capital – Atlanta (426,600; 3.6 million in the metro area)

Birthplace of – Martin Luther King Jr, Jimmy Carter (39th US President), Little Richard, Ray Charles

Famous for – *Gone with the Wind*, a tale of survival and a romanticized version of the Civil War-era South; official state song 'Georgia on My Mind'

First home for – Girl Scouts (Savannah, 1912), newspaper in a Native American language (Cherokee, New Echota, 1828), Coca-Cola (Atlanta, 1886), 24-hour news channel (CNN, Atlanta, 1980), US college to grant degrees to women (Wesleyan College, Macon), female US Senator (Rebecca L Felton, 1922)

Highlights – Strolling Savannah's historic district, canoeing the Okefenokee Swamp, hiking the North Georgia mountains

Most likely overheard – Adults calling their parents 'Daddy' and 'Mama'; 'y'all'; complaints about Atlanta traffic

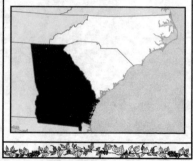

1513, and other Spanish expeditions certainly visited the area over the next two decades, including Hernando DeSoto in 1540. The Spanish constructed a fort on St Catherine's Island and established missions on many other islands.

Permanent English settlement dates from 1733 when James Edward Oglethorpe and 20 other trustees founded Savannah. Tomochichi, a Creek chief, persuaded other tribes to permit the colonists to settle. The settlement was intended as a buffer between the Spanish in Florida and the English colony of South Carolina. A battle on St Simons Island in 1742 ended Spanish hopes of colonizing the area and established English dominance over the eastern part of North America.

An enduring myth is that the colony – last of the original 13 – was settled by prison convicts. Oglethorpe, in fact, planned to provide a refuge for the penniless released from debtors' prison and for dissident Protestant sects. This noble goal, however, was subverted by the practical need for soldiers, farmers and merchants; of the 5,500 settlers that arrived in 21 years, only a handful had spent time in debtors' prison. (Native Georgian historian James Cobb wrote: 'When I heard anyone repeat the outrageous falsehood that Georgians are descended from thieves and murderers, it made me so mad that I wanted to shoot him or at least take his wallet.')

Hard liquor, Catholicism, and slavery were initially banned in the colony. Slavery was prohibited because Oglethorpe believed it would make the settlers lazy and he feared a slave uprising. Plans for silk production and many other commercial schemes failed, settlers were unhappy over the restrictions (especially the ban on slavery, which was lifted in 1750), and the trustees turned the colony over to the King in 1752.

Once the slavery ban was lifted, the colony grew rapidly. By the time of the Revolutionary War, almost half the population was slaves. Smaller-scale farming and industry in the more mountainous north complemented the lowland agricultural cotton society. Rice plantations were common along the coast.

During the Revolutionary War, the British captured Savannah in December 1778, and eventually nearly all of Georgia. They were driven out in 1782, and Georgia became the second largest of the new United States of America in 1788.

After Eli Whitney invented the cotton gin outside Savannah in 1793, cotton farming based on slavery expanded rapidly. Although most slaves worked on large plantations, most farms were small operations.

Georgia initially extended westward to the Mississippi River. Lands west of the Chattahoochee River were sold to the Federal government in 1802 in exchange for a promise to settle contentious land claims and to remove Native Americans from the state. By 1827, the Creek had sold their land in Georgia and moved to the Arkansas Territory. In 1828, gold was discovered near Dahlonega, which became one of north Georgia's main population centers. This sped up the dispossession of North Georgia's Cherokee population during the first half of the 19th century, culminating in their forced removal to Oklahoma along the 1838 Trail of Tears.

Georgia was the fifth state to secede from the Union in 1861, though many Georgians remained Unionist, especially in the north. Though far removed from the Civil War's early phases, Georgia was one of the most important battlefronts in the latter part of the war. Union troops were defeated at Chickamauga, but fought their way to Atlanta, which they defeated and burned; they then marched through Georgia to Savannah (see the boxed text 'War in Georgia'). After the war, the US Congress set up an agency to distribute the fabled '40 acres and a mule' to freed slaves along the coast in an attempt to economically equalize whites and blacks, but most lands were eventually returned to plantation owners or sold to speculators. Atlanta, the South's major transportation hub, was rebuilt with startling speed.

The state's economy continued to be dominated by cotton, but weaving became

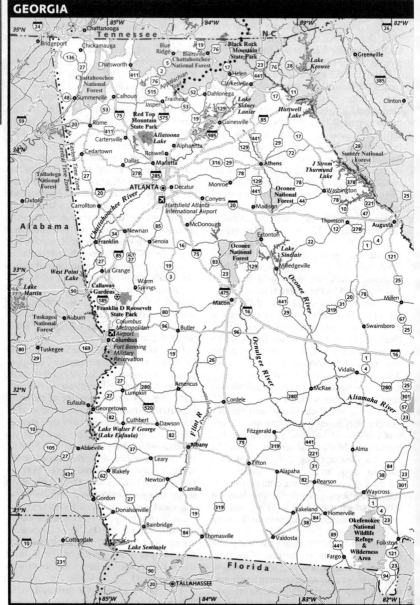

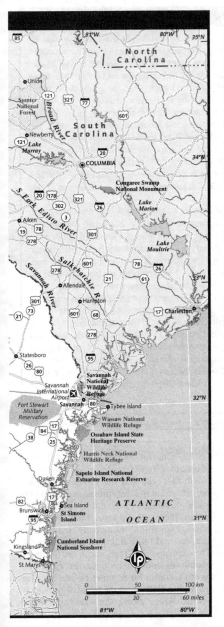

as important as growing, and the textile industry expanded. Manufacturing and trade grew, and many plantations were divided into smaller lots. In the early 20th century, agriculture became more diversified, expanding into corn, fruit and tobacco. Defense expenditures during WWII helped the economy significantly by increasing industrialization, and also led to a migration of farm workers to cities.

After WWII, Georgia's passage through the civil rights era was less traumatic than that of some other Southern states, in part because business leaders recognized the futility of fighting the inevitable. In early 2001, the Georgia state flag, which had incorporated the Confederate battle flag – to some a symbol of Southern heritage, to others a symbol of slavery and racism – was changed in an attempt to decrease racial divisions.

In the 20th century the state vaulted to national prominence on the back of an eclectic group of events and images: the wildly popular film (and novel) *Gone With the Wind;* Martin Luther King Jr and the Civil Rights protest marches; Jimmy Carter; and Atlanta's rise as a global media and business center, culminating in the 1996 Summer Olympics.

GEOGRAPHY

Like other East Coast states, Georgia has a coastal plain, a central upland plateau and a portion of the Appalachian Range farther inland. The mountains, though they can provide some lovely views, are not particularly high. The state's highest point is Brasstown Bald, in northeast Georgia, at 4784 feet above sea level. The central plateau, known as the Piedmont, has gently rolling hills and the state's largest cities. The drop in height between the central plateau and the southern coastal plains is known as the 'fall line.' The flat coastal plain has fertile soil good for growing peanuts, onions, tobacco and watermelons. The Okefenokee Swamp covers a large portion of the state's southeast corner. Georgia has many rivers, including the Chattahoochee and Altamaha; many are dammed to create artificial lakes.

War in Georgia

In 1862, the Union bombarded and defeated the Confederates at Fort Pulaski near Savannah, effectively blocking this vital port from shipping its cotton cash crop and receiving military supplies. The Union soon controlled all the sea islands, and many slaves escaped to the coast during the war.

The first significant land battle on Georgia soil was at Chickamauga in September 1863, when the Confederates won a rare victory and pushed the Yanks back to Chattanooga. In the spring of 1864, General William Tecumseh Sherman began moving his forces inexorably toward Atlanta, usually outflanking the Confederates in superior numbers rather than meeting them head-on. Battles were fought at Resaca, New Hope Church, Kennesaw Mountain and Pickett's Mill. Upon reaching Atlanta, the forces fought four more battles and Sherman laid siege to the city, pounding it with artillery and forcing many civilians to flee. Ultimately, the Confederate Army evacuated, and Sherman's troops marched in. Sherman ordered the remaining 1600 white civilians (and uncounted blacks) out of the city; when the mayor submitted a formal protest, Sherman replied, 'War is cruelty, and you cannot refine it…. You might as well appeal against the thunderstorm as against these terrible hardships of war.'

After 10 weeks in the city, Sherman set fire to all major buildings, destroying Atlanta's railroad and industrial centers. He then began his famous (infamous if you're a Southerner) March to the Sea. His goal was to 'make Georgia howl' by breaking the spirit of its citizens and destroying the economic and transportation resources that supported the Confederate Army. He left Atlanta with 62,000 troops and cut a path 60 miles wide through the countryside, destroying all factories, mills, bridges, public buildings and railroads – more than $100 million in property. His troops lived off the land, looting the countryside and stealing food from plantations, towns and even slave cabins. More than 25,000 slaves freed themselves by flocking to the Union lines; Sherman was more annoyed than appreciative of this civilian army that ate up his supplies and got in his way.

As the Union troops neared Savannah, the outnumbered Confederates abandoned the city to avoid being encircled. Sherman entered the city on December 21, 1864, but refrained from annihilating it. He telegraphed President Lincoln: 'I beg to present you as a Christmas gift the city of Savannah, with 150 heavy guns and plenty of ammunition, also about 25,000 bales of cotton.' He rested his troops, then headed north to South Carolina. Because of his focus on breaking the will of the civilian population instead of fighting enemy soldiers, Sherman's name remains anathema to many Southerners to this day.

NATIONAL PARKS & PROTECTED AREAS

Georgia has no full-blown National Parks, but does have many protected areas. The Okefenokee National Wildlife Refuge & Wilderness Area in southeast Georgia protects the 650-sq-mile Okefenokee Swamp, the largest in the US; canoeing here is one of the state's highlights. The Cumberland Island National Seashore on Georgia's southernmost barrier island is accessible only by ferry and offers beachcombing, armadillo seeking, hiking and camping.

The Chattahoochee National Forest blankets 750,000 mountainous acres in North Georgia, and the Oconee National Forest encompasses more than 113,000 acres of rolling hills in central Georgia. Together, these contain more than 500 developed campsites, numerous lakes and streams, and more than 500 miles of trails. The Appalachian Trail starts on Springer Mountain and climbs over the ridges of North Georgia for 80 miles before heading for Maine. Rafting on the Chattooga Wild & Scenic River along the Georgia–South

Carolina border may be the most thrilling activity in the state.

The Feds also operate the Chatta-hoochee River National Recreation Area between Atlanta and Lake Sidney Lanier; the Chickamauga & Chattanooga National Military Park in northwest Georgia; a few National Historic Sites (Jimmy Carter in Plains, Martin Luther King Jr in Atlanta, and Andersonville, where you can see the old Camp Sumpter Confederate prison); and three National Monuments (Fort Fred-erica on St Simons Island; Fort Pulaski near Savannah; and Ocmulgee near Macon).

Georgia has an excellent system of 48 state parks, with the greatest concentration in the North Georgia mountains. Recreational opportunities include hiking, mountain biking, fishing, boating, canoeing, swimming, backpacking, and sometimes horseback riding, golfing, miniature golfing, pedal-boat rental and tennis. Entry to each park requires a $2 ParkPass or an annual $25 parking pass; Wednesdays are free.

Most state parks have well-run camp-grounds with hot showers and flush toilets; rates are about $13 to $18. Some parks have cheaper walk-in campsites ($6 to $12) or primitive campsites ($3 to $8 per person) and many parks have one- to three-bedroom cottages equipped with kitchens and cooking utensils. Pets are not allowed. Rates range from $55 to $115, depending on the park, cottage size and time of year. Five parks have hotel-style lodges. The Department of Natural Resources (☎ 404-656-2770), 1352 Floyd Tower East, 205 Butler St SE, Atlanta, GA 30334, distributes brochures, operates a useful Web site (www.gastateparks.org) and sells a comprehensive travel guide.

Reservations for almost all park accommodations – including camping – can be made by calling a central reservations number (☎ 800-864-7275, in metro Atlanta ☎ 770-389-7275), and are accepted from 11 months to the day in advance of your stay. Minimum stays often apply when making

Kudzu

Throughout the South, you'll often see areas with large trees completely covered by a leafy green vine, like impossibly large topiaries. This is kudzu, brought by the Japanese to Philadelphia in the late 19th century as a decoration. Southerners adopted it as a fragrant, shady porch vine. The US Soil Conservation Service discovered that it stopped erosion and planted it throughout the South.

Oops. Growing as much as a foot a day in the hot, moist Southern climate, kudzu took over farmers' fields, climbed electric poles and created electrical outages, derailed trains on steep grades, smothered trees and swallowed porches, billboards, road signs and abandoned automobiles. This 'savior of Southern soil' – as it was once called – blankets 7 million acres from Florida to Maryland and as far west as Louisiana (an area the size of Massachusetts). Once established, the tough vines are difficult to get rid of – the root of a 20-year-old plant can weigh 250 pounds. Construction and road building help spread kudzu – a single root buried in fill material can create an infestation.

Not everyone sees kudzu as completely useless. The Japanese use it in tea, as a health tonic and to make kimono fibers. The Chinese use it to make rope and as a hangover remedy. Enterprising Southerners turn it into art or food – making woven-kudzu baskets, kudzu-blossom jelly, or french-fried kudzu. Festivals celebrating the weed are popping up in small towns. Cattle and sheep love it, but there's more of it than them.

So while in Georgia, grab a sharp machete and go looking for your next art project or meal. Just don't fall asleep next to it.

reservations for cabins, so be sure to ask. For example, most cabin accommodations in the summer must be booked in advance, and the minimum stay is seven nights (waived if you call within 30 days of your visit).

The Department of Natural Resources also operates about 15 State Historic Sites; 11 are covered in this book. These are closed on Mondays. And finally, 79 wildlife management areas where you can hike or walk are scattered around the state.

GOVERNMENT & POLITICS

Like many Southern states, Georgia was solidly Democratic from shortly after the Civil War until the mid-1960s; in fact, every Governor since 1872 has been a Democrat, though other elected officials have been Republican. From 1872 until 1964, there were *no* Republican US representatives. The Democratic party primary dominated the elections and determined the winner of the general elections. African Americans were effectively disenfranchised because they were banned from voting in the Democratic primary until 1946, when the US Supreme Court overturned the ban. The primary was dominated by the county-unit system, in which the candidate winning the most counties won the election; this system maximized the rural vote and minimized the urban vote. The county-unit system was ruled unconstitutional in 1962, giving more equal representation to urban (and black) voters. It wasn't until 1968 that there were more representatives from urban areas than rural areas.

Since the '60s, Georgia's politics have drifted to the right as white voters became disenchanted with the Civil Rights leanings of the Democratic Party. As is so often the case in the South, race remains a major political fault line: after the 1998 elections all of Georgia's Republican congressmen were white and all of its Democrats were black, though its current governor, Roy Barnes, is white and a Democrat.

ARTS

Atlanta dominates the arts scene in Georgia, with the respected Atlanta Sym-phony Orchestra and the High Museum of Art. The theatre scene is very active here as well, and venues such as the Fox Theater support a range of Broadway musicals and other entertainment.

For architecture, Savannah clearly reigns supreme, with its large Historic District of stately, Regency-style houses, used as models for Greek Revival homes throughout the state. The 6000-student Savannah College of Art and Design (SCAD) is renowned for its programs on the visual and performing arts, design, building arts, and the history of art and architecture.

Georgia has a strong musical tradition, from composer Johnny Mercer to soul man James Brown. The Georgia Music Hall of Fame in Macon celebrates the state's musical history. Country and gospel can be heard throughout the state, and bluegrass is popular in the northern mountains. Music of the area is covered in the special section in the Facts About the Region chapter.

Literature

Georgia has a rich legacy of literature. *Georgia Voices – Volume 1: Fiction,* edited by Hugh Ruppersburg, is an excellent collection of stories and novel excerpts by Georgia writers, from Sidney Lanier to most of the writers mentioned later in this section. *Georgia Voices – Volume 2: Nonfiction* does the same for nonfiction, from James Oglethorpe to Martin Luther King Jr and Jimmy Carter.

Joel Chandler Harris (1848–1908), born in Eatonton, grew up listening to African folk tales told by plantation slaves. He later published many of these stories as told by 'Uncle Remus.' His first two books – *Uncle Remus: His Songs and His Sayings* (1880) and *Nights with Uncle Remus* (1883) – recite the tales in their purest forms; later books contain larger elements of Harris' own imagination. Harris has become controversial largely due to the character of Uncle Remus – a docile ex-slave who has fond memories of the days of slavery. The books are written in a strong dialect that is also controversial and moreover makes the books quite difficult to read. Nevertheless,

Harris' role in helping save authentic African folk tales is undeniable. Several recent children's books tell the tales themselves without using the controversial character of Uncle Remus, and recordings provide an easy introduction. The antics of Brer Rabbit and the Tar Baby were later featured in Disney's 1946 movie *Song of the South;* continuing controversies over racial stereotyping keep this film from being available.

Gone with the Wind (1936), by Margaret Mitchell (Atlanta; 1900–49), is the second best selling novel of all time (after the Bible). With the success of the 1939 movie, this is *still* the image many people (including Southerners) have of Georgia during and after the Civil War. An epic romance and enduring tale of survival, it immortalized stereotypes of the Georgia belle, the Southern lady and gentleman, and the contented slave.

Carson McCullers (1917–67), from Columbus, wrote several novels and stories addressing loneliness, adolescence, social ostracism and racial divisions. She achieved worldwide fame at the age of 23 with the publication of her stunning novel *The Heart is a Lonely Hunter,* about a deaf-mute and a teenage girl, isolated in a small mill town. *A Member of the Wedding* is a coming-of-age story made into a successful Broadway play. Both novels also made good films.

Flannery O'Connor (1925–64), born in Savannah, is the master of Southern gothic fiction. Her characters are often alienated psychopaths, deformed in both body and spirit, who seek redemption. Her influential output consists of two novels and two short-story collections.

Alice Walker (born 1944, in Eatonton) is one of the nation's preeminent African-American writers and poets. *The Color Purple* (1982), popular as a novel and a film, is the story of the growth and awakening of an abused farm woman in the first half of the 20th century.

For lighter reading, *Cold Sassy Tree* (1984), by Olive Ann Burns (1924–1990), is a humorous, tender story of a recently widowed grandfather who creates a scandal in a small 1906 Southern town by marrying a Yankee suffragist half his age.

Bailey White's wry stories of South Georgia life have been broadcast on National Public Radio. An elementary school teacher near Thomasville, her stories are collected in *Mama Makes Up Her Mind* (1993) and *Sleeping at the Starlite Motel* (1995). To appreciate her slow, Southern drawl, try to find a recording.

Former US President and Plains native Jimmy Carter has written 15 books, tackling subjects that include Middle East peace, conflict resolution, his presidential memoirs, poetry and fly fishing. His latest, *An Hour Before Daylight* (2001), describes his memories of growing up during the Depression on a South Georgia farm, including an eye-opening account of race relations before Civil Rights.

For general information, *The New Georgia Guide* (1996) follows in the footsteps of the depression-era Federal Writers' Project of the Works Progress Administration, presenting a combination of history, travelogue and social analysis of each region in Georgia. It's enlightening but sometimes long-winded.

INFORMATION

The Georgia Department of Industry, Trade & Tourism (☎ 800-847-4842, 404-656-3590), PO Box 1776, Atlanta, GA 30301, will send you an excessively thick travel guide, or you can check their Web site at www .georgia.org. There is a Georgia Welcome Center off all the interstates as they cross into the state (as well as at Plains, and before Hwy 301 crosses into South Carolina). Local Chambers of Commerce also operate welcome centers in many towns. For a listing of tourist offices in other countries, turn to the Facts for the Visitor chapter.

Tourist areas can be busy in spring, summer and fall, especially on weekends. Rates for accommodations vary widely with the season.

The state sales tax is 4%; cities add 1% to 3% on top of this. In addition, cities impose a 4% to 7% bed tax, so that the total hotel tax adds up to a steep 9% to 14%.

Legal Matters

Georgia's liquor laws vary by county. Alcohol can be purchased from state liquor stores Monday through Saturday, but not on Sundays, election day, Thanksgiving or Christmas. Grocery stores often sell beer and wine. Some rural counties prohibit alcohol sales totally, while others may restrict sales to beer and wine only. In some counties, you may be able to buy a drink in a restaurant only with food, and in some resorts, you can drink only if you bring your own.

Motorcycle helmets are required, as are seat belts for drivers and all passengers. Child restraints are mandatory for ages three and under, as are bicycle helmets for ages 16 and under.

BOOKS

A large number of specialist hiking, biking and other books on the Blue Ridge Mountain area in North Georgia have been published. The *Highroad Guide to the Georgia Mountains,* by the Georgia Conservancy, is the best overall guide to outdoor opportunities offered in the mountains. It includes plenty of geology and natural descriptions, plus good maps. *The Hiking Trails of North Georgia,* by Tim Homan, describes 124 trails of various lengths and degree of difficulty.

Mountain Biking Georgia, by Alex Nutt, provides the needed details for a biking vacation. *Mountain Bike: The Southern Appalachian and Smoky Mountains,* lists 16 rides in Georgia. *Biking the Trails of Rabun,* by Lester Raney, focuses on the trails of Rabun County. *Road Bike North Georgia,* by Jim Parham, has 25 rides for bicyclists without knobby tires.

SPECIAL EVENTS

For a list of non-Georgia-specific public holidays, see the Facts for the Visitor chapter.

For more special events related to individual cities, see the various Georgia chapters.

January

Martin Luther King Jr Holiday – Atlanta; a week of arts, entertainment, speeches and church services celebrates the national holiday centered around the Atlanta Civil Rights leader

March

St Patrick's Day – Savannah; second largest Irish celebration in the US

Cherry Blossom Festival – Macon; celebrates the blossoming of 250,000 flowering Japanese Yoshino cherry trees (more than are in Washington DC)

April

Classic City Brew-Fest – Athens; the South's largest indoor beer festival

Riverfest – Columbus; folk artists, five stages of entertainment, and a barbecue contest

Masters Golf Tournament – Augusta; one of the country's most prestigious tournaments

Atlanta Dogwood Festival – Atlanta; the city's largest festival, featuring blooming dogwoods

June

Bicycle Ride Across Georgia (BRAG) – location varies; a week-long ride through Georgia in the sweat of summer (☎ 770-921-6166, www.brag.org)

July

Peachtree Road Race – Atlanta; held on the Fourth of July every year with 50,000 runners, this is the world's largest 10km road race

September

Helen's Oktoberfest – Helen; German food and polkas, through early November

October

Georgia State Fair – Macon; Americana: everything from rides to hog shows to eating contests

Gold Rush Days – Dahlonega; arts and crafts, food, gold-panning contests

Atlanta

pop 426,600

The 'Capital of the New South,' Atlanta is one of the nation's fastest-growing metropolitan areas. Internationally known as the host of the 1996 Olympics and the home of CNN, Atlanta is one of the country's top business destinations, with more than 3000 conventions held here annually. While some Southerners consider Atlanta to be too big, new, foreign and fast to be truly Southern, the entire South follows Atlanta Braves baseball.

Atlanta covers 131 sq miles in the city proper; the metropolitan area sprawls over 6126 sq miles in 20 counties and contains 3.6 million people. Nearly 45% of Georgia's population lives in the Atlanta metro area; an average of 110,000 people moved here annually throughout the 1990's. Atlanta has the highest per-capita income in the state, but also the largest discrepancies between rich and poor. Ethnic neighborhoods,

Highlights

- Soak up the crowning moments of the Civil Rights era at the Martin Luther King Jr National Historic Site.

- Line up for a taste of heaven at the Flying Biscuit Café.

- Catch a show for the at the Center for Puppetry Arts.

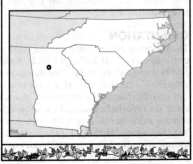

booming with Chinese, Korean and Hispanic newcomers, are popping up everywhere, along with transplants from throughout the US. The influx creates a tension: Some traditionalists complain that if the Yankees don't like the way things are done, they can just go home; others point out that Southern hospitality ought to include making newcomers feel more welcome.

Atlanta's population is 61% African American within the city limits, 29% overall in the metro area. Ebony Magazine in 1997 named it the number one city in the US for African Americans.

Today, freeways slice through the city, high-rise buildings abound, and the suburbs spill ever farther north and east. But Atlanta is appealing for its diverse and progressive population and its widely varied neighborhoods. It has lots of young people and students, an active gay community and a prosperous black middle class. It's also the South's cosmopolitan center for the arts, education, sports and fine dining.

Of course, Atlanta has its big-city problems of crime, pollution and nightmarish traffic, and the universal American problem of racial tension, but people on the street still meet your eyes and say hello.

HISTORY

Atlanta was created as a railroad junction in 1837, connecting a new line from Chattanooga, Tennessee to several existing lines. It was originally called Terminus, later Marthasville, and eventually Atlanta. A railroad town quickly sprang up, disproving the conventional wisdom that major cities could grow only on coastal harbors and navigable rivers (the Chattahoochee River was not navigable above Columbus). By 1861, when the Civil War started, Atlanta had grown to 9,000 inhabitants.

Because of its rail links and relatively safe location, the town became a major Confederate industrial, transportation and munitions center. This made the city a prime objective for the Union forces. Union General William T Sherman invaded Georgia in 1864; Atlanta was besieged from mid-July until its surrender on September 2.

Much of the city was destroyed in the siege, and still more was destroyed when retreating Confederates blew up their own ammunition and explosives. Then Sherman ordered the remaining people evacuated, escorted them outside the city and left them in the countryside. His army remained in the city about 10 weeks. When they left in mid-November, they burned everything that might be of any use to the Confederates. By the time they were done, more than 90% of Atlanta's buildings lay in ruins.

After the war, Atlanta became the epitome of the 'New South,' a concept that entailed reconciliation with the north, the promotion of industrialized agriculture, and a progressive business outlook. Its railroads were rebuilt within a year after the Civil War ended. The state capital was moved from Milledgeville to Atlanta in 1868. The city became a center of cotton processing. The railroads continued to grow, helping the local economy, affecting the city's layout, and providing connections to the rest of the country.

Atlanta's relentless boosterism led to civic improvements and energetic business partnerships. In the late 1800s, the city's oldest institutions were created – Coca-Cola, the *Atlanta Journal* and *Atlanta Constitution,* the public school system, and several separate colleges for whites and blacks, including Spelman, Morehouse and Emory Colleges. Suburbanization started when the town of Inman Park was connected to downtown by streetcar service. A 1920s campaign launched by the Chamber of Commerce lured 762 new businesses into town.

Parallel black and white societies developed, completely separate from each other. Racial tensions erupted in 1906 when white mobs attacked African Americans. Nevertheless, black businesses developed, segregated by whether they served white or black clientele. Sweet Auburn Avenue was a particularly energetic area of black businesses serving black customers.

Atlanta and the rest of the South were helped by increased government spending during World War II. Afterwards, Atlanta embarked on another improvement plan, annexing surrounding suburbs, establishing the rim-and-spoke highway system and expanding the local airport. This era was dominated by an elite power structure consisting of a few white men.

After public sit-ins and demonstrations in the early 1960s led by Atlanta native Reverend Martin Luther King Jr, the city's business leaders signed a joint agreement to desegregate public accommodations. This relatively painless transition was lauded by President John F Kennedy as a model for other communities facing integration. By 1970, Atlanta's population was predominantly African American.

Atlanta continues its explosive growth. Construction cranes are everywhere; the Atlanta approach is to tear down the old and put up something new made of steel and glass. Without natural boundaries, the city continues to expand. Increased suburbanization has increased racial segregation and dependence on the automobile. Atlanta's century of boosterism culminated when it hosted the 1996 Summer Olympic Games. The final Olympic financial records have never been made public, but the boost to the city's morale and status are unquestioned. With the Carter Center working worldwide for peace and civil rights, Ted Turner's 24-hour Cable News Network (CNN) beamed throughout the country and world, and numerous global conglomerates with local offices, Atlanta has become a truly international city.

ORIENTATION

The sprawling Atlanta metropolitan area is crisscrossed by I-20, I-75 and I-85. I-75 and I-85 become a single road – 'the downtown connector' – as they pass through the city center. I-285 forms 'the perimeter,' though there are suburbs beyond it. Peachtree St is a main north-south artery through town but be aware that 100 other streets, avenues, roads, circles, courts, boulevards, places, parkways etc, are also called

'Peachtree.' Atlanta's bizarre street-naming quirks mean that it's important to be precise with the street name: W Peachtree St, for example, is a separate street running parallel but west of Peachtree St; W Peachtree St merges into Peachtree St, which promptly changes its name to Peachtree Rd north of I-85. Several other major streets follow this odd naming convention or change names periodically after crossing a major intersection. Two streets are unimaginatively named 'Boulevard' and 'North Ave.'

Addresses specify NE, SE, SW or NW, with W Peachtree St (and, farther north, Peachtree Rd) dividing east from west, and Martin Luther King Jr Dr/Edgewood Ave dividing north from south. It's pretty clear once you get used to it (and with the LP maps in hand) where each quadrant is; for example, 'NE' is north of Underground Atlanta and to the east of W Peachtree St.

The city is also oriented around its rapid transit system, known as MARTA (Metropolitan Atlanta Rapid Transit Authority), which divides the city in quadrants running roughly along compass lines. Attractions may note their proximity to the nearest MARTA stop.

Downtown is centered on Five Points and Centennial Park and is bordered on the east by the I-75/85 downtown connector. East of downtown, Sweet Auburn was a progressive black district in the 1920s. Auburn Ave is now being revived around sites associated with Martin Luther King Jr and the Civil Rights movement. Northeast of Auburn is Little Five Points (L5P), with bars, bookstores, cafes and clubs for Atlanta's students and grunge set. Farther east – and further upmarket – is Virginia Highland. Also to the east is Decatur, an independent city, but still well inside the perimeter, and the home of several good nightspots.

Turner Field (formerly Olympic Stadium), Grant Park – with its Zoo and nearby family neighborhoods – and East Atlanta are south and southeast of downtown. The West End, west of downtown, is Atlanta's oldest neighborhood and has a lively black community.

North of downtown, Midtown is another upmarket entertainment and nightlife area, the center of the arts scene and a focus of gay life. Ralph McGill Boulevard is its southern boundary. The posh suburb of Buckhead, with high-rise office towers, shopping and nightlife, is farther north.

Northeast, Buford Highway near Doraville is called the International Corridor for its ethnic population and concentration of Asian and Latino businesses.

Maps

Many free maps are available at tourist centers, hotels and the like, usually with a detailed map of downtown and a usable map of surrounding areas. For detailed explorations, the ADC Street Map Book ($11), available in local bookstores, is a worthy investment.

Be aware that new construction and constant neighborhood renewals may make many maps out of date. (A developer recently petitioned the city to change the street name for his new office tower because a major law client wanted to be 'on Peachtree.' Thus, Atlanta ended up with yet another street named Peachtree.) As in the rest of Georgia, maps may retain older Interstate exit numbers, which were changed in 2000. Most remain usable, if occasionally confusing.

INFORMATION
Tourist Offices

The Atlanta Convention and Visitors Bureau (☎ 404-222-6688, fax 404-521-6562), 233 Peachtree St, Suite 100, Atlanta, GA 30303, mails out comprehensive visitor brochures and operates a good Web site (www.atlanta.com). The *Atlanta Now* magazine published by the Bureau has the best organized listings of events, restaurants and hotels (including price ranges). The downtown map they give out is decent.

The Bureau also runs information centers at the airport (North Terminal, ☎ 404-305-8426); at Lenox Square (☎ 404-266-1398); and at Underground Atlanta (☎ 404-577-2148), 65 Upper Alabama St. The Underground Atlanta office, at the intersection of

Alabama and Pryor Sts, is the most comprehensive; it's open until 6 pm daily.

The Bureau also has brochures in Spanish, French, Portuguese and German and specific-interest brochures tailored to ethnic tourism (mostly African American).

Money

Currency Exchange Thomas Cook Currency Services (☎ 800-287-7362, 404-350-8750) has counters at the Hartsfield Atlanta International Airport in the main atrium and on Concourse E (the international concourse).

American Express can exchange foreign currency at its two offices: 3384 Peachtree Rd (Map 6; ☎ 404-262-7561), near Lenox Square in Buckhead; and in Perimeter Mall (Map 2; ☎ 770-395-1305).

Main downtown offices of major banks can exchange foreign currency, as can some top-end hotels. Most banks are open 9 am to 4 pm weekdays, and sometimes on Saturday until noon.

ATMs You won't have a problem finding an ATM in Atlanta. In most locations, you're probably within a block of one. Besides the usual places (banks, shopping malls), ATMs are found in some museums, hotels and restaurants. Peachtree Center has three full-service banks.

Taxes

The basic sales tax in Atlanta is 7%, which incorporates the state sales tax of 4% plus an additional 3% local option. The hotel tax is an additional 7%, for a total of 14%.

Post & Communications

Mail All General Delivery mail must be sent to the post office (Map 3; ☎ 404-521-9843) at Federal Center, 41 Marietta St NW, Atlanta, GA 30301. For general information, call ☎ 800-275-8777. Other branches in business and tourist areas that may be of interest are:

Buckhead – 1 Buckhead Loop Rd, Map 6
CNN Center – 1 CNN Center, Map 3
Little Five Points – 457 Moreland Ave SE, Map 5

Main Post Office – 3900 Crown Rd SW, Map 2
Midtown – 1072 W Peachtree St, Map 4
North Highland – 1190 N Highland Ave NE, Map 5
Peachtree Center – 240 Peachtree St NW, Map 3
Pharr Road (Buckhead) – 575 Pharr Rd NE, Map 6

Most post offices are open 8:30 am to 5 pm weekdays and 8:30 am to noon Saturday.

Telephone Three area codes – 404, 678 and 770 – serve the Atlanta and metro area. You must dial all 10 digits (with a 1) when making local calls, even when dialing between numbers with the same area code. Hotels might charge exorbitant fees for calls from their rooms.

Email & Internet Access Internet access is provided for free at many branches of the public library (see the Libraries section later in this chapter). Some hotels are beginning to add Internet access, either in the lobby or in rooms.

The e-Bar Cyber Café (☎ 404-221-9825), 84 Peachtree St, in the Flatiron Building across from Woodruff Park, offers 10 computers with Internet access at $10 an hour, a full coffee bar, basic business services (fax, copier) and an ATM in a hip atmosphere with background jazz. You can check your email for five minutes with the purchase of a coffee. It's open starting 6 am weekdays, 10 am weekends, and closes at 9 pm weekdays, 1 am weekends, and 6 pm Sunday.

Newspapers & Magazines

The *Atlanta Journal-Constitution* is Atlanta's major newspaper by far, with a Sunday circulation of 700,000 readers. Cartoonist Mike Luckovich is distributed widely throughout the country. The daily Vent column will give you a quick summary of what Atlantans whine about.
Web site: www.ajc.com

The *Atlanta Business Chronicle* is the major newspaper for local business news, with a circulation of 40,000.
Web site: www.amcity.com/atlanta

[Continued on Page 126]

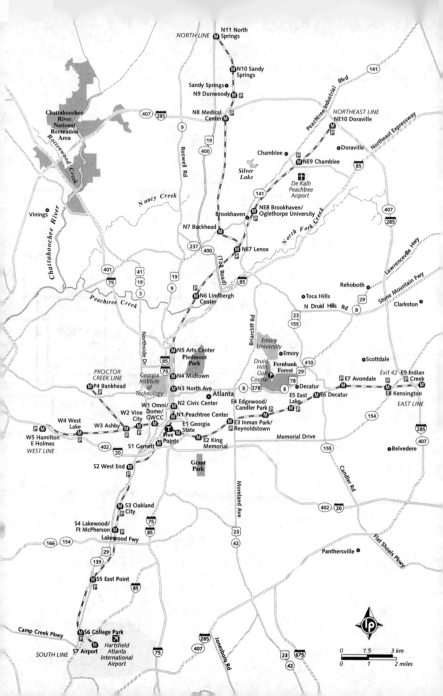

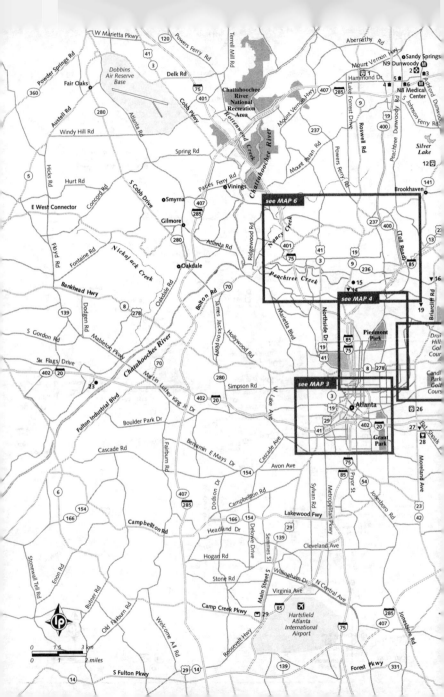

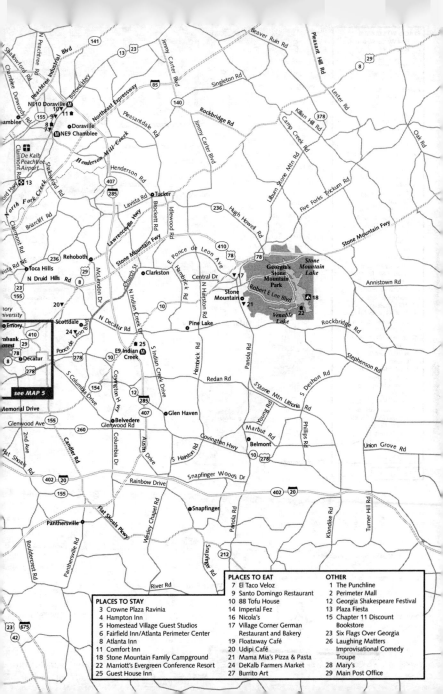

PLACES TO STAY
3 Crowne Plaza Ravinia
4 Hampton Inn
5 Homestead Village Guest Studios
6 Fairfield Inn/Atlanta Perimeter Center
8 Atlanta Inn
11 Comfort Inn
18 Stone Mountain Family Campground
22 Marriott's Evergreen Conference Resort
25 Guest House Inn

PLACES TO EAT
7 El Taco Veloz
9 Santo Domingo Restaurant
10 88 Tofu House
14 Imperial Fez
16 Nicola's
17 Village Corner German Restaurant and Bakery
19 Floataway Café
20 Udipi Café
21 Mama Mia's Pizza & Pasta
24 DeKalb Farmers Market
27 Burrito Art

OTHER
1 The Punchline
2 Perimeter Mall
12 Georgia Shakespeare Festival
13 Plaza Fiesta
15 Chapter 11 Discount Bookstore
23 Six Flags Over Georgia
26 Laughing Matters Improvisational Comedy Troupe
28 Mary's
29 Main Post Office

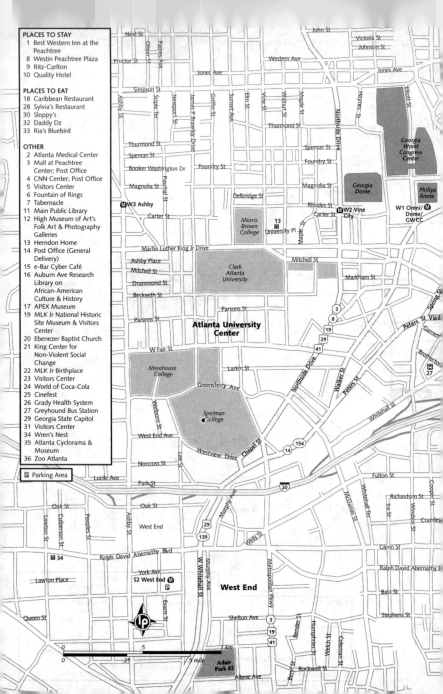

PLACES TO STAY
1 Best Western Inn at the Peachtree
8 Westin Peachtree Plaza
9 Ritz-Carlton
10 Quality Hotel

PLACES TO EAT
18 Caribbean Restaurant
28 Sylvia's Restaurant
30 Sloppy's
32 Daddy Dz
33 Ria's Bluebird

OTHER
2 Atlanta Medical Center
3 Mall at Peachtree Center; Post Office
4 CNN Center; Post Office
5 Visitors Center
6 Fountain of Rings
7 Tabernacle
11 Main Public Library
12 High Museum of Art's Folk Art & Photography Galleries
13 Herndon Home
14 Post Office (General Delivery)
15 e-Bar Cyber Café
16 Auburn Ave Research Library on African-American Culture & History
17 APEX Museum
19 MLK Jr National Historic Site Museum & Visitors Center
20 Ebenezer Baptist Church
21 King Center for Non-Violent Social Change
22 MLK Jr Birthplace
23 Visitors Center
24 World of Coca-Cola
25 Cinefest
26 Grady Health System
27 Greyhound Bus Station
29 Georgia State Capitol
31 Visitors Center
34 Wren's Nest
35 Atlanta Cyclorama & Museum
36 Zoo Atlanta

🅿 Parking Area

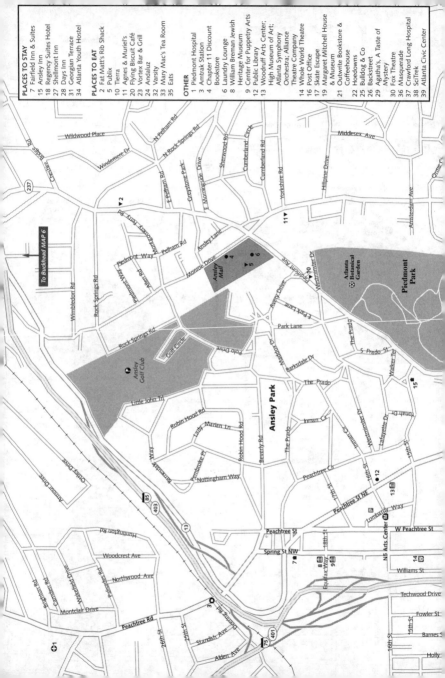

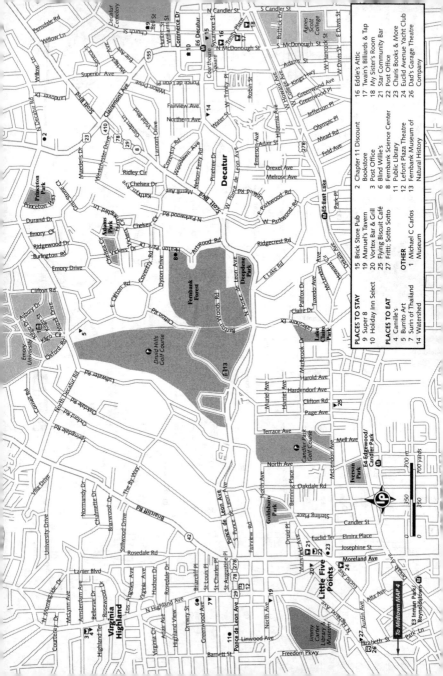

PLACES TO STAY
9 Super 8
10 Holiday Inn Select

PLACES TO EAT
4 Camille's
5 Burrito Art
7 Surin of Thailand
14 Watershed
15 Brick Store Pub
19 Manuel's Tavern
20 Vortex Bar & Grill
25 Flying Biscuit Café
27 Fritti; Sotto Sotto

OTHER
1 Michael C Carlos Museum
2 Chapter 11 Discount Bookstore
3 Post Office
6 Blind Willie's
8 Fernbank Science Center
11 Public Library
12 Lefont Plaza Theatre
13 Fernbank Museum of Natural History
16 Eddie's Attic
17 Twain's Billiards & Tap
18 My Sister's Room
21 Star Community Bar
22 Post Office
23 Charis Books & More
24 Euclid Avenue Yacht Club
26 Dad's Garage Theatre Company

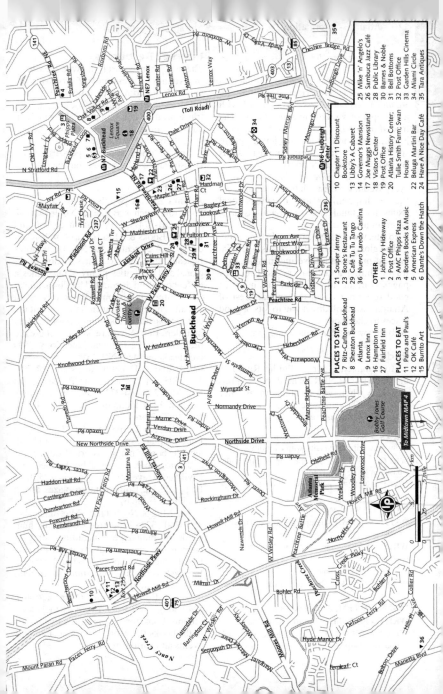

PLACES TO STAY
7 Ritz-Carlton Buckhead
8 Sheraton Buckhead Atlanta
16 Lenox Inn
19 Hampton Inn
27 Fairfield Inn

PLACES TO EAT
11 Pano and Paul's
12 OK Café
15 Burrito Art

21 Souper Jenny
23 Bone's Restaurant
29 Café Tu Tu Tango
36 Nuevo Laredo Cantina

OTHER
1 Johnny's Hideaway
2 Post Office
3 AMC Phipps Plaza
4 Borders Books & Music
5 American Express
6 Dante's Down the Hatch

10 Chapter 11 Discount Bookstore
13 Libby's Cabaret
14 Governor's Mansion
17 Joe Muggs Newsstand
18 Visitors Center
19 Post Office
20 Atlanta History Center; Tullie Smith Farm; Swan House
21 Beluga Martini Bar
24 Have A Nice Day Café
25 Mike 'n' Angelo's
26 Sambuca Jazz Café
28 Public Library
30 Barnes & Noble
31 Bell Bottoms
32 Post Office
33 Garden Hills Cinema
34 Miami Circle
35 Tara Antiques

[Continued from Page 116]

The *Atlanta Daily World* is the nation's oldest African-American weekly. The *Atlanta Maccabiah Press* is a monthly Jewish newspaper (www.maccabiahpress.com). The free *Mundo Hispánico* serves the burgeoning Latino population, and lets English-speakers practice their Spanish skills (www.mundohispanico.com).

The free *Creative Loafing,* published every Wednesday, lists all the music, arts and theater happenings and discusses local issues. Its annual 'Best of Atlanta' issue is entertaining reading.
Web site: www.atlanta.creativeloafing.com

The glossy *Atlanta Magazine* is a general interest publication covering lifestyle, arts, travel, dining and local issues. The back pages contain an excellent summary of good restaurants, and the annual 'Best of Atlanta' issue will direct you to lots of good places to check out.
Web site: www.atlantamagazine.com

Radio

Unfortunately, Georgia Public Radio (a major carrier of NPR) is hard to get in this city. But when you're stuck in another Atlanta traffic jam, here are a few stations that might be of interest:

WRAS – 88.5 FM, rock station produced at Georgia State University, with a lot of variety

WRFG – 89.3 FM, eclectic community radio based in Little Five Points

WABE – 90.1 FM, public radio with NPR news, jazz music

WCLK – 91.9 FM, jazz

WSTR – 94.1 FM, contemporary hits and modern rock

WBTS – 95.5 FM, standard pop with some rap and R&B

WFOX – 97.1 FM, oldies

WHAT – 97.5 FM, urban station that plays local artists

WNNX – 99.7 FM, alternative rock

WKHX – 101.5 FM, high-watt country station

WGST – 105.7 FM, mixed classic rock and modern rock/pop

Internet Resources

The best place to start is the Web site run by the Atlanta Convention & Visitors Bureau, www.atlanta.com, with links to arts and culture, hotels, dining, museums, sports, transportation and shopping. Many individual attractions listed later in this chapter have their own Web sites.

The Web sites of newspapers, listed previously, can also be a good starting place.

Bookstores

Atlanta is well populated by the mega-bookstores such as Barnes & Noble (Map 4; ☎ 404-261-7747), 2900 Peachtree Rd, and Borders Books & Music (Map 4; ☎ 404-237-0707), 3637 Peachtree Rd NE. These stores typically have an excellent selection of regional and local titles, plenty of magazines, a coffeehouse and discounted hardback books.

Chapter 11 Discount Bookstore is an Atlanta chain with branches throughout the city specializing in discounted books and remainders. Bestsellers are 30% off. There are branches at the following locations: 3509 Northside Parkway NW (Map 6; ☎ 404-841-6338); 2091 N Decatur Rd (Map 5; ☎ 404-325-1505), in Decatur; 2345 Peachtree Rd NE (Map 2; ☎ 404-237-7199); and in Ansley Mall, at 1544 Piedmont Ave NE (Map 4; ☎ 404-872-7986).

C Dickens Books (☎ 404-231-3825), in Lenox Square, specializes in rare and collectible books, maps, historical documents and autographs. For travel books, check out Civilized Traveller (☎ 404-264-1252), in Phipps Plaza. Both of these plazas are in Buckhead (Map 6).

Joe Muggs Newsstand (Map 6; ☎ 404-364-9290), 3275 Peachtree Rd NE, has hundreds of magazines, including some in foreign languages. It also carries international Sunday papers, such as the *Australian,* the *Irish Times* and the *Montreal Gazette.* It's open 6 am until late.

Charis Books & More (Map 5; ☎ 404-524-0304), 1189 Euclid Ave, is the oldest feminist bookstore in the South. In addition to the books, the 'more' is music, community events and various readings.

Other bookstores with a good selection of fiction and travel books, as well as readings and other events, are near Emory University, including Tall Tales Bookshop (☎ 404-636-2498), 2999 N Druid Hills Rd, and Druid Hills Bookstore (☎ 404-727-2665), 1401 Oxford Hills Rd.

Libraries

The main branch of the Atlanta-Fulton Public Library System (Map 3; ☎ 404-730-1700) is downtown at Margaret Mitchell Square, corner of Forsyth St and Carnegie Way, where they intersect at Peachtree St. Free Internet access is available. A Margaret Mitchell exhibit featuring memorabilia of her famous book and movie is on the 5th floor. The library is open 9 am to 8 pm Tuesday to Thursday, 9 am to 6 pm Monday, Friday and Saturday, and 2 to 6 pm Sunday. The closest MARTA station is Peachtree Center N1.

Web site: www.af.public.lib.ga.us

Several other branches are scattered throughout the city, including:

Auburn Avenue Research Library on African-American Culture and History, ☎ 404-730-4001, 101 Auburn Ave, Map 3

Buckhead Branch, ☎ 404-814-3500, 269 Buckhead Ave, Map 6

Peachtree Branch, ☎ 404-885-7830, 1315 Peachtree St NE, Map 4

Ponce de Leon Branch, ☎ 404-885-7820, 980 Ponce de Leon Ave, Map 5

The Jimmy Carter Library (☎ 404-331-0296) contains many historical documents on the Carter presidency; see the section on the Jimmy Carter Library & Museum later in this chapter.

Universities

The Atlanta area has plenty of universities and colleges. The four largest are:

Georgia State University (Map 3; ☎ 404-651-2000), with 32,000 students, is the 2nd largest in the state university system. It's located in the center of downtown.

Georgia Institute of Technology (Map 4; ☎ 404-894-2000, 225 North Ave) – or 'Georgia Tech' – is one of the top technical universities in the nation; over 12,000 students are enrolled. It is also the South's largest industrial and engineering research agency.

Emory University (☎ 404-727-6123), 1380 S Oxford Rd NE, near N Decatur Rd NE in Druid Hills, is one of the top universities in the country. It's known for its medical and law schools. Its scenic campus includes the Michael C Carlos Museum.

Atlanta University Center (Map 3; ☎ 404-522-8980) is the largest and oldest African-American academic center in the nation. The center is composed of several distinct universities and colleges, including Clark Atlanta University, Morehouse College, Morehouse School of Medicine, Spelman College, Morris Brown College and the Interdenominational Theological Center. These colleges have played a significant historic role as centers of higher learning in the segregated South since reconstruction.

Laundry

Hotels will sometimes have a washer and dryer in a guest laundry room stuck in a hidden corner somewhere, even if they don't advertise it. Ask the front desk staff before trudging out into the city, or before paying high hotel laundry bills.

Coin laundromats are listed in the Yellow Pages. A few convenient to some of the tourist haunts are:

Laundry Lounge, ☎ 404-876-3517, 1544 Piedmont Ave (Map 4; in Ansley Mall, behind Publix)

Midtown Laundry Center, ☎ 404-875-5872, 670 Myrtle St NE, Midtown

Splash, ☎ 404-262-9707, 2459 Piedmont Ave NE, Buckhead

All of these have drop-off and self service. Some accept dry cleaning as well.

Medical Services

Crawford Long Hospital of Emory University (Map 4; ☎ 404-686-4411), 550 Peachtree St NE in Midtown, offers 24-hour emergency services, as does Grady Health System (Map 3; ☎ 404-616-4307), 35 Butler St in the Georgia State University campus.

Other conveniently located hospitals, depending on where you are, are:

Atlanta Medical Center, ☎ 404-265-4000,
303 Parkway Dr NE, Map 3
Piedmont Hospital, ☎ 404-605-5000,
1968 Peachtree Rd, Map 4

An alternative to the emergency room is Doc-on-Call (☎ 404-874-0432), a service of the Midtown Medical Center. For minor problems, a physician will come to your hotel room with the necessary medicines. The cost is $175 during waking hours, or $225 if you wake the doctor up. You may want to check with your insurance if you hope to recover some of the charge.

Dangers & Annoyances

Atlanta has the usual big-city crime problems. Most of downtown Atlanta is safe enough during the day, but as businesspeople go home to the suburbs and conventioneers go north to the hot restaurants and nightspots, it becomes rather deserted. Stay in populated areas and be careful. There are also a fair number of panhandlers in Atlanta, who can make some people uncomfortable.

The Atlanta Ambassador Force, created for the Olympic Games, patrols downtown and Midtown. The members of this force help the police department by reporting suspicious activities, and can help visitors with directions, emergency assistance and even hailing a cab. They are recognizable by their distinct uniforms and helmets.

Due to Atlanta's repetitive street names (see the Orientation section) it's easy to get lost.

Atlantans love their automobiles to death, and the city is *not* pedestrian friendly. Many drivers seem to be shocked at the very idea that other people can breathe outside an automobile. These oblivious drivers don't yield to pedestrians, even when crossing with a light or crossing a restaurant driveway. Trying to reach the other side of a wide street can be an exercise in frustration and prayer. Buckhead is especially well known for car-pedestrian accidents.

Out on the Interstates, local drivers make up for the awful gridlock by going as fast as they can. Speeding truckers like to get within 3 feet of your rear bumper and flash their lights, expecting *you* to move over into another lane that you can't see because the truck is blocking your view. Be careful out there.

Atlanta also has a nasty rush hour. If you don't want to spend your vacation sitting in traffic, avoid the freeways on weekdays between 7 and 9 am and 4 and 7 pm. Frequent traffic accidents can snarl traffic at any time.

DOWNTOWN & SWEET AUBURN (MAP 3)

Centered around Peachtree St and International Blvd, downtown is Atlanta's focus of conventions, sports arenas, universities and businesses such as CNN. A recent spate of loft apartments is beginning to reintroduce the radical idea of living here. The area known as Sweet Auburn lies to the east of downtown; historically it was the cultural and commercial center of Atlanta's black community; today it houses many of the city's monuments to Martin Luther King Jr and the Civil Rights movement.

Downtown

Centennial Olympic Park, on the west side of downtown, is a 21-acre legacy of green space from the 1996 Olympic Games. It features the Fountain of Rings, the world's largest fountain that uses the Olympic symbol of five interconnecting rings; it has 25 water jets and is popular for family splash events. The park is also popular for picnicking and occasional outdoor concerts. The nearest MARTA station is Omni/Georgia Dome/GWCC (W1).

Next to Centennial Olympic Park is **CNN Center** (☎ 877-266-8687, 404-827-2300), headquarters of the worldwide cable TV news service owned by philanthropist media mogul Ted Turner. Frequent 45-minute tours give you a look at the newsrooms of CNN Headline News and CNN International; you can watch bored news anchors fidget when they are off the air. A

Fishing boats at sunset in Lazaretto Creek, Tybee Island, GA

East Broad St, historic Savannah

The Atlanta skyline at dusk

Phoenix Rising from the Ashes

Chickamauga & Chattanooga National Military Park, GA

Reflections on downtown Atlanta

Georgia State Capitol

Atlanta's Centennial Park fountain celebrates the Olympics.

mock control room provides an introduction to the technology that makes it all work. The tours are offered 9 am to 5 pm daily; $8/5. You can also sign up for the daily audience participation issues show *Talk-Back Live,* filmed 3 to 4 pm weekdays. Call ☎ 800-410-4266 for free tickets, or just stop by. The Dome MARTA station (W1) is closest.

Woodruff Park, at Peachtree St and Edgewood Ave, is a small park with a fountain and waterfall that features the bronze statue 'Phoenix Rising from the Ashes,' representing Atlanta's comeback after the Civil War.

The oldest part of the city is the area around Alabama St. As the city grew, bridges and viaducts were built over the railroad tracks to make life easier for horses, pedestrians and, later, cars. Eventually, an entire level of shops and storefronts vanished beneath street level. An imaginative 1960s renewal program rescued six dingy blocks of these 'lost' streets to construct **Underground Atlanta** (☎ 404-523-2311), an enclosed, air-conditioned, multilevel maze of shops, restaurants and street-cart merchants incorporating a few of the original brick streets and storefronts. Underground Atlanta closed in the early 1980s, was reinvented, and reopened in 1989. Billed as the 'center of it all,' Underground Atlanta is not much more than a struggling mall set in a historic atmosphere. Most of its nightspots have moved to more happening locales. The Peach Drop on New Year's Eve is modeled after the countdown in Times Square. The information desk near the food court has a free guide to the historical markers scattered around the complex. Enter from the Five Points MARTA station.

Next to Underground Atlanta, **World of Coca-Cola** (☎ 404-676-5151), 55 Martin Luther King Jr Dr, strives mightily to convince you that Coca-Cola is not just a soft drink, but rather one of the world's major cultural icons (this might in fact be true). One of Atlanta's most overrated attractions, its exhibits feature memorabilia and historic advertising stretching back to Coke's origins in 1886 Atlanta. Like the product itself, this attraction focuses on style and advertising over substance. The highlight is near the end of the tour, where you can try Coke products from around the world: a watermelon soda from China, a bitter apéritif from Italy or a ginger drink from South Africa. It's open 9 am to 5 pm daily (noon to 6 pm Sunday), until 6 pm in summer (from 11 am Sunday). Admission is $6/3 adults/children.

The **Georgia State Capitol** (☎ 404-651-6996), on Washington Street between Martin Luther King Jr Dr and Mitchell St, is an Atlanta landmark, with its gold dome easily visible. Constructed in 1889, its Classical Renaissance architecture is similar to the US Capitol in Washington DC. The dome is plated with 85oz of gold leaf. Outside the building, 14 monuments and memorials depict people and events in Georgia history. Inside, a small but entertaining museum has exhibits on the history of Georgia and the capitol building, the natural history of the region, and oddities such as a two-headed snake and a two-headed calf. Photos of the all-white-male legislature of 100 years ago contrast with photos of today's diverse legislature for a capsule summary of how much Georgia has changed. The Senate and House meet starting the second Monday of January for 40 legislative days; the galleries are open to the public. Guided tours (☎ 404-656-2844) are offered free of charge at 10 am, 11 am, 1 pm and 2 pm weekdays; morning tours are 30 minutes earlier when the legislature is in session. Admission is free. The building itself is open 8 am to 6 pm Monday through Friday. From the MARTA Georgia State station (E1), walk one block south on Capitol Ave, or it's a short walk from Underground Atlanta.

Web site: www.sos.state.ga.us/museum/

In an attempt to bring some culture downtown, the **High Museum of Art's Folk Art & Photography Galleries** (☎ 404-577-6940), at 30 John Wesley Dobbs Ave in the Georgia-Pacific Center, have rotating exhibits. A short way from the Peachtree Center MARTA station (N1), the museum is open 10 am to 5 pm Monday through Saturday. It's small, but free.

Web site: www.high.org

Interesting examples of modern architecture include the **Peachtree Center**, a vast complex of shops, offices and restaurants diagonally across from the 73-story Westin Peachtree Plaza hotel – check out the aerial walkways and revolving rooftop restaurant with great views.

Sweet Auburn

For decades, Auburn Ave was the heart of black Atlanta – the cultural and commercial center of the city's bustling African American community. Today many of the street's sights are associated with its most famous son: Martin Luther King Jr, who was born

on Auburn and preached on Auburn and whose grave now looks out onto the street.

The National Park Service's **Martin Luther King Jr National Historic Site** (☎ 404-331-6922) encompasses several blocks of Sweet Auburn. The **Visitors Center**, 450 Auburn Ave, will help you get oriented, with a map and brochure of the area sites and exhibits on King and the Civil Rights movement. It's open 9 am to 5 pm daily; admission is free. From here, guided tours leave for the **Martin Luther King Jr Birthplace**, 501 Auburn Ave. This Queen Anne–style house, built in 1895, was the birthplace of King and his home until 1941. Web site: www.nps.gov/malu

Heading back toward town, you come to the **Ebenezer Baptist Church**, 407 Auburn

---

In Pursuit of a Dream

Martin Luther King Jr was born on January 15, 1929, in the middle-class Atlanta neighborhood of Sweet Auburn. He attended Atlanta's Morehouse College at age 15 and was ordained three years later as a Baptist minister. He attended Crozer Theological Seminary in Pennsylvania and went on to earn a PhD from Boston University.

King intended to live a quiet life as an intellectual teaching theology. Influenced by the teachings of Mahatma Gandhi, he espoused principles of nonviolence and redemption of adversaries through love. In 1955, he was chosen to lead the bus boycott in Montgomery, Alabama. After a year of boycotting, the US Supreme Court struck down the laws that enforced segregated buses. From this successful beginning, King emerged as an inspiring moral voice in civil rights, motivating African Americans with his extraordinary oratorical ability.

In 1957, King and 115 other black leaders formed the Southern Christian Leadership Conference (SCLC) to expand the Montgomery success across the South. He returned to Atlanta in 1960, served as co-pastor of the Ebenezer Baptist Church (where his father was pastor), and helped form the Student Nonviolent Coordinating Committee (SNCC). King was arrested during a sit-in at a segregated snack bar and released only when Democratic presidential nominee John F Kennedy interceded (thereby winning enough black votes to carry the election).

King's strategy was to select a notoriously segregated city, mobilize the local black residents,

Ave, where King, his father and grandfather were all pastors, and where his mother was murdered in 1974. The church is open daily; admission is free. The congregation has moved across the street and the church is being restored.

Next door to the church, the **King Center for Non-Violent Social Change** (☎ 404-893-9882), founded in 1968 by King's widow, Coretta Scott King, and currently headed by one of King's sons, Dexter Scott King, continues working toward economic and social equality for all. The facility has more information on King's life and work, and a few of his personal effects, including his Nobel Peace Prize. It's open 9 am to 5 pm daily. King's **grave site**, between the church and center,

is surrounded by a long reflecting pool and can be viewed at any time.

All of the King sites are a few blocks' walk from MARTA's King Memorial station (E2). MARTA bus No 3 from the Five Points station goes by all the sites on Auburn Ave.

For more on black history, visit the **APEX Museum** (African-American Panoramic Experience; ☎ 404-523-2739), 135 Auburn Ave, closer to downtown Atlanta. The museum shows two films – one on the history of blacks from Africa to America, and the other on the history of Sweet Auburn. Rotating displays include African Art and African-American heroes. It's open 10 am to 5 pm Tuesday to Saturday. In summer and February, it's also open 1 pm to

---

In Pursuit of a Dream

then lead nonviolent protest marches. The demonstrations would force the white authorities to either negotiate or resort to violence; if the latter, the scenes of violence would arouse the national conscience and force the federal government to act. This worked according to plan in 1963 in Birmingham, Alabama (followed by the 1964 Civil Rights Act), and in 1965 in Selma, Alabama (followed by the 1965 Voting Rights Act). This approach failed in Albany, Georgia, in 1962 because white authorities treated the marchers with impeccable decorum and refused to resort to violence.

King's most often remembered speech, delivered in 1963 to an interracial crowd of 250,000 in Washington, DC, refers to his home state:

I have a dream that one day on the red hills of Georgia, sons of former slaves and sons of former slave-owners will be able to sit down together at the table of brotherhood… I have a dream that my four little children will one day live in a nation where they will not be judged by the color of their skin but by the content of their character. I have a dream today!

In 1964, King was awarded the Nobel Peace Prize, at age 35 its youngest recipient in history. By 1965, King began addressing racial problems in the urban North, and he made speeches denouncing the Vietnam War. The SNCC renounced King's nonviolent teachings, advocating 'black power' instead. On a trip to Memphis, Tennessee, in support of sanitation workers' right to unionize, he was assassinated by James Earl Ray on April 4, 1968. Ray confessed to the crime but three days later recanted his guilty plea, claiming that he was but a pawn in a murder conspiracy. He died in prison in 1998, without ever receiving the new trial he sought

King remains one of the most recognized and respected figures of the 20th century. In a span of 10 years, he led a movement that essentially ended a system of statutory discrimination in existence since the country's founding. His letters and speeches reflect some of the greatest American prose and a great vision still to be fulfilled. The National Historic Site and the King Center for Non-Violent Social Change in Atlanta are testaments to his life, his moral vision, his ability to inspire others and his lasting impact on the fundamental fabric of American society.

5 pm Sunday; admission costs $3. APEX is about a 15-minute walk west from the historic district; as you go, look for the purple and yellow signs posted along Auburn Ave identifying historically significant buildings. Georgia State (E1) is the closest MARTA stop.
Web site: www.apexmuseum.org

Grant Park

This park, like its neighbor to the north, Piedmont Park, is a large oasis of green on the edge of the city center. An old area just southeast of downtown, the neighborhood of Grant Park is slowly undergoing a revival.

The park is home to the **Atlanta Cyclorama** (☎ 404-658-7625), one of Atlanta's most famous attractions. The Cyclorama is a circular painting measuring 358 feet long and 42 feet high, depicting the Battle of Atlanta in July 1864. Painted in 1886, the interesting painting is the largest in the world and is one of only three such Victorian-era circular paintings remaining in the USA. A three-dimensional diorama was added in 1935, and includes figures (such as the image of Clark Gable as a dead Union soldier) and scenery that blend seamlessly into the painting. Visitors sit on a revolving platform during the showings while listening to the narration and sounds of battle. Even folks tired of the whole Civil War thing will enjoy the historic diorama. The building also contains a Civil War museum with artifacts, weapons, displays, maps and photographs. On the ground floor is the *Texas,* a steam locomotive used by the Confederates in April, 1862, to chase down the *General,* a locomotive seized by Union soldiers in a daring attack known as Andrews' Raid. The bookstore has an extensive collection of Civil War books. Brochures and translation devices are available in French, German, Spanish and Japanese. The painting and accompanying museum are open from 9:30 am to 5:30 pm daily (until 4:30 pm October through May), with showings every half hour. You can view the museum while waiting for the show. Admission is $5/3.

Nearby, **Zoo Atlanta** (☎ 404-624-5600) provides naturalistic environments for many African and Asian animals. Highlights include two giant pandas, four gorilla families, large animals from the plains of Kenya, orangutan families, Sumatran tigers and a reptile house. Small for a city of this size, the zoo still has almost 1000 animals. Admission is pricey, at $15/10 adults/children; open 9:30 am to 4:30 pm daily, and until 5:30 pm on weekends during daylight savings time. Web site: www.zooatlanta.org

The only place to eat inside Grant Park is at an overpriced McDonalds at the zoo entrance, or a few snack shops inside the zoo.

From the Five Points MARTA station, take bus No 31. You can also reach Grant Park by walking south from Sweet Auburn or the King Memorial MARTA station (E2). The route under the MARTA tracks on Boulevard is seedy; take Hillard/Grant St instead.

Gone With the Wind author Margaret Mitchell and golf great Bobby Jones are buried in the **Oakland Cemetery** (☎ 404-688-2107), 248 Oakland Ave at Martin Luther King Jr Dr. The 88-acre cemetery was the city's only burial place from 1850 to 1884 and contains the remains of 100,000 people of all races and classes. Markers in the Jewish section are tightly spaced, many in Hebrew. Nearly 3000 Confederate dead (and 20 Union dead) are buried here, as are many prominent African Americans. Many interesting Victorian and neo-classical monuments and mausoleums are scattered throughout the site. A complete tour of the cemetery would be about a 1½-mile walk. The cemetery is open 8 am to 6 pm daily (until 7 pm in summer). Stop at the visitors center (open 9 am to 5 pm weekdays) for information and a walking brochure ($1). Admission is free. Guided tours cost $3/1 adults/children and are offered March through October at 10 am and 2 pm Saturday and at 2 pm Sunday. Enter at Martin Luther King Jr Dr and Oakland Ave. From the MARTA King Memorial station (E2), turn left, left again on Hillard/Grant St, go under the tracks, and take another left on Martin Luther King Jr Dr. Bus No 18 will

also take you there from either the Five Points or King Memorial stations.
Web site: www.oaklandcemetery.com

West End

Older than the city of Atlanta itself and a long-established African-American community, West End was home to Alonzo Herndon, who was born a slave but who went on to found Atlanta Life Insurance and become one of the country's first black millionaires. The **Herndon Home** (☎ 404-581-9813), 587 University Place NW, is an impressive beaux-arts mansion, built and decorated by black workers in 1910. Admission is free but donations are requested. It is open for hourly tours 10 am to 4 pm Tuesday to Saturday. The house sits on the edge of the campus of **Morris Brown College**, a three-block walk from the Vine City MARTA station (W2).

South of I-20, the **Wren's Nest** (☎ 404-753-7735, wrensnest@mindspring.com), 1050 Ralph David Abernathy Blvd SW, was the 1881 to 1908 home of Joel Chandler Harris, the white Atlanta journalist (born in Eatonton, Georgia) whose newspaper columns and Uncle Remus books retold and popularized African-American folktales of Brer Rabbit, Brer Fox and Brer Bear. The house has been restored to the early 1900s. A slide show only touches on the controversy that Harris has generated in modern reinterpretations (see literature in the Facts about Georgia section). Storytelling sessions are held on Saturday during the spring and summer and after Christmas, or you may be able to join a program scheduled for a school group; call for times. The house is open 10 am to 4 pm Tuesday to Saturday and 1 pm to 4 pm Sunday. Admission is $7/3. The Wren's Nest is about half a mile west of the MARTA West End station (S2); bus No 71 passes the house.

The West End is also home to the **Atlanta University Center,** including historic African-American colleges such as Clark Atlanta University, Morehouse College, Morehouse School of Medicine, Spelman College and Morris Brown College.

MIDTOWN (MAP 4)

Midtown is considered to be the arts district, with the city's largest choice of cultural activities. Undergoing a renaissance along with seemingly everything else in the area, it's defined by multipurpose development, offices, condos, retail and even a new Federal Reserve Bank.

Closest to downtown, **SciTrek** (☎ 404-522-5500), 395 Piedmont Ave, is a child-oriented science and technology museum with 150 interactive, hands-on exhibits on electricity, magnetism, robotics, computers and other cool stuff. It's open 10 am to 5 pm daily, Sunday from noon. Admission is $7.50/5 adults/children. It's about five blocks from the MARTA Civic Center station (N2), or you can take bus No 16 from Five Points. Web site: www.scitrek.org

The **Fox Theatre** (☎ 404-881-2100), 660 Peachtree St NE, in the center of Midtown, is a 1929 movie palace with fanciful Moorish and Egyptian designs such as minarets and onion domes. One of the few remaining movie palaces of the 1920s, it was saved from destruction in the 1970s, and today hosts Broadway shows, film festivals and concerts in a 5,000-seat auditorium. The Atlanta Preservation Center (☎ 404-876-2041) offers guided tours year-round at 10 am Monday, Wednesday and Thursday, and at 10 am and 11 am Saturday; $5/3 adults/students.

The **Margaret Mitchell House & Museum** (☎ 404-249-7015), at 10th and Peachtree Sts, is a shrine to the author of *Gone With the Wind.* Mitchell wrote her epic in a small apartment in the basement of this house, which she referred to as 'The Dump' because it was cold, dark and drafty. The apartment is not of particular interest other than the fact that Mitchell lived there; you'll need to be a true fan to appreciate the celebrity-focused tours. The attached movie museum has exhibits on the making of the movie and its premiere in Atlanta. The more interesting issues of why the book and movie have been so popular and how they reflect (or don't reflect) the views of Southerners are only addressed in one storyboard. The visitors center, house and museum are open 9 am to

4 pm. Admission is an expensive $10/7. Take MARTA to Midtown station (N4), exit onto 10th St and turn right.
Web site: www.gwtw.org

The **Woodruff Art Center** (☎ 404-733-4200), 1280 Peachtree St NE at 15th St, is named for Coca-Cola king Robert W Woodruff, who gave so much to local causes that he was nicknamed Mr Anonymous Donor. The center includes a theater, concert hall and art school, but the highlight is the **High Museum of Art** (☎ 404-733-4444), in a stunning modern building designed by Richard Meir. The museum was picked by the American Institute of Architects as one of the 10 best works of American architecture during the 1980s. Its collection includes European and American contemporary art, decorative arts and furniture, European painting and sculpture from the 14th through the 19th centuries, and first-class African exhibits. Special, high-quality traveling exhibits are major events. The museum often has lectures and shows classic films (☎ 404-733-4570). A coffee shop serves sandwiches, soups, salads and gourmet coffee. The museum is open 10 am to 5 pm Tuesday to Saturday and noon to 5 pm Sunday; $6/2 adults/children, free on Thursday from 1 pm to 5 pm. Additional charges usually apply to traveling exhibits. Take MARTA to Arts Center station (N5). Web site: www.high.org

The **Center for Puppetry Arts** (☎ 404-873-3391), 1404 Spring St NW at 18th St, is a wonderland for both kids and adults. The permanent collection consists of over 1000 puppets from around the world. Try to see one of the well-produced, full-stage puppet shows – the Family Series is geared to children and kids at heart, while the New Directions series is aimed at an adult audience. Workshops for every age, from preschool to adults, are also offered frequently. The museum is open 9 am to 5 pm Monday through Saturday. Admission is $5/4; shows cost $8/7 and include museum admission. Free parking is available at the rear of the building. The MARTA Arts Center station (N5) is three blocks to the south and east. Web site: www.puppet.org

Next to the puppet museum, the **William Breman Jewish Heritage Museum** (☎ 404-873-1661), 1440 Spring St NW, is an exploration of Atlanta's Jewish experience. The core galleries include the Holocaust as seen by survivors who moved to Atlanta and the history of Jews in Atlanta. Hours are 10 am to 5 pm Monday through Thursday, 10 am to 3 pm Friday, and 1 pm to 5 pm Sunday; $5/3.

A few blocks east of the High Museum of Art is the Olmstead-designed **Piedmont Park**, which includes playgrounds, a pool, bike/walking paths, a tennis center, softball fields and two lakes (fishing permitted with Georgia license only). The 185-acre park is the oldest and largest in the Atlanta metro area, and recently underwent a $66 million renovation. A visitors center is located inside the Piedmont Ave entrance at 12th St. Bicycles can be rented at Skate Escape (☎ 404-892-1292), 1086 Piedmont Ave NE, at 12th St; see Activities later in this chapter for details. The park is a favorite people-watching and picnicking hangout as well.

The 30-acre **Atlanta Botanical Garden** (☎ 404-876-5859), 1345 Piedmont Ave NE, in the northwest corner of Piedmont Park, features a Japanese garden and diverse collections of roses, native wildflowers, herbs and ornamental grasses. Visitors can walk through a 15-acre hardwood forest, one of the few remaining within the city limits. The 16,000-sq-foot, glass-walled Dorothy Chapman Fuqua Conservatory houses threatened tropical and desert plants; look for poison dart frogs. Children can romp through the delightful Children's Garden, featuring a caterpillar maze and a tree house. It's open 9 am to 7 pm (until 6 pm October through February) Tuesday through Sunday; $7/4. A cafeteria serves lunch in summer. Piedmont Park and the botanical garden are a few blocks east of the MARTA Arts Center station (N5); walk or take bus No 36.
Web site: www.atlantabotanicalgarden.org

POINTS EAST & DECATUR (MAP 5)

The **Jimmy Carter Museum** (☎ 404-331-0296) on Freedom Parkway displays arti-

Gay Atlanta

Atlanta is one of the few places in Georgia – perhaps in the South – with a noticeable and active gay and lesbian population. Midtown is the center of gay life – Piedmont Park is a popular hangout, and there are several gay bars here. The town of Decatur, east of downtown Atlanta, also has a significant gay and lesbian community, including an openly lesbian city council member.

The Atlanta Gay/Lesbian Center (☎ 404-523-7500), 159 Ralph McGill Blvd, 6th floor, is a clearinghouse for organizations and information. The weekly newspaper *Southern Voice* contains regional news relevant to gays and lesbians (www.sovo.com).

Out & Active has a comprehensive listing of clubs, churches, health services, social activities and organizations. The *etcetera magazine* also has some information on Atlanta's gay scene. You can view an online version, including a calendar of events, at www.etcmag.com.

The **Atlanta Pride Festival** is a celebration of the city's gay and lesbian community; it's held at the end of June every year and is centered around Piedmont Park in Midtown.

Outwrite Bookstore & Coffeehouse (Map 4; ☎ 404-607-0082, 991 Piedmont Ave), at 10th St in Midtown, is a cheerful gay and lesbian bookstore with a full coffee bar and wonderful desserts. Although the clientele is mostly gay men, the atmosphere seems welcoming for others as well. Their Web site (www.outwritebooks.com) includes online ordering, reviews and a list of store events.

In the Little Five Points neighborhood, Charis Books & More (☎ 404-524-0304), 1189 Euclid Ave NE, is a crowded, well-stocked feminist and lesbian bookstore that also sells music, cards, t-shirts and jewelry (http://charis.booksense.com).

More than 30 gay clubs are listed in *Out & Active*. The Gay Guide to Atlanta Web site (www.gayguides.com/atlanta/) also has comprehensive listings of clubs and places to hang out.

Backstreet (Map 4; ☎ 404-873-1986, 845 Peachtree St NE), in Midtown at 6th St, is Atlanta's top gay club, but it gets a good mix of everyone else as well. A risqué female impersonation cabaret show is always standing room only Thursday through Sunday starting at 11pm. Several bars and a crowded dance floor with a massive sound and light show complete this complex. Amazingly, it's open 24 hours a day, 365 days a year, so those who can't stop the motion head here after the other bars close at 4 am. The cover is $10 your first visit for a membership card; afterwards, with your card, it's $5 on the weekends, free weekdays.

Nearby, ***Bulldog & Co*** (Map 4; ☎ 404-872-3025, 893 Peachtree St NE) is a staple for gay men over 30. It draws a racially mixed crowd and plenty of leather.

You can practice your boot-scootin' boogie at ***Hoedowns*** (☎ 404-876-0001, 931 Monroe Dr). Mostly men in tight jeans and cowboy hats, it's also popular with the ladies on Thursday and Sunday. Free dance lessons are offered at 8 pm Thursday and 4 pm Sunday.

Mary's (Map 1; ☎ 404-624-4411, 1287 Glenwood Ave) is a laid-back video bar in East Atlanta. Weekends are crowded, and Thursday is all-request night.

My Sister's Room (☎ 404-370-1990, 222 E Howard St), next to the railroad tracks in Decatur, is a popular hangout for area lesbians. A spacious covered patio, intimate garden hideaways and a stage and dance floor attract a growing clientele.

---

facts from Carter's 1977–1981 presidency, including a replica of the Oval Office and gifts received from the leaders of other countries: a lace doily from Belgium and a carved elephant tusk from Nigeria. Displays explain the highlights and lowlights of Carter's years in office (see the boxed text 'From Peanuts to President' in the South Georgia chapter). The library, containing 27 million pages of documents and 1.5 million photos, is of interest mainly to historians and other researchers. A bookstore sells all of Carter's many books. A cafe serves lunch.

The Carter Presidential Center (☎ 404-420-5100) is a nonprofit organization devoted to preventing and resolving conflicts worldwide and fighting disease. The center is not open to the public, and the museum next door unfortunately does not contain any exhibits on its important and interesting work. From the Carter Center, **Freedom Park** extends east for walkers, joggers and bikers.

The museum and center are located on 35 acres of a hilltop with a marvelous view of downtown Atlanta, from which Sherman once watched the burning of the city. The grounds include formal gardens, a wildflower meadow, a Japanese garden, a cherry orchard and a rose garden. Visitors can wander the grounds without paying admission. They are open 6 am to 9 pm. From the Five Points MARTA station, take bus No 16. If you're driving, take I-75 or I-85 south to exit 248C, which says 'Freedom Parkway, The Carter Center'; follow the signs.

The museum is open 9 am to 4:45 pm Monday through Saturday and noon to 4:45 pm Sunday. Admission is $5, free for people age 16 and under.
Web site: www.cartercenter.org

Opened in 1992, the **Fernbank Museum of Natural History** (☎ 404-929-6300), 767 Clifton Rd NE, features permanent collections on Georgia's natural wonders, from its physical connection to West Africa 200 million years ago to its diverse ecosystems today. *Sensing Nature* is a gallery of interactive exhibits that plays with your perceptions. Separate rooms are geared toward children aged 6 to 10 and those aged 3 to 5. Movies are shown on the six-story IMAX screen. The museum is open 10 am to 5 pm Monday through Saturday and noon to 5 pm Sunday, with additional IMAX shows on Friday nights. Rates are $9/7 for the museum only, $7/5 for IMAX only, and $14/10 for combination tickets. Temporary exhibitions often have an additional cost. A cafeteria serves soup and sandwiches.
Web site: www.fernbank.edu/museum

The nearby **Fernbank Science Center** (☎ 404-378-4311) has smaller exhibits on Georgia's ecosystems and on outer space, but its main draw is its planetarium. Call for show times. The center is open 8:30 am to 5 pm Monday, 8:30 am to 10 pm Tuesday through Friday, 10 am to 5 pm Saturday, and 1 pm to 5 pm Sunday. Admission to the center is free; planetarium shows cost $2/1.
Web site: http://fsc.fernbank.edu/

For the separate museum or science center stops, take bus No 2 from the North Avenue MARTA station (N3).

Rotating exhibits at the excellent **Michael C Carlos Museum** (☎ 404-727-4282), 571 S Kilgo St, are selected from a permanent collection of 16,000 objects of art from ancient South and North America, Africa, Egypt, Greece and Rome – the largest such collection in the Southeast. Housed in an impressive 1993 building of white and rose marble designed by Michael Graves, highlights include Egyptian mummies, sarcophagi and other ancient Egyptian funerary art. A well-stocked bookstore and a cafe are on site. The museum is open 10 am to 5 pm Monday through Saturday, noon to 5 pm Sunday; $5 suggested donation.

The Carlos Museum is located on the main quadrangle of the Emory campus, near the intersection of Oxford and N Decatur Rds. Take MARTA bus No 6 from the Edgewood/Candler Park (E4) or Lindbergh Center (N6) station, or take bus No 36 from the Arts Center (N5) or Avondale (E7) station.
Web site: www.emory.edu/CARLOS/

BUCKHEAD (MAP 6)

The 'Beverly Hills of the South,' Buckhead is a neighborhood full of upscale shopping malls and homes (median house price of $430,000), high-rise condos, good restaurants and diverse nightlife. The neighborhood was named for a buck's head that hung in a tavern in 1839.

The **Atlanta History Center** (☎ 404-814-4000), 130 W Paces Ferry Rd NW, is an excellent museum that covers the history of Atlanta from railroad junction to modern suburban metropolis. The DuBose Gallery features *Turning Point: The American Civil War*, a balanced approach to a defining moment in the South's – and Atlanta's – history (though it could use more information on the Battle of Atlanta). Unlike some museums that focus on artifacts or military strategy, the exhibits give good coverage to the reasons Americans went to war against each other. For lovers of artifacts, however, there are displays such as a comprehensive Civil War ordnance collection. *Metropolitan Frontiers: Atlanta, 1835-2000* completes the story, covering Atlanta's rise from the ashes after the Civil War, the Civil Rights struggles, and its modern boosterism and commercialism. *Shaping Traditions: Folk Arts in a Changing South* is a quiet celebration of handmade crafts in the South and their adaptation to modernization.

On the History Center's landscaped grounds, the **Tullie Smith Farm** is an 1845 homestead typical of Georgia's Piedmont region. The **Swan House** is a 1928 European-style manor designed by famous architect Philip Shutze in the Classical style using 18th-century European elements.

A museum cafe downstairs serves sandwiches, desserts and ice cream. The Swan Coach House restaurant serves lunch Monday through Saturday. The bookstore has a comprehensive selection of history books.

Museum hours are 10 am to 5:30 pm Monday through Saturday, noon to 5:30 pm Sunday. Tours of the Swan House and Tullie Smith Farm are offered every 30 minutes from 11 am to 4 pm Monday through Saturday, 1 pm to 4 pm Sunday. Admission is $10/8 adults/children. Tours of the house and farm cost an additional $1 each.
Web site: www.atlantahistorycenter.com

To reach the museum by MARTA, take bus No 23 from the Lenox station to Peachtree and W Paces Ferry Rd. Walk 3 blocks west on W Paces Ferry Rd to the museum's pedestrian entrance. The bus runs daily every 11 minutes. By car, take I-75 to exit 255, W Paces Ferry Rd, go left and follow signs east. Free parking is available.

The nearby **Governor's Mansion** (☎ 404-261-1776), 391 W Paces Ferry Rd NE, completed in 1968, is a Greek Revival–style house, rich with 19th-century furniture, paintings and porcelain. It's open to the public 10 am to 11:30 am Tuesday through Thursday. Admission is free.

SCENIC NEIGHBORHOODS

Several neighborhoods in Atlanta do not have any specific sites, but are pleasant to walk around. Near Emory, Druid Hills is an elegant neighborhood of Tudor mansions and magnolia trees; part of *Driving Miss Daisy* was filmed here. Ansley Park, about three miles north of downtown (Map 4), is a neighborhood constructed starting in 1905 and containing renovated homes of early American heritage, with cobblestone walkways. The entire neighborhood is a National Historic District.

Two miles from downtown Atlanta, Virginia Highland is popular with Atlanta's young professionals and has a pleasant neighborhood of 60- to 80-year-old homes, a popular shopping district and numerous

---

Atlanta for Children

Atlanta has plenty of activities to keep kids entertained, delighted, thrilled and – perhaps against their will – educated. Here are some of the major sites that work at being kid-friendly (see the main text for full information):

Center for Puppetry Arts – puppet shows for the young and young at heart

Zoo Atlanta – introduce your little animals to much bigger ones

Atlanta Botanical Garden – features a special Children's Garden

Fernbank Museum of Natural History – the huge IMAX screen and the toddler play area are favorites

SciTrek – offers fun yet educational, hands-on science exhibits

Six Flags Over Georgia – a favorite amusement park

White Water Theme Park – 50 ways to get wet in Marietta

restaurants. Nearby Little Five Points is more alternative. West of Little Five Points, Inman Park was Atlanta's first planned suburb. Once the home of wealthy residents, it was restored beginning in the 1970s and features Victorian-style homes and tree-shaded streets.

The Atlanta Preservation Center offers walking tours in many of these neighborhoods; see the Organized Tours section, below. The book *Atlanta Walks*, by Ren and Helen Davis, describes 45 walks in the Atlanta area.

SIX FLAGS OVER GEORGIA

This huge 331-acre theme park (☎ 770-948-9290) is 12 miles west of downtown Atlanta off I-20. Six Flags has eight roller coasters, whitewater rafting, a 10-story free-fall ride and musical shows. The new Georgia Scorcher is the Southeast's tallest and fastest stand-up roller coaster.

The park is open daily at 10 am Memorial Day through Labor Day; it's also open on weekends in the spring and fall. Closing times vary. Prices are $37 for adults and $19 for children under 48 inches tall. Two-day admission is $48/$29. Parking is an additional $7 to $12.

The Six Flags shuttle (bus No 201) leaves from the Hamilton E Holmes MARTA station (W5) every 36 minutes when the park is open. The bus ride is $2.50. If you're driving, take I-20 to the Six Flags exit (either 46B or 47, depending on the direction you're coming from).

BICYCLING

Riding a bike on streets within the city can be dangerous, but there are a couple of dedicated paths where you can escape the traffic. In **Piedmont Park**, you'll share a lazy six-mile bike path with joggers, rollerbladers, dog walkers and romancing couples. The park provides lots of opportunities for people watching. Bikes and in-line skates are available for rent at Skate Escape (☎ 404-892-1292), 1086 Piedmont Ave NE at 12th St. Bikes can be rented for $6 an hour, in-line skates for $5; pads and helmets cost a one-time $1.

Freedom Park is a 45-acre park with biking and jogging paths adjacent to Freedom Parkway near the Jimmy Carter Library & Museum in southeast Atlanta. It forms a section of the Atlanta/Stone Mountain Trail, an 18-mile path that connects the Georgia Institute of Technology to Stone Mountain Park via Freedom Park, the Martin Luther King Jr National Historic Site, the Jimmy Carter Library & Museum and the Fernbank Museum of Natural History. Maps of the trail can be purchased for $3 from most local bike shops, including Skate Escape (see above), across from Piedmont Park. However, part of the trail is shared with automobiles. The portion next to Freedom Parkway, near the Carter Center, is the best.

ORGANIZED TOURS

Gray Line of Atlanta (☎ 800-965-6665, 404-767-0594, fax 404-765-1399, american.coach@coachusa.com) offers somewhat expensive bus tours of various parts of Atlanta, departing from their office near the visitors center in Underground Atlanta. Most of the tour is on a bus while your guide outlines the history of Atlanta and describes the sites you're driving by. The rest of the tour consists of visiting selected sites. The 'Atlanta's Past and Present' tour includes admission to Margaret Mitchell's house and the Atlanta Cyclorama. Rates are $35/30 adults/children. The 'All Around Atlanta' tour includes admission to the Jimmy Carter Museum & Library, the Martin Luther King Jr National Historic Site and the World of Coca-Cola museum. Rates are $40/32. Web site: www.amebus.com

More intriguing are the walking tours offered by the Atlanta Preservation Center (☎ 404-876-2041), 537 Peachtree St NE. Volunteer-led tours lasting one to two hours are regularly scheduled for the historic downtown area, Sweet Auburn, Ansley Park, Druid Hills, the Fox Theatre and Inman Park. Tours are offered March through November, except for the Fox Theatre, which is offered all year. The cost is $5/4 adults/students. Reservations are not required, but you'll need to call or check the

Web site (www.preserveatlanta.com) for the schedule and directions to the starting point.

Classic Tours & Destinations (☎ 888-767-8687, 404-589-1002) focuses on Atlanta's rich African-American heritage.

SPECIAL EVENTS

Dates of special events may shift from year to year, so if any of these events are essential to your plans, confirm the dates with the Atlanta Convention and Visitors Bureau (☎ 404-222-6688), check their Web site at www.atlanta.com, or call individual event organizers. Atlanta has many more events than those listed below; a calendar is available from the visitors bureau.

January

Martin Luther King Jr Holiday – a week of arts, entertainment, speeches and church services celebrates the national holiday centered around the Atlanta civil rights leader.

March/April

Park Fest (☎ 404-223-7275) – held in Centennial Olympic Park, with 200,000 visitors a year; it features concerts, water shows and arts.

Atlanta Dogwood Festival (☎ 404-329-0501) – held in Piedmont Park, this is Atlanta's largest festival, featuring blooming dogwoods and hot air balloons. Web site: www.dogwood.org

Inman Park Spring Festival and Tour of Homes – one of the city's best neighborhood celebrations, with a colorful parade, a huge street market and a tour of homes.

May

Music Midtown (☎ 770-643-8696) – a three-day musical event with more than 130 local and nationally known bands on nine outdoor stages, plus regional arts and crafts. Web site: www.musicmidtown.com

Atlanta Jazz Festival (☎ 404-817-6851) – this laid-back festival in Piedmont Park is the country's largest free jazz festival.

Decatur Arts Festival & Garden Tour - Memorial Day event held around Decatur Square, featuring art exhibitions, a film festival, tours of area homes and gardens and live music, dance and theater on outdoor stages.

June

Virginia Highland Festival (☎ 404-222-8244) – a two-day neighborhood arts and food festival with a more local feel.

Atlanta Pride Festival – centered around Piedmont Park, this is a celebration of the city's gay and lesbian community, culminating in a parade up Peachtree Street.

Atlanta Film & Video Festival – produced by IMAGE Film & Video Center, this festival consists of modern films shown in theaters around Atlanta; it's often considered the Sundance of the South.

July

Peachtree Road Race – held on the Fourth of July every year with 50,000 runners, this is the world's largest 10km road race.

September

Atlanta Greek Festival (☎ 404-633-7358) – at the Atlanta Greek Orthodox Cathedral, 30,000 people celebrate Greek culture through food, music and dance.

Yellow Daisy Festival (☎ 770-498-5633) – held at Stone Mountain Park, this is one of the region's top arts and crafts shows.

October

Sweet Auburn Festival – five stages of gospel, jazz, blues and hip-hop, a classic car show and soul food, held in conjunction with the Atlanta Football Classic weekend, a competition at the Georgia Dome of historically African-American college and university teams.

PLACES TO STAY

Metro Atlanta is aptly served by more than 81,000 hotel rooms. A full range is offered, from a decent youth hostel well located in Midtown to blow-your-budget luxury hotels. Your budget and choice of neighborhood should help you decide among them.

The rates quoted here are the normal midweek rates during the high season; weekend rates are sometimes provided where available. Use them for comparison purposes only, since they can vary widely from day to day and hour to hour. Many maps and other tourist literature distributed around town have good coupon values.

You'll also find coupon books at rest stops outside town on I-75 and I-85.

Because Atlanta is primarily a city of business, hotel rates often decrease on the weekend. A $99 hotel during the week might cost $69 on a weekend. On the other extreme, rates can soar when a convention is in town, and you may need to head farther out to get a decent price.

Beware of the steep 14% hotel tax, which is not included in the rates quoted here.

Downtown hotels are most convenient to downtown business towers, many tourist sites and MARTA stations. You probably won't want to wander around after dark, when the streets are deserted. Midtown is enjoying a renaissance, and hotels are close to such popular sites as the Fox Theatre. Buckhead is a good choice if you want to sample the many late-night entertainment spots. Streets are more lively at night – so lively, in fact, that the chief danger is from the heavy traffic.

Decatur's courthouse square has a more relaxed feel than other parts of Atlanta, and it has good restaurants and entertainment options as well. A MARTA station keeps it in easy contact with the rest of Atlanta.

North of Atlanta, the area on the north side of I-285, known as Perimeter North, is a booming business area near the popular Perimeter Mall. Stay here if you have business in the area or outside the perimeter, or if the hotels are cheaper during a large downtown event. MARTA stations provide convenient access to other parts of Atlanta (see Map 1).

A good option for budget lodging is to stay somewhere along the perimeter and to take MARTA into the city for sightseeing. There are several cheap hotels at or near the end of MARTA lines, and you can park at the stations. The trip by train to downtown should take 30 to 40 minutes, depending on where you start. Options included here are on the east perimeter, within striking distance of Stone Mountain Park; and in the northeast along Buford Highway, an area populated by a wide variety of immigrant groups.

Finally, plenty of chain and budget lodgings are available on the interstates beyond the perimeter. These are typically cheaper than those found closer to town. Look for the signs, especially on I-75 and I-85 headed north and south, and on I-20 headed east and west.

See the Stone Mountain Park section later in this chapter for lodging within the park.

Budget
Camping The closest camping is at Stone Mountain 16 miles east of Atlanta; see the Around Atlanta section. *Atlanta South KOA* (☎ 770-957-2610), a good 25 miles south of downtown at I-75 exit 222, charges $23 for tent sites (two people) and $26/28 for partial/full RV hookups. The generator noise near the tent area may bother some. At *Atlanta North KOA* (☎ 770-427-2406), about 25 miles north of the city at I-75 exit 269, rates are $28 for tents or RVs.

Downtown Two blocks from Peachtree Street and three blocks from the MARTA Peachtree Center station (N1), the *Quality Hotel* (☎ 800-228-5151, 404-524-7991, 89 Luckie St) is nothing special, but has acceptable modern hotel rooms in a convenient downtown location. Rates start at $59 and can zoom up to $129 when a convention is in town. A continental breakfast is included, but parking in a secure garage next door is $9 extra.

Midtown The *Atlanta Youth Hostel* (☎ 404-872-1042, 223 Ponce de Leon Ave), at Myrtle St, is in a Victorian house three blocks east of the Fox Theatre. The lively hostel has 80 beds in dorm rooms containing three to five bunk beds each. There are separate men's and women's rooms as well as coed rooms. Common areas include a TV room with a pool table, a small outside courtyard, and downstairs and upstairs screened porches. A kitchen, laundry, lockers, free morning coffee and donuts, and Internet access ($1 for 10 minutes) are available. Reservations may be needed in the summer, when it can get crowded. The office is closed noon to 5 pm. Beds cost $17 for members of Hostels America and $19 for nonmembers, plus $1 for linens. Four private rooms are available for $44/49 shared/private baths. The hostel is four fairly long blocks east of the MARTA North Avenue station (N3).

Decatur *Super 8* (☎ *800-800-8000, ☎/fax 404-378-3765, 917 Church St*) is ⅓ mile from quaint downtown Decatur and the MARTA station (E6). Basic modern hotel rooms are $55/60 weekdays/weekends, including breakfast donuts and cereal. The cemetery next door makes for a good stroll.

Buford Highway The *Atlanta Inn (Map 2; ☎ 770-452-8500, 5114 Buford Hwy)* is located in the midst of a long strip of businesses catering to Chinese, Vietnamese and Hispanic immigrants in Doraville, a mile south of the MARTA Doraville station (NE10); bus No 39 runs in front of the hotel to the station. The basic rooms are worn and only moderately clean. Rates are $45/50 singles/doubles.

The *Comfort Inn* (☎ *888-816-0924, 770-455-3700*) offers shuttle service to the MARTA Doraville station, an outdoor pool, and microwave ovens and VCRs (with videos for rent) in all rooms. Standard chain hotel rooms are $69/74, including breakfast, though lower rates are sometimes available on the weekends. The hotel is at I-285 exit 32; follow the signs to a side road.
Web site: www.comfortinnatl.com

Perimeter East One of the best values for hotels near a MARTA station, the *Guest House Inn* (☎ *404-836-8100, 4649 Memorial Dr*) opened in 1997. It offers singles/doubles from $41/46 and has weekly rates from $197. All rooms have a small kitchenette and coffeemaker. The hotel is along an unattractive strip of Hwy 10 (Memorial Dr), a third of a mile east of I-285 exit 41 and about one mile from the Kensington MARTA station (E8). MARTA bus No 121 passes the hotel and goes to the MARTA station. Stone Mountain Park is about 6 miles east.

Mid-Range

Downtown Near the northern edge of downtown and within striking distance of Midtown, *Best Western Inn at the Peachtree* (☎ *800-242-4642, 404-577-6970, fax 404-659-3244, 330 W Peachtree St)* has 110 nice, cozy rooms in a well-done renovation of an older hotel. Amenities include an exercise room and a coin laundry. Some rooms have microwaves and coffeemakers; suites have a refrigerator and stove. Rates from $80 include a hot breakfast; parking on site or across the street is $8 extra. The hotel is three blocks from the MARTA Civic Center (N2) or Peachtree Center (N1) station.

Midtown The older *Days Inn* (☎ *800-329-7466, 404-874-9200, fax 404-873-4245, 683 Peachtree St NE)* is a bit worn, but adequate. Its saving feature is its location one block from the Fox Theatre and a few blocks east of the MARTA North Avenue station (N3). Standard rates are $89/99 singles/doubles, including a continental breakfast. Parking is $7 extra.

Fairfield Inn & Suites (☎ *800-818-9745, 404-872-5821, fax 404-874-3602, 1470 Spring St)*, at 19th St, is on the northern edge of Midtown, next to the William Breman Jewish Heritage Museum, and four blocks from the High Museum of Art and the Woodruff Arts Center. A predictable, mid-range business hotel, it includes a fitness center and outside pool. Standard rooms starting at $79 are a good value and include a continental breakfast and parking.
Web site: www.fairfieldinn.com

The *Ansley Inn* (☎ *800-446-5416, 404-872-9000, fax 404-892-2318, 253 Fifteenth St)* is on a quiet residential street in the prestigious neighborhood of Ansley Park, right down the road from Piedmont Park. This restored 1907 yellow-brick English Tudor mansion has 22 rooms featuring four-poster beds, period furnishings and Jacuzzis. Rooms in the main house start at $129 doubles, while the smaller rooms in the separate corporate building start at $109. Rates include a full hot breakfast and afternoon hors d'oeuvres.
Web site: www.ansleyinn.com

Decatur In downtown Decatur near the MARTA station, *Holiday Inn Select* (☎ 800-225-6079, 404-371-0204, fax 404-377-2726, 130 Clairemont Ave), near W Ponce de Leon Ave, is a business-class hotel with 185 modern, business-style rooms. Views are either outward toward the surrounding town or inward toward the five-story enclosed atrium. Amenities include an indoor pool, fitness center, a restaurant and lounge and van service to nearby areas. Rates are $89 to $139, plus $5 for parking.

Buckhead The *Lenox Inn* (☎ 800-241-0200, 404-261-5500, fax 404-261-6140, 3387 Lenox Rd NE) is a rare, older-style motel in the midst of Buckhead's upscale shopping and gleaming office towers. The two-story inn has 176 so-so rooms, an outdoor pool, free parking and a pleasant outside courtyard good for a retreat from Buckhead's frantic pace. Rates are $79 to $125, including continental breakfast. The inn is two blocks north of the MARTA Lenox station (NE7). It has been known to close in winter when business is slow.
Web site: www.lenoxinnbuckhead.com

The *Fairfield Inn* (☎ 800-228-2800, 404-846-0900, 3092 Piedmont Rd), at E Paces Ferry Rd, is your standard mid-price business hotel, built in 1997. No surprises here, it's next to the Sambuca Jazz Café (see Entertainment), within a few long blocks of the MARTA Buckhead station (N7) and within driving distance to the Lindbergh Center station (N6). It has an indoor pool and hot tub. Rates are $99 to $119, including a continental breakfast and free parking.
Web site: www.fairfieldinn.com

Similar is the *Hampton Inn* (☎ 800-426-7866, 404-233-5656, fax 404-233-5656, 3398 Piedmont Rd), with rates from $109 to $119 doubles. The local hotel staff seem to quote lower rates and are more polite than the people answering the 800 number.

Perimeter North The *Fairfield Inn Atlanta/Perimeter Center (Map 2; ☎/fax 770-350-0000, 1145 Hammond Dr)*, between Peachtree Dunwoody Rd and Ashford-Dunwoody Rd, is convenient to the office towers and business parks on the north perimeter, as well as to Perimeter Mall. Standard mid-class hotel rooms are $99 weekdays, and $59/$69 singles/doubles on weekends, including breakfast. It's close to the MARTA Dunwoody station.
Web site: www.fairfieldinn.com

Similar is the *Hampton Inn* (☎ 800-426-7866, 404-303-0014, 769 Hammond Dr), in the same area but farther from MARTA, with rates of $105/69 weekdays/weekends.

Across from the Concourse Office Park, the *Homestead Village Guest Studios* (☎ 888-782-9473, 770-522-0025, fax 770-522-0033) is designed for long-term business travelers. Studios with a fully equipped kitchen and work area rent from $77 a night. Weekly rates start at $53/day.
Web site: www.stayhsd.com

Top End

Downtown *Westin Peachtree Plaza* (☎ 800-937-8461, 404-659-1400, fax 404-589-7424, 210 Peachtree St NW), at International Blvd, is in the heart of downtown. The sleek cylindrical glass makes it one of Atlanta's most recognizable buildings, and at 723 feet and 73 stories, it's the tallest hotel in the Western Hemisphere. The 1068 comfortable rooms have great views of the city. Comprehensive amenities include an indoor pool and business and fitness centers. Scenic glass elevators whiz you to the revolving Sun Dial Restaurant at the top. Standard rates start at $209, but discounts are often possible. Parking costs an additional $18. The hotel is adjacent to the MARTA Peachtree Center station (N1).
Web site: www.westin.com

Also located near the MARTA Peachtree Center station, the *Ritz-Carlton* (☎ 800-241-3333, 404-659-0400, fax 404-221-6578, 181 Peachtree St NE), at Ellis St, has a warmer, Victorian tone to its decorations. The usual luxury business amenities are provided. Its 444 rooms start at $225.
Web site: www.ritzcarlton.com

Midtown If you want to spread out, the *Regency Suites Hotel* (☎ 800-642-3629,

404-876-5003, 975 W Peachtree St) is a converted apartment building with 96 efficiencies, each with a king or two double beds, couch and kitchen. The hotel is overpriced at $139 to $159, including breakfast, but you may find special deals in tourist literature. Parking is an additional $9 in a poorly designed garage. The hotel is well located adjacent to the MARTA Midtown station (N4).
Web site: www.regency-suites.com

The **Georgian Terrace** (☎ 800-651-2316, 404-897-1991, fax 404-724-0642, 659 Peachtree St NE) is right across the street from the Fox Theatre. Built in 1911 and remodeled in 1997, the hotel is on the National Register of Historic Places. Many of the Gone With the Wind stars stayed here during the film's debut in 1939. The 326 rooms include small standard rooms and one-, two- and three-bedroom suites. The spacious suites have a washer and dryer and a fully stocked kitchen. An elaborate health center, rooftop swimming pool, restaurant and lounge mean you never have to leave the hotel. Rates start at $170 for the tiny standard rooms and at $230 for the one-bedroom suites. Penthouse suites can exceed $1000 – ouch. Parking is an additional $17.
Web site: www.thegeorgianterrace.com

The **Shellmont Inn** (☎ 404-872-9290, fax 404-872-5379, 821 Piedmont Ave NE), at 6th St, is a comfortable retreat in an 1891 classic Victorian home on the National Register of Historic Places, complete with Tiffany stained-glass windows, great carved woodwork, wall stenciling and authentic period furnishings. A beautiful veranda overlooks a garden and fish pond. The house may be classic, but the new granite bathrooms – some with Jacuzzis – are modern. Rates start at $135, including a full gourmet breakfast.
Web site: www.shellmont.com

Buckhead The **Sheraton Buckhead Atlanta** (Map 6; ☎ 800-325-3535, 404-261-9250, fax 404-848-7391, 3405 Lenox Rd NE), across from Lenox Square shopping center, is popular for business travelers and shoppers alike. Recently renovated, the 369 medium-size rooms feature large sleigh beds and large writing desks. The hotel has a new health and fitness center, outdoor swimming pool, business center and restaurant. The lobby bar with cozy fireplace is popular for heightening that post-shopping buzz. Rates are $159 to $199 weekdays, $139 to $159 weekends, plus $10 parking.
Web site: www.sheraton.com

Money burning a hole in your pocket? You can spend it all at the **Ritz-Carlton Buckhead** (☎ 800-241-3333, 404-237-2700, fax 404-239-0078, 3434 Peachtree Rd), a 22-story hotel in the heart of Buckhead. One of the most elegant hotels in Atlanta, it's expensively decorated in marble, hardwood, antiques and paintings. Expect all the amenities, including 24-hour room service, a business center, good views, a concierge and private meeting lounges. Designed to be offices, the standard rooms are a bit smaller than the Ritz-Carlton norm, but the international headquarters next door ensures everything is kept first class. The hotel restaurant is considered one of the finest in the city. Standard rooms start at $255/195 weekdays/weekends; club-level rooms start at $330; penthouse suites cost somewhere around $1500.
Web site: www.ritzcarlton.com

Perimeter North The **Crowne Plaza Ravinia** (Map 2; ☎ 800-227-6963, 770-395-7700, fax 770-392-9503) is in the middle of the perimeter center business area, and close to Perimeter Mall. This upscale hotel is also popular for weddings, and features a comfortable lobby and large, cheerful rooms. Amenities include a health club, business center, heated indoor/outdoor swimming pool, tennis court, valet parking (extra) and bell captains who could be more attentive. It's set on 10 acres of greenery, with walking paths and pools of Japanese fish. A courtesy van transports guests to nearby areas, including the Perimeter Mall and the MARTA station. Rates start at $219.
Web site: www.crowneplaza.com

GEORGIA

PLACES TO EAT

With more than 8000 restaurants, from fast-food joints to the finest of fine dining, Atlanta has plenty of places to eat. The restaurants here are grouped by neighborhood and, within each section, listed in roughly ascending order of price.

Downtown

A cheap choice is the huge cafeteria nicknamed **Sloppy's** in the basement of the James H 'Sloppy' Floyd Veterans Memorial Building (the two big, brown towers at 2 Martin Luther King Jr Dr), catty-corner from the State Capitol. Always crowded with government workers, there's no atmosphere to speak of, but the Southern specialties are decent, and everything is cheap. Sandwiches, soups and salads are also available. Full meals can easily be had for about $5. It's open 6:45 am to 2:30 pm weekdays.

Ria's Bluebird (☎ 404-521-3737, 421 Memorial Dr SE), at the corner of Cherokee Ave across from Oakland Cemetery, is a cheerfully eclectic, small cafe, focusing on an all-day breakfast ($5 to $7) and gourmet sandwiches ($7) such as roasted eggplant and tarragon chicken salad. It's popular with locals and an alternative crowd and is open 8 am to 4 pm daily.

Daddy Dz (☎ 404-220-0206, 264 Memorial Dr SE), at Hill St, is a ramshackle shack in a rugged light-industrial neighborhood west of Oakland Cemetery. Skip the appetizers and go straight for the ribs ($10 a half slab) and sides (baked beans and fried okra). It's open for lunch and dinner. There's live blues here on Thursday, Friday and Saturday nights.

The **Caribbean Restaurant** (☎ 404-658-9829, 180 Auburn Ave), near Piedmont Ave in the Sweet Auburn district, serves West Indies cuisine with a definite Jamaican slant such as kingfish, conch, snapper, plantains, oxtails, curry goat and jerk chicken. It's open for lunch and dinner, but closed Sunday.

Sylvia's Restaurant (☎ 404-529-9692, 241 Central Ave), across from City Hall at the corner with Trinity Ave, is an upscale, elegant soul food restaurant that started out in Harlem. Specialties include fried chicken, catfish, ribs (though ours were a bit tough) and very good cornbread. Extra touches include a full bar, jazz at noon on Friday and on weekend nights, and an all-day Sunday brunch with gospel entertainment from noon to 3 pm.

Midtown

The **Varsity** (☎ 404-881-1706), on the northwest corner of Spring St and North Ave, is hectic, crowded, dirty, loud and rude, yet it's *still* an Atlanta tradition. Nearly everyone who eats here has the chili dog ($1.50), and the onion rings are good and greasy. If you don't want to walk inside and be hollered at, carhops will come to your car.

The **Vortex Bar & Grill** (☎ 404-875-1667), on Peachtree St between 7th and 8th Sts, is known for offering some of the city's best burgers ($6). Open until 2 am (until midnight on Sunday), it draws students and other night prowlers. The extensive, fun menu includes pub-style sandwiches, wings, and quesadillas, and you can always substitute a veggie burger or black bean veggie burger for the beef patty. Another branch is in Little Five Points (see Map 5).

Eats (☎ 404-888-9149, 600 Ponce de Leon Ave NE), at Lakeview Ave (across from City Hall East), is one of the most popular cheap eateries in the city, offering home-cooked food at fast-food prices. The environment is energetic, the décor marginal. Eats offers mix and match pasta, chicken and vegetables and little else, but a full meal can be had for under $5; the black beans and rice are especially good. Beer and wine are available.

The *Flying Biscuit Café*, in Midtown at the corner of Piedmont Ave and 10th St, opened at the end of 2000 to long lines of people waiting for the all-day breakfasts of omelets, organic oatmeal pancakes, fried green tomatoes and tasty grits, all accompanied by their justifiably famous huge, fluffy biscuits. Ah, heaven. A diverse, happy crowd enjoys the rest of the vegetarian-friendly menu of black bean quesadillas and veggie burgers. Meals are about $6 to $8.

Mary Mac's Tea Room (☎ 404-876-1800, 224 Ponce de Leon Ave), three blocks east of the Fox Theatre, serves tasty Southern food in a bright, cheery, grandmotherly atmosphere. Vegetarian-friendly veggies are marked on the menu. The fried okra, cream corn, and sweet potato soufflé are all good. Prices are moderate ($9 lunch; $10 dinner). It's open for lunch and dinner daily except Sunday, when it's open for lunch only.

Andaluz (☎ 404-875-7013, 903 Peachtree St NE), at 7th St, draws a sophisticated crowd looking for a snack before or after theater performances, after work or as a late-night outing. Serving Spanish *tapas* such as tortilla española or tomatoes on bread, full meals are also available (including *paella*). A full selection of beer, wine, sangria, coffee and tea is served. Individual items are $1.50 to $12. It's open 5 pm to midnight (until 2 am on weekends), but closed Monday.

Atlanta's barbecue aficionados will direct you to *Fat Matt's Rib Shack* (☎ 404-607-1622, 1811 Piedmont Ave NE), less than a mile north of Piedmont Park. The unpretentious, nonsmoking atmosphere complements the wonderful barbecue ribs ($9 a half slab), sandwiches ($5) and sides. Up-and-coming blues acts start around 8:30 pm every night (see the Entertainment section later in this chapter).

Agnes & Muriel's (☎ 404-885-1000, 1514 Monroe Dr NE), at Piedmont Ave just north of Piedmont Park, serves old-fashioned food with a modern twist, comfort food that goes beyond merely Southern. An eclectic crowd chows down in this bright, cheerful brick bungalow, with 1950s décor inspired by Jane Jetson, June Cleaver and Pee Wee Herman. Main dishes of barbecue fried catfish, buttermilk fried chicken, Louisiana barbecue shrimp over grits and grilled salmon pot pie are $9 to $15; sandwiches $6 to $8. It's open for lunch and dinner.

Tierra (☎ 404-874-5951, 1425-B Piedmont Ave), near the northern tip of Piedmont Park, serves tasty, unusual Latin American specialties: Salvadoran cheese *pupusa* (turnover), chicken *molé* (a spicy Mexican reddish-brown sauce with a hint of chocolate), plantains and *calabaza* (a sweet, pumpkinlike squash). The elegant atmosphere is complemented by attentive, polite service, and by Chilean wines. Main dishes are $14 to $19. It's open for dinner only; closed Monday.

Points East & Virginia Highland

The original *Flying Biscuit Café* (☎ 404-687-8888, 1655 McLendon Ave) is in the Candler Park neighborhood, just southeast of Candler Park (the park, not the neighborhood); see the listing under Midtown.

Surin of Thailand (☎ 404-892-7789, 810 N Highland Ave), among the string of pubs on N Highland Ave in the Virginia Highland neighborhood, is often crowded and noisy with diners packed around long tables in one big room. The reason: reasonably priced Thai dishes. Meat and vegetable dishes are $8; special creations are about $14.

Among the most popular bars in Virginia Highland is *Manuel's Tavern* (☎ 404-526-3447, 602 N Highland Ave), a longtime political hangout. Jimmy Carter announced his candidacy for governor here. It has a good range of salads and sandwiches for $6 to $10, a friendly pub atmosphere and even a nonsmoking room. The standard bar food is supplemented by more unusual choices, such as pita, hummus and veggie burgers. Carter claims they have the best wings in the South ($10 for 20 pieces).

The *Vortex Bar & Grill* (☎ 404-688-1828, 438 Moreland Ave NE) has a branch in Little Five Points (see the Midtown listings). Look for the huge skull.

Camille's (☎ 404-872-7203, 1186 N Highland Ave NE) is another place in Virginia

GEORGIA

Highland with long waits. It's a traditional, homey Italian restaurant with family photos covering the walls and red-and-white checkered plastic tablecloths, and the calzones are a favorite. Dishes cost $14 to $16.

Fritti (☎ 404-880-9559, 311 N Highland Ave NE) specializes in delightful gourmet Neapolitan pizzas with a very thin crust. A second-floor loft overlooks the downstairs. As pizzas go, they're rather expensive at $14 for a 10-inch pie.

Next door, **Sotto Sotto** (404-523-6678, 313 N Highland Ave NE), at Elizabeth St, is a subdued but closely packed trendy restaurant serving authentic Italian dishes from $14 to $20. It serves dinner only; closed Sunday.

Decatur

The **Brick Store Pub** (☎ 404-687-0990, 125 E Court Square), in a brick building in downtown Decatur, has a pleasant, warm atmosphere that appeals to a variety of ages. Pub food includes munchies, salads, burgers and sandwiches ($6). An extensive beer list is available.

Watershed (☎ 404-378-4900, 406 W Ponce de Leon Ave) is a trendy but bright and pleasant restaurant serving creative New American food in a converted garage. The menu has plenty of dishes incorporating pasta, Italian sausage, fish and mussels, complemented by an extensive wine selection. Sandwiches cost $7 to $12; main dishes are $9 for lunch, $14 to $18 for dinner. It's closed Sunday.

Buckhead

Souper Jenny (☎ 404-239-9023, 56 E Andrews Dr) serves up a variety of simple and hearty low-fat soups with ingredients such as spinach, kale, chicken, lentils, pumpkin, wild mushrooms and beans. Its popularity and small size make finding a seat difficult. You can get a cup of soup, side salad, roll and fruit for about $6. It's located in Andrews Square; enter from Cains Hill Rd. It's open 11 am to 6:30 pm Tuesday through Friday; closed the month of August.

Burrito Art (☎ 404-237-0095, 3365 Piedmont Rd NE) dishes out gourmet 'Ameri-canized' burritos in a colorful, funky, non-smoking atmosphere. The unusual creations include jerk chicken, Thai chicken, barbecue chicken and eggplant burritos. Lunch is about $7; dinner is $1 more. It's closed on Sunday. There are additional branches at 1259 Glenwood Ave (Map 2; ☎ 404-627-4433, between Flat Shoals and Moreland Aves) and in Emory Village (Map 5; ☎ 404-377-7786, 1451 Oxford Rd), near N Decatur Rd NE.

In far southwest Buckhead, the **Nuevo Laredo Cantina** (☎ 404-352-9009, 1495 Chattahoochee Ave NW) is out of the way, but diners in search of home-cooked authentic Mexican food eagerly make the effort. This unassuming cantina is consistently picked as Atlanta's best Mexican restaurant, serving quesadillas, enchiladas, tacos, chorizo, *chile relleno, chimichangas, chalupas* and martinis; dishes cost $6 to $12. It's closed Sundays.

OK Café (☎ 404-233-2888, 1284 W Paces Ferry Rd), at Northside Parkway on the western side of Buckhead near I-75, is a tremendously popular cafe serving filling Southern, soul and other comfort food, with fast and attentive service. Blue plate specialties include chicken pot pie, country fried steak and pot roast ($10 to $11), accompanied by two fresh veggies (baked sweet potato, collard greens, Waldorf salad). Sandwiches and burgers are also available ($7). It's open 7 am to 11 pm daily, later on weekends.

Café Tu Tu Tango (☎ 404-841-6222, 220 Pharr Rd), in the midst of Buckhead's entertainment district, is a hangout for a young artsy crowd. Along with its close-packed tables and an artist's basement look, you'll find local art on the walls and Tarot card readings in the corner. Not particularly cheap, the food consists of creative multi-ethnic tapas that cost $4 to $8 each.

Pano and Paul's (☎ 404-261-3662, 1232 W Paces Ferry Rd), in the shopping center behind the OK Café, is an elegant, classy restaurant where waiters in tuxes serve classic Continental cuisine. The menu is heavy on seafood – lobster tails, salmon, sea bass etc. Dishes cost $22 to $38.

GEORGIA

Bone's Restaurant (☎ 404-237-2663, 3130 Piedmont Rd NE) has gotten the votes for best steaks in Atlanta every year since 1988. Atlanta's most New Yorkish setting, with lots of wood and brass, the restaurant is defined by he-man ambience, where people exuding power pheromones meet to scarf down huge steaks. A steak sandwich (lunch only) is $17; steaks are $23 to $38. Dinner is served daily; lunch on weekdays only.

The *Imperial Fez (Map 2; ☎ 404-351-0870, 2285 Peachtree Rd NE)*, in South Buckhead, is decorated like a Moroccan potentate's tent. Guests remove their shoes at the door and sit on layered silk cushions placed on the thick Berber carpets. While diners munch on a six-course Moroccan feast, belly dancers entertain. Dinner and show are offered for a fixed price of about $45. It's open for dinner only.

Greater Atlanta

The *DeKalb Farmers Market (☎ 404-377-6400, 3000 E Ponce de Leon Ave)* is a huge, 140,000-sq-foot inside market crowded with international customers, workers and ingredients. Here you can find the normal – as well as the unusual – fruits and vegetables, fresh shellfish, dairy products and fresh herbs. If you've just *got* to have fresh rabbit, quail, beef tongue, bison, lamb kidneys, durian or Chinese eggplant, you'll find it here. You can watch the workers catch and prepare live farm-raised catfish. At the cheap cafeteria, you can load up on hot foods and salads for $3/pound, or $3.50 a sandwich. The market is open 9 am to 9 pm daily.

As an expanding mecca for Atlanta's burgeoning immigrant population, Buford Highway in Doraville has an increasing number of authentic ethnic restaurants. Korean noodle houses, Vietnamese *pho* shops, Salvadoran *pupusa* eateries and Asian and Latino food markets vie for the multiethnic palates. Although these places aren't necessarily big on décor and atmosphere, the food is always interesting.

El Taco Veloz (☎ 770-936-9094, 5084 Buford Hwy) is like home to the local immigrant Hispanic population. It serves authentic tacos and burritos from a cinderblock box, and the food is fast and inexpensive. Another location is at 5670 Roswell Rd, a few miles to the west.

The *Santo Domingo Restaurant (☎ 770-452-3939, 5310 Buford Hwy)* is an unpretentious little place inside a former donut shop that serves Dominican-style *sancocho* and stews; vegetarians are stuck with rice, beans and plantains. Dishes are $6 to $9.

The *88 Tofu House (☎ 770-457-8811, 5490 Buford Hwy NE)* serves Korean-style vegetable tofu and spicy *kim-chi* soup in a cafeteria setting. Dishes cost about $9, with $6 lunch and dinner specials. They're open 24 hours.

The area around Emory University is also a good place to go for a variety of reasonably priced meals. There's a branch of *Burrito Art (Map 5; ☎ 404-377-7786, 1451 87 Rd)* here in Emory Village, near N Decatur Rd NE. See the Buckhead listing, earlier, for a description.

The *Udipi Café (☎ 404-325-1933, 1850 Lawrenceville Hwy)*, north of downtown Decatur, is somewhat out of the way but worth the trip. Authentic vegetarian South Indian Cuisine such as the eggplant curry is spicy but good, and is served with rice and *pachadi* (yogurt sauce). The *Uthappam* (Indian-style pancakes) were also recommended. Huge dishes cost about $7, combo dinners $12 to $15.

At *Nicola's (☎ 404-325-2524, 1602 Lavista Rd NE)*, the fun-loving owner provides the entertainment, with periodic spasms of folk dancing, sometimes convincing the diners to join in. The filling, meaty dishes such as *kibbee, kafta* and stuffed grape leaves are moderately priced at $10 to $11.

The *Floataway Café (☎ 404-892-1414, 1123 Zonolite Rd)*, a bit northwest of Emory University, is a trendy French-Italian bistro that's fashionable without being fancy. In a converted warehouse, dishes are $15 to $25. It serves dinner only; closed Sunday and Monday.

ENTERTAINMENT

Atlanta has big-city nightlife, with most venues concentrated in several areas. The free weekly *Creative Loafing* has the best listings. The Saturday edition of the *Atlanta Journal-Constitution* has less comprehensive but still easy-to-use listings.

Buckhead has a concentrated strip of bars and dance clubs in an area bounded by Peachtree, E Paces Ferry and Pharr Rds (Map 6). You can walk around and find what looks and sounds good (be aware of the oblivious drivers). Some folks in the neighborhood, however, think that things have gotten a bit *too* wild. Buckhead also has the area's more sophisticated options, from martini bars to lively jazz supper clubs.

Little Five Points has a young/college/punk scene. Start around the intersection of Euclid and Moreland Aves to explore the options.

North of Little Five Points, Virginia Highland draws a more affluent yuppie crowd. Bars and restaurants are concentrated on N Highland Ave.

Decatur is another place to explore, with a few pubs, a pool hall and a good acoustic music venue near the courthouse square and MARTA station.

Bars & Pubs

Mike 'n' Angelo's (☎ 404-237-0949, *312 E Paces Ferry Rd*), in the main Buckhead bar district, is a friendly bar that draws a youthful crowd (late '20s–'30s) who have moved past the rowdy stage. You can actually hear yourself talk here. There's a game room with pool and darts.

The *Beluga Martini Bar* (☎ 404-869-1090, *3115 Piedmont Rd NE*), also in Buckhead (Map 6), offers martinis (duh), wine and single-malt scotch in a cozy, upscale atmosphere.

Twain's Billiards & Tap (☎ 404-373-0063, *211 E Trinity Place*), in Decatur, has a limited menu but a huge selection of beer. It is becoming one of the city's more popular pool halls, and features both smoking and nonsmoking rooms.

In Little Five Points, the *Euclid Avenue Yacht Club* (☎ 404-688-2582, *1136 Euclid Ave*), with its huge beer selection, is a hangout for the friendly alternative crowd, from tattooed bikers to pierced goths.

Turn back to the Places to Eat section for additional pubs that serve food.

Dance Clubs

Johnny's Hideaway (Map 6; ☎ 404-233-8026, *3771 Roswell Rd*), in Buckhead, is often packed with dancers from 30 to 70 grooving to mixed '40s big band music, '50s doo-wop, '70s disco and '80s rock on a moderate-size dance floor. There's a two-drink minimum, but no cover. The cigarette smoke is very thick.

At *Bell Bottoms* (Map 6; ☎ 404-816-9669, *225 Pharr Rd*), in the main Buckhead strip, a racially mixed crowd of dancers who believe hip-huggers are back in style swing those hips to disco, '70s and '80s music. It's open Thursday through Saturday starting at 8 pm; $5 cover. Nearby, the *Have a Nice Day Café* (☎ 404-261-8898, *3095 Peachtree Rd*), open Thursday through Sunday, has a similar theme, complete with a glittering disco ball.

In Midtown, *Masquerade* (Map 4; ☎ 404-577-8178, *695 North Ave*) is a mammoth dance place that supposedly gets popular after midnight. Before then, it can resemble a high school dance, with young lookers-on gaping at one or two hip movers on the floor. You only have to be 18 to get in. The complex includes the dance floor, a quieter bar area with pool tables, and a live music stage with local music acts (tending toward heavy metal and punk). The cover is typically $5 (no re-entry), $10 for the live acts.

North of the perimeter in Kennesaw, *Cowboy's* (☎ 770-426-5006, *1750 N Roberts Rd*) is a large, rowdy dance hall packed on the weekends with line dancers and mechanical bull riders.

Backstreet (see the Gay Atlanta boxed text) has 24-hour dancing.

Jazz

The *Sambuca Jazz Café* (Map 6; ☎ 404-237-5299, *3102 Piedmont Rd NE*), in Buckhead, has 20 to 25 live jazz acts every month. It's often packed with a well-dressed and racially mixed crowd. Mediterranean cuisine is served; main dishes start at $20. There's no cover, but there is a $17 per person food minimum for those seated. You can also enjoy the jazz from the crowded bar (two drink or $10 minimum). Sambuca opens at 6 pm, with jazz at 7:30 pm every night. Reservations are recommended. Check the current schedule on their Web site, www.sambucajazzcafe.com.

Dante's Down the Hatch (Map 6; ☎ 404-266-1600), on Peachtree St across from Lenox Square in Buckhead, features sentimental, contemporary jazz nightly starting at 7:30 pm. Its unusual sailing ship décor includes plenty of antiques and a moat containing live crocodiles. Fondue dinners are the specialty; they're pricey at $14 to $28.

Cabaret

Libby's A Cabaret (Map 6; ☎ 404-237-1943, 3401 Northside Parkway), tucked away in a shopping center just south of W Paces Ferry Rd near I-75, is a supper club featuring cabaret shows Wednesday through Sunday. The pricing structure may change, but a weeknight with a top-quality touring act costs around $75 for dinner and a show; a weekend night might cost $90. A cheaper late-night alternative consisting of the show, dessert and coffee might be offered on Saturday for $50. Reservations are recommended. See their Web site at www.libbyscabaret.com for a schedule and prices.

Blues

For serious blues, try *Blind Willie's* (Map 5; ☎ 404-873-2583, 828 N Highland Ave), in Virginia Highland, a well-established blues bar with pub food, local and occasional big-name acts. The cover is typically $6 weeknights, $10 weekends. The door opens at 8 pm; the show starts at 9 pm.

Fat Matt's Rib Shack (☎ 404-607-1622, 1811 Piedmont Ave NE) is another good place, with up-and-coming blues acts playing nightly starting about 8:30 pm. In a very small space, expect the music to be loud, and you may come out of the bathroom (next to the stage) to applause. Smoking is allowed only outside on the patio. There's no cover, but be sure to try the ribs (see the Places to Eat section, earlier).

Other Live Music

The *Star Community Bar* (Map 5; ☎ 404-681-9018, 437 Moreland Ave), in Little Five Points, draws a funky crowd to its live acts four nights a week. The music ranges from disco funk to rockabilly, blues and swing, and includes local and national touring acts. Be sure to check out the infamous Elvis shrine in the old bank vault. It opens at 9 pm, with music typically starting around 10:30 pm. The cover is $5 to $7.

Eddie's Attic (Map 5; ☎ 404-377-4976, 515-B N McDonough St), on the main square in Decatur (and convenient to MARTA Decatur station E6), is one of the city's best places to hear folk and acoustic music seven nights a week. The intimate performance hall is nonsmoking and non-talking. For popular performances, numbers are given out starting at 4 pm. There's also tavern food and an area with pool tables. The cover is $3 to $20, depending on the act; there's no cover for the nonperformance area.

The *Tabernacle* (Map 3; ☎ 404-659-9022, 152 Luckie St), downtown, is one of the best venues for live music. Funky and popular, it has five floor levels, two performance stages and nine bars.

See Masquerade under Dance Clubs previously for more live music.

Classical Music & Opera

For a schedule of cultural events, see the *Atlanta Now* magazine or call the Bureau of Cultural Affairs at ☎ 404-817-6815.

The Woodruff Arts Center (Map 4) hosts the *Atlanta Symphony Orchestra* (☎ 404-733-5000, 1293 Peachtree St NE). Check their Web site (www.atlantasymphony.org) for a current schedule.

The *Atlanta Opera* (☎ 404-817-8700, 728 W Peachtree St NW) performs full-stage grand opera at the Fox Theatre (Map 4). Web site: www.atlantaopera.org

The *Atlanta Ballet* (☎ 404-873-5811, 1400 W Peachtree St) is the oldest ballet company in the US. Classical and contemporary performances are staged at the Fox Theatre. Web site: www.atlantaballet.com

The **Atlanta Civic Center** *(Map 4; ☎ 404-523-6275, 395 Piedmont Ave)* hosts Broadway and other traveling shows.

Theater

Atlanta has a wide range of theatrical experiences to choose from, including dinner audience-participation mysteries, Shakespeare, and just pure goofiness.

Agatha's, A Taste of Mystery *(☎ 404-875-1610, 693 Peachtree St NE)*, across from the Fox Theatre, specializes in campy, audience-participation murder shows. The $40 to $50 price includes a five-course dinner and wine.

The **Alliance Theatre Company** *(☎ 404-733-5000, 1280 Peachtree St NE)*, at the Woodruff Arts Center (Map 4), is Atlanta's premier professional theater. Productions include some that appeal to children. Check their Web site, www.alliancetheatre.org, for current productions; tickets start at $17.

The **Georgia Shakespeare Festival** *(Map 2; ☎ 404-264-0020, email boxoffice@ gashakespeare.org, 4484 Peachtree Rd)*, at the Conant Performing Arts Center in Oglethorpe University, serves up the traditional Shakespeare, but isn't afraid to put on modern-dress performances as well.
Web site: www.gashakespeare.org

A bit less serious, **Dad's Garage Theatre Company** *(Map 5; ☎ 404-523-3141, 280 Elizabeth St)* offers everything from comedy to musicals, including improvisational, audience-participation skits. Snacks and beverages are available.

Tickets can be purchased at Ticketmaster (☎ 404-279-6400). AtlanTIX (☎ 770-772-5572) sells half-price tickets the day of a show by phone, through their Web site at www.atlantatheaters.org, and at the visitors center at Underground Atlanta (Map 3; open 11 am to 3 pm Tuesday; 11 am to 6 pm Wednesday to Saturday, and noon to 3 pm Sunday).

Cinemas

It should be no surprise that Atlanta offers plenty of movie theaters. **AMC Phipps Plaza 14** *(☎ 404-816-4262)*, at Phipps Plaza in Buckhead, is one of the few multiscreen theaters to show an occasional independent film. The **Regal Cinemas Hollywood 24** *(☎ 770-936-5737, 3265 Northeast Expressway Access Rd)*, in Chamblee, is the largest, with 24 screens. The **Lefont Plaza Theatre** *(☎ 404-873-1939, 1049 Ponce de Leon Ave)* is the ultimate urban art house.

The **Garden Hills Cinema** *(Map 6; ☎ 404-266-2202, 2835 Peachtree Rd NE)*, in Buckhead, plays unusual, independent and artistic films. The Sunday Cinema Club meets here to watch and discuss independent films.

Cinefest *(Map 3; ☎ 404-651-2565, 66 Courtland St)*, in the University Center of Georgia State University, shows artsy, campy and classic movies at reasonable prices ($3 before 6 pm; $5 after). Call for a schedule and directions. The MARTA Georgia State station (E1) is less than 3 blocks away.

The High Museum of Art in Midtown (Map 4) also has a good art film series.

Comedy

Atlanta has a number of comedy venues, including:

Dad's Garage Theatre Company *(Map 5; ☎ 404-523-3141, 280 Elizabeth St)*

Laughing Matters Improvisational Comedy Troupe *(Map 2; ☎ 404-874-4050, 173 Cleveland St)*, Atlanta's longest running improv comedy troupe, with weekly shows
Web site: www.laughingmatters.com

The Punchline *(Map 2; ☎ 404-252-5233, 280 Hilderbrand Dr)*, providing stand-up comedy for more than 15 years

Whole World Theatre *(Map 4; ☎ 404-817-7529, 1214 Spring St NW)*, in Midtown

SPECTATOR SPORTS

With four professional sports teams, Atlanta has plenty of sports action. The Atlanta Braves professional baseball team plays just south of downtown at Turner Field (☎ 404-577-9100), formerly Olympic Stadium (after the games, the stadium was reconfigured into a baseball-only facility). In the 1990s, the Braves won eight consecutive division titles, five National League Championships, and the World Series in 1995. Tickets cost $5 to

$40; a few $1 seats are available only on the day of the game.

You can see the Braves Museum or take one of the Turner Field Tours (☎ 404-614-2311) year-round for $7/4 adults/children.

Turner Field is not near a MARTA station, but you can get there by taking buses No 17, 55, 90 or 97 from the Five Points station. Dedicated shuttle buses run between the Five Points station and the stadium starting 90 minutes before games.

Web site: www.atlantabraves.com

The Atlanta Falcons pro football team (☎ 404-223-8000) plays in the 71,200-seat Georgia Dome, on the western side of downtown next to the Georgia World Congress Center (a huge convention center). They played in, but lost, the Superbowl in January 1999. Tickets start at $25. Take the MARTA to the Omni/Dome/GWCC station (W1).

Web site: www.atlantafalcons.com

The Atlanta Hawks basketball team (☎ 404-827-3800) plays at the new (1999) Philips Arena, next to the Georgia Dome. Regular ticket prices range from $10 to $65.

Web site: www.hawks.com

A new ice hockey team, the Atlanta Thrashers (☎ 404-584-7825) also plays in the Philips Arena. The team is named after the brown thrasher, Georgia's state bird, and is owned by Ted Turner (who also owns the Braves and the Hawks). Ticket prices range from $10 to $55.

Web site: www.atlantathrashers.com

In collegiate football, the Georgia Tech Yellow Jackets (☎ 404-894-5447) play in the 46,000 seat Bobby Dodd Stadium, North Ave and Techwood Dr. The Chick-fil-A Peach Bowl (☎ 404-586-8500), an elite post-season football game in Midtown that is often sold out, and the Atlanta Football Classic are played each year at the Georgia Dome.

Web site: www.peachbowl.com

Tickets can be ordered through Ticketmaster by phone (☎ 800-326-4000, 404-249-6400) or from their Web site (www.ticketmaster.com).

SHOPPING

In Atlanta, shopping is more than a hobby, it's a lifestyle. With more than 53 enclosed malls, it's no wonder that these grand examples of American plenty are often used as landmarks. Lenox Square (☎ 404-233-6767), 3393 Peachtree Rd, in Buckhead, is the largest in the city, with more than 240 shops, anchored by the department stores of Neiman Marcus, Macy's and Rich's. Nearby Phipps Plaza (☎ 404-261-7910), 3500 Peachtree Rd, is the most upscale, with stores such as Tiffany & Co, Gucci, Saks Fifth Avenue, Lord & Taylor and Parisian.

The Mall at Peachtree Center (☎ 404-654-1296) is the downtown attempt at a mall, with more than 60 shops, restaurants and business services. Note that there is a full range of services here, including three full-service banks, a print shop, Federal Express and UPS.

Perimeter Mall (Map 2; ☎ 770-394-4270), 4400 Ashford Dunwoody Rd, is a major mall beyond the perimeter with almost 200 shops, including Ann Taylor, Eddie Bauer, Nordstrom, Macy's, Rich's and JC Penney.

You'll forget you're in Atlanta when you visit Plaza Fiesta (Map 2; ☎ 678-596-6605), 4166 Buford Hwy. This Hispanic-focused mall provides a glimpse of Atlanta's growing Latino community along Buford Hwy. You can buy *santos* and cowboy boots here.

Besides malls, Atlanta contains several neighborhoods with interesting browsing. Many of these areas have been mentioned in other sections of this chapter. East of downtown, Virginia Highland has lots of boutiques and galleries selling expensive designer fashions, home furnishings and art. Little Five Points is the place for cheap vintage clothing, ethnic imports, incense and body piercings. Both these neighborhoods are shown on Map 5.

Atlanta is also one of the top antiques markets in the country. Chamblee Antique Row, in the neighborhood of Chamblee northeast of town, has the greatest concentration of antique and collectibles stores, with over 200 dealers in 20 buildings on Peachtree Rd and Broad St. The city of Marietta has a couple of dozen antiques stores within walking distance of the town square, including DuPre's Antique Market. Miami Circle in Buckhead (Map 6) is stuffed with upscale antique stores; it's off Piedmont Rd just north of the Lindbergh MARTA station (N6). Tara Antiques (☎ 404-325-4600), 2325 Cheshire Bridge Rd, is one of the larger antique shops and offers everything from pop-culture collectibles to furniture.

GETTING THERE & AWAY
Air
Atlanta's huge Hartsfield International Airport, 12 miles south of downtown, is a major regional hub and an international gateway. With nearby 80 million visitors a year, it recently surpassed Chicago as the busiest airport in the world in overall passenger traffic. Georgians say that 'whether you go to heaven or hell, you have to go through Atlanta first.' Its tremendous growth reflects Atlanta's exploding economy and population.

The complex consists of the North and South Terminals, five domestic concourses, an international concourse (Concourse E) and an underground transit system. A full-service bank, currency exchange and ATM machines are located in the atrium. Two currency exchanges are located in the international terminal. Public transportation (MARTA), taxis, limousines, rental cars and shuttle service are near the baggage claim.

The airport's 32 airlines provide direct service to more than 180 US cities and 29 countries. Delta has the most flights, with most other national – and many international – carriers represented.

The airport Web site (www.atlanta-airport .com) has a real-time listing of on-time, delayed and canceled flights.

Bus
The Greyhound bus terminal (Map 3; ☎ 404-584-1731), 232 Forsyth St, is conveniently located next to the MARTA Garnett station (S1). The company has buses to all points in North America. Sample fares with service frequency and travel time are shown in the following table.

destination	distance (miles)	cost	length (hrs)	frequency
Chattanooga, TN	126	$18	2–3½	7 daily
Savannah	285	$47	5½	5 daily
New Orleans	533	$71	9–14	7 daily
Washington, DC	718	$77	13–17	10 daily
Miami	721	$94	16–21	9 daily
New York, NY	956	$98	18–24	11 daily

Lockers at the bus terminal can be used for up to 48 hours.

Train
Atlanta's Amtrak station (Map 4; ☎ 800-872-7245, 404-881-3062), 1688 Peachtree St NW at Deering Rd, is 3 miles north of downtown. Take bus No 23 for about 0.8 miles from the MARTA Arts Center station (N5). The *Crescent* passes through Atlanta daily between New York ($107 to $191 for a one-way ticket; 19 hours) and New Orleans ($50 to $89; 11 hours).

GETTING AROUND
Public transit in Atlanta is decent by American standards. The MARTA rail line goes near many tourist sites, and dedicated public transportation users can find a bus to most parts of the city. Signage is pretty good. Using a taxi to fill in the gaps could be cheaper than a rental car. However, if you plan to hit multiple sites away from the rail lines – in Buckhead and neighborhoods east of downtown – a car will definitely save you time.

To/From the Airport
A MARTA rail line goes from the airport to downtown ($1.75; 15 to 20 minutes). The station is located next to baggage claim.

Atlanta Airport Shuttle (☎ 800-842-2770, 404-524-3400) transports passengers to hotels all over the city in a minibus; reservations are required for most destinations. The fare is $12 per person to downtown hotels, and $18 per person to Buckhead hotels. For two or more people, a taxi is cheaper.

Flat taxi fares are $18 between the airport and downtown ($20 for two, $24 for three passengers) and $28/$30 for one or two people between the airport and Buckhead.

Public Transportation

MARTA (Metropolitan Atlanta Rapid Transit Authority; ☎ 404-848-4711) operates a small but efficient rail system and a very extensive bus network in Atlanta and some of the surrounding communities. There are 36 rail stations (see Map 1), 46 miles of rail, and over 700 buses in the system. MARTA riders number 155 million per year, 552,000 on an average weekday.

The rail system has only two major lines (with a couple of branches), but manages to get close to many of the major sites. The two lines intersect at the Five Points station in downtown Atlanta. The North-South Line heads south to the airport and north to parts of downtown, Midtown, Buckhead and other locations close to the northern perimeter. The line branches near Buckhead into a North Line and a Northeast Line, so be sure to get on the appropriate rail car. The East-West Line goes east to Sweet Auburn and Decatur, and west to the Georgia Dome and the west side of the city. Stations are designated by letters and numbers: N1 for the first stop north of Five Points, E6 for the sixth stop east of Five Points, and so forth.

Use the white courtesy phones at the rail stations to find out which train or bus will take you to your destination; you can also call the MARTA number given previously for directions, or to have a route map and schedule mailed to you. Multilingual operators are available. The Web site also has complete route and schedule information in seven languages.

All fares are $1.75. Exact change or a token is required on the buses, but the token machines in the stations make change. Free transfers are available between bus routes and between the rail and the bus. If you plan to transfer from rail to a bus, you must press the transfer button on top of the faregate before you board the train, and a transfer slip will pop up. To transfer from bus to train, tell the bus driver when you pay your fare.

Weekly passes, accepted on all buses and trains, cost $13. Weekend passes, good for travel Friday through Sunday, are $9. Passes can be purchased only at the RideStores in the Five Points, Lindburgh Center (N6), Lenox (NE7), Georgia State (E1) and Airport (S7) stations. They can also be purchased at local Kroger stores and other retail outlets.

The trains run from about 5 am to 1 am on weekdays, 5 am to 12:30 am on weekends. They run every 4 to 8 minutes on weekdays, every 10 minutes on Saturday, and every 15 minutes on Sunday and holidays. Most buses also start early in the morning, around 5 am, and run until midnight or 1 am. Some stop running much earlier, so be sure to check if it's critical for your return trip. The bus frequency varies widely, from 10 to 20 minutes during rush hour, every 15 to 60 minutes midday, and every 30 to 60 minutes in the evening.

All buses and trains are completely accessible for people who use wheelchairs. For more information on accessibility, call MARTA handicapped services (☎ 404-848-5389). MARTA's TDD telephone number for the hearing impaired is ☎ 404-848-5665.

Bicycles are allowed on the trains at any time, although there are no special compartments for bicycles.

Free parking is available at most stations beyond downtown. If you're heading into Atlanta for the day and don't want to deal with parking or driving hassles, you can park on the perimeter and take MARTA to town. The Indian Creek station (E9) has its own exit, No 42, on the eastern side of I-285. The Dunwoody (N9; exit 29) and Doraville (NE10; exit 32) stations are also convenient park-and-ride places on the northern and northeastern sides of the perimeter.

Web site: www.itsmarta.com

Car

Most major car rental companies have offices at the airport, and many also have offices scattered around the downtown area. Rental car companies at the airport include:

Alamo	☎ 800-327-9633
Avis	☎ 404-530-2725
Budget	☎ 404-530-3000
Dollar	☎ 404-766-0244
Hertz	☎ 404-530-2925
National	☎ 404-530-2800
Payless	☎ 404-768-2120
Thrifty	☎ 770-996-2350
Value	☎ 404-763-0220

If you're planning to stay downtown for a convention, consider using the MARTA rail system, supplemented by the occasional taxi for hitting the nightspots.

Atlanta is known throughout Georgia and other states for its bad traffic. The 12-lane interstates can become crammed with impatient drivers trying to close their next business deal, get home or just make it through the city in one piece. Accidents can snarl traffic even worse. If possible, it's best to avoid the interstates during rush 'hour,' from about 7 to 9 am, and 4 to 7 pm.

Street parking is limited downtown. Parking lots and garages are plentiful, but rates are steep, about $1 to $2 an hour, or sometimes a fixed fee of $3 to $10.

Taxi
Atlanta taxis have the unfortunate reputation of being dirty, in need of maintenance and manned by unprofessional drivers. In 2000, Atlanta attempted to improve taxi safety by passing an ordinance requiring that taxis cannot be more than eight years old.

To find a cab on the street, look near large hotels, on corners of major shopping or office areas, or near MARTA stations. The downtown Ambassador Force will also help you hail cabs. Rapid Taxi Co (☎ 404-222-9888) or Yellow Cab Co (☎ 404-521-0200) are two you might call.

A flat fare zone applies to downtown (and quite a bit of Midtown) and Buckhead, so there are no cheap fares. The flat rate is $5 plus $1 each additional passenger, plus

tax. The downtown flat fare zone is bounded by Boulevard, Fourteenth St, Northside Dr and Turner Field. In other locations, the metered fare is $1.60 for the first $1/7$ mile, then 23 cents each additional $1/7$ mile, plus $1 each additional passenger. The 7% sales tax is added to all fares.

Around Atlanta

STONE MOUNTAIN PARK
This 3200-acre park (☎ 800-317-2006, 770-498-5690), 16 miles east of downtown, is home to 825-foot high Stone Mountain, the world's largest outcropping of exposed granite. It is best known for the huge carving of Confederate heroes Jefferson Davis, Stonewall Jackson and Robert E Lee. The carving took more than a half century to complete. This is the largest high-relief sculpture in the world (larger than Mount Rushmore), covering three acres.
Web site: www.stonemountainpark.com

The Ku Klux Klan was revived here in 1915, and the mountain was used for 40 years as the 'sacred soil' on which they held rallies. Today, however, families of all races flock to the park to picnic, take a skylift to the top of the mountain, ride the train and watch the laser show in summer. More than 4 million visitors a year come to the park.

The best place to start a tour is **Memorial Hall**, which has a visitors center with information on the park, a 12-minute film and exhibits on the history of the mountain. You can buy tickets here to all the park's attractions. Tickets are also sold at the Main Ticket Center in front of the railroad depot.

A **skylift** whizzes visitors to the top of the rounded monolith, from which Atlanta's skyline can be seen. A 1.3-mile hiking trail starts near the West Gate entrance and winds through trees to the top of the mountain. You can cheat by taking the skylift up and then walking down. Note that if you park near the skylift, ride to the top, and then walk down, you will be a mile from your car when you reach the bottom. You could then walk back or catch the hourly train at Confederate Hall.

The **Antebellum Plantation** is a collection of 19 original buildings built between 1790 and 1845, including the Thornton House, which is the oldest restored house in the state. Early plantation mansions are shown as well as slave cabins. Crafts and cooking demonstrations are often featured.

At **Confederate Hall**, the Battle of Atlanta is shown on a huge Georgia relief map in a so-so presentation. There's also an incomplete photo history of the Civil War. A gift shop here has books on the Civil War and slavery.

The **Stone Mountain Scenic Railroad** takes a 5 mile journey around the base of the mountain. It operates every hour on the hour. The **Antique Car & Treasure Museum** showcases classic cars and memorabilia.

The **laser show** is presented from the lawn between Memorial Hall and the Confederate carving. A conglomeration of laser lights, fireworks and patriotic music, it is shown daily Memorial Day through Labor Day, and Saturday only in March, April, May, September and October. The show is at 8:30 pm or 9:30 pm; call for a current schedule.

As if all this weren't enough, the park also offers paddlewheel riverboat cruises on the lake, an authentic grist mill, pontoon boats for rent, 10 miles of hiking and nature trails, miniature golf, tennis courts, a top-rated golf course, a beach and waterslide complex and a playground.

Entrance to the park costs $7 per car (free for cyclists and pedestrians). Individual activities cost around $5. Passes to all six major attractions are the best deal, at $17/14 for adults/children. Georgia residents pay a few dollars less.

The park is open 6 am to midnight daily. Attractions are open 10 am to 8 pm in the summer, 10 am to 5 pm in winter.

Places to Stay

The **Stone Mountain Family Campground** (☎ 800-385-9807, 770-498-5710, fax 770-413-5082) is set among hardwoods and pines in a pretty location on the lake, but doesn't offer much privacy. With more than 400 sites, it's the largest campground in the state and the best camping option near Atlanta. Rates are $20 to $26 for tents and pop-ups, $25 to $30 for sites with water and electricity and $30 to $35 for full hookups. A laundry and grocery store are available. A water taxi in the summer will take you across the lake to the riverboat complex, from where you can access all the park's attractions.

Stone Mountain Inn (☎ 770-858-1859) is a two-story brick hotel located inside the park with 92 rooms, an outdoor pool and a restaurant. Rates are $79 to $109, plus 12% tax. The lobby looks nice, but the staff refused to show us a room.

More isolated and luxurious is **Marriott's Evergreen Conference Resort** (☎ 770-879-9900), off Stonewall Jackson Dr in the southern portion of the park, with 249 rooms, a health club, tennis facilities and conference space. Summer weekends can be sold out months in advance. Rates start at $159 in summer.

Web site: www.evergreenresort.com

Places to Eat

Six restaurants serving everything from barbecue to seafood are scattered throughout the park. Outside the park in the nearby Stone Mountain Village is **Mama Mia's Pizza & Pasta** (Map 2; ☎ 770-469-1199, 961 Main St), an Italian eatery serving New York–style pizza baked in a stone oven. A 12-inch vegetarian costs $12. The restaurant also has a full range of good pasta dishes ($8 to $11).

The **Village Corner German Restaurant & Bakery** (Map 2; ☎ 770-498-0329), at the corner of Main St and Memorial Dr, serves dishes of bratwurst or sauerbraten for about $11 to $16. Lighter options are available for $7 to $9. You could buy fresh bread here for your Stone Mountain picnic. It's closed Monday.

Getting There & Away

Stone Mountain Park is located off Highway 78 (I-285 exit 39), which will dump you at the east gate entrance. Highway 10 is the more leisurely path, passing by the village of Stone Mountain and directing you to the west gate entrance.

Bus No 120 can take you from the MARTA Avondale station (E7) to the village of Stone Mountain, where some buses continue into the park.

Bikers should note that there is an 18-mile bike path that winds its way from downtown Atlanta through Decatur, ending at the park's west gate (maps are available at bike shops).

CHATTAHOOCHEE RIVER NATIONAL RECREATION AREA

This sprawling national recreation area consists of 16 units (areas within the park) and 9300 acres of land along a 48-mile stretch of the Chattahoochee River north of Atlanta. The land was acquired starting in 1978, as environmental groups sought to protect some of the last remaining wild lands from zealous developers. Recreational activities include fishing, hiking, picnicking, canoeing and rafting.

For basic information and maps, contact the National Park Service (☎ 770-399-8070, 770-952-4419), 1978 Island Ford Parkway, Atlanta, GA 30350-3400. You can also stop by the visitors center in the Island Ford Unit; however, it's only open 8 am to 4:30 pm weekdays. A $2 daily parking fee is required for all units.

Web site: www.nps.gov/chat

'Shooting the Hooch' is a popular summertime activity. **Canoes** and **rafts** can be put in at several points on the Class I/II river; the Johnson Ferry and Powers Island units are most common. The Chattahoochee Outdoor Center (☎ 770-395-6851, info@chattahoocheerafting.com), 1990 Island Ford Parkway, offers canoe and raft rentals, plus shuttle service, for trips lasting one to four hours. Canoe rentals are $40, a four-person raft is $45. Shuttle service is $2.50/1.25 adults/children for renters, and $3/1.50 for those who bring their own boat. The season is May through September (weekends only in May and September). Reservations are recommended on weekends. Be forewarned that the water is very

cold, since it is released from the bottom of the Buford Dam.

Web site: www.chattahoocheerafting.com

More than 70 miles of **hiking trails** crisscross the recreational areas. Try the Palisades unit for upland ridge trails; Sope Creek and Vickery Creek units for wooded areas and historic mill ruins; Cochran Shoals, Johnson Ferry and Gold Branch units for marshland and open fields; and Island Ford and Jones Bridge units for trails to the river's edge.

The **Cochran Fitness Trail**, in the Cochran Shoals unit, is a paved, fully accessible path.

The **Chattahoochee Nature Center** (☎ 770-992-2055), 9135 Willeo Rd in Roswell, is an environmental education facility, with forest trails, a wetland boardwalk, live animal exhibits, native plant gardens and indoor education exhibits.

Getting There & Away

To reach the Island Ford visitors center, go north on GA 400, take exit 6 (Northridge) to the right, continue onto Dunwoody Place, turn right at the second light onto Roberts Dr, then go a mile and turn right into the park entrance. The Web site (www.nps.gov/chat) also provides information and maps.

MARIETTA

Activity in the quaint town of Marietta, 15 miles northwest of downtown Atlanta (see the North Georgia map, later in this book), is concentrated around the main square, which has museums, shops, restaurants, a professional theater and summertime festivals. The town has five National Register Historic Districts; you can get driving/walking brochures from the **Welcome Center** (☎ 770-429-1115), near the main square in the old train depot. It's open 9 am to 5 pm weekdays, 11 am to 4 pm Saturday and 1 pm to 4 pm Sunday. Highlights include the **Confederate Cemetery** and the **Marietta Museum of History**, where Sherman had his headquarters while bombarding Atlanta. The town is also known for the **Big Chicken**, a local landmark with funky '60s design and rolling eyes.

Web site: www.mariettasquare.com

The **White Water Theme Park** (☎ 770-424-9283), 250 Cobb Parkway N, has 50 ways to get wet on 50 acres, including a 750,000-gallon wave pool, tube slides, body flumes and raft rides. It's open weekends in May, daily late-May through mid-August, then weekends only through Labor Day. Hours are 10 am to 8 pm in peak season. Regular admission (for people over 4 feet tall) is $27, and $17 for kids above age 3. From Atlanta, take I-75 to exit 265 and follow the signs.

Web site: www.whitewaterpark.com

KENNESAW MOUNTAIN NATIONAL BATTLEFIELD PARK

The site of two Civil War battles during the siege of Atlanta, this pretty park (☎ 770-427-4686) west of Marietta (see the North Georgia map, later in this book in the North Georgia chapter) covers 2900 acres and has 11 miles of original earthworks – mounds of soil soldiers piled up to hide behind. The visitors center distributes brochures, has a good Civil War bookstore and shows a 20-minute film explaining the battle action and the context in which it was fought. Behind the visitors center, Kennesaw Mountain Drive leads to an overlook near the summit of the mountain. The fiercest battle raged at Cheatham Hill, where a trail leads to monuments, Confederate earthworks and markers. Various popular trails starting at the visitors center offer hikes of 2, 5, 10 and 16 miles.

The park is open from dawn until dusk; the visitors center is open 8:30 am to 5 pm daily (until 6 pm on weekends during daylight savings time).

To get there, take I-75 to exit 269 (Barrett Parkway), turn west, go on Barrett Parkway for approximately 3 miles, turn left at the light onto Old Hwy 41, then turn right at the next light, Stilesboro Rd. The visitors center is on the left. Look for brown and white signs located along the roads.

PICKETT'S MILL STATE HISTORIC SITE

In one of the few Confederate victories during Sherman's campaign in Georgia, the Union lost 1600 men and the Confederates 500 in only a few hours of battle here on May 27, 1864. This battlefield is one of the best preserved – with original roads, earthworks and ravines – and has none of the monuments that were put up after the war at other battlefields. The park features hiking trails of 1.1 to 2 miles, a film explaining the action and a few exhibits.

The historic site (☎ 770-443-7850) is open 9 am to 5 pm Tuesday through Saturday, noon to 5 pm Sunday; admission is $2.50/1.25 adults/children. To get here, take I-75 north from Atlanta to Hwy 92 south (exit 277), then follow the signs (see the North Georgia map, later in this book).

RED TOP MOUNTAIN STATE PARK

Located 35 miles north of downtown Atlanta near Cartersville, this park (☎ 770-975-4226, reservations ☎ 800-573-9658) is set on 12,000-acre Lake Allatoona, and named for the color of the iron-laden soil. Activities include boating, fishing, picnicking and hiking, plus there's an 1869 reconstructed pine log cabin. Deer are everywhere.

The pretty campground is set among dense pines. Tent/RV sites cost $19/23. The standard 33 rooms at the lodge and conference center are $85/95 weekdays/weekends for doubles. Cottages overlooking the lake rent from $109; two-night minimum stay. Dining is available at the lodge.

Take I-75 north from Atlanta to exit 285 (see the North Georgia map, later in this book).

ETOWAH INDIAN MOUNDS STATE HISTORIC SITE

Between about AD 1000 and 1550, several thousand Native Americans lived in the Great Valley between the Armuchee Ridges and the Cohutta Mountains, where the rich soils could be worked with primitive tools. This 54-acre state historic site (☎ 770-387-3747), 5 miles southwest of I-75 exit 288 (see the North Georgia map, later in this book), is the most intact Mississippian Culture site in the Southeast.

A museum here contains exhibits and artifacts, including two well-preserved stone effigies; a 15-minute film on the Mississippian culture is also shown. After this orientation, visitors can see the remains of three earthen platform mounds (which can be climbed), a plaza, a village area, borrow pits (places where soil was 'borrowed' to make the mounds) and a defensive ditch. One mound was used as a platform for the home of the priest-chief; nobility were buried in another mound. A nature trail leads to the Etowah River.

The site is open 9 am to 5 pm Tuesday through Saturday, 2 pm to 5:30 pm Sunday, closed Monday; admission is $3/2.

LAKE SIDNEY LANIER

About 45 miles northeast of Atlanta's urban sprawl, off I-985, is Lake Sidney Lanier (see the North Georgia map, later in this book), the site of the Olympic rowing competitions in 1996. The 38,000-acre lake has 540 miles of shoreline and holds 350 billion gallons behind Buford Dam, give or take a few billion based on water conditions.

More than 20,000 boats populate the area, and on a busy summer weekend, thousands of them will be on the water. Summer water temperatures in the 80s make swimming comfortable. The Chattahoochee River, however, receives its water from the bottom of the lake, where the temperature is much colder.

The Corps of Engineers (COE) operates the dam as well as 10 fully developed campgrounds and 38 day-use areas. Several areas have beaches for swimming, picnicking spots, hiking trails and boat ramps. The best place to get a grip on the activities is at the COE Resource Management Office (☎ 770-945-9531), 1050 Buford Dam Rd, or see their Web site (www.sam.usace.army.mil/op/rec/lanier). The visitors center here, open 8 am to 4:30 pm daily, has basic information. The office is just south of Buford Dam off Buford Dam Rd.

Near the Resource Management office, **Buford Dam** is worth a view. The nearby 3.8-mile **Laurel Ridge Trail** will take you by the dam and lake, along the river and through woodlands with mountain laurel growing along the hillsides. Get brochures from the Resource Management Office.

The *COE campgrounds* cost $14 for campsites without hookups and $22 for sites with full hookups.

To get here from Atlanta, take I-85 north to Highway 20 (exit 115), go west to Suwanee Dam Rd, then north (right) to Buford Hwy, then left. From the other (west) side, GA 400 also takes you to Hwy 20, then go east to Suwanee Dam Rd.

Lake Lanier Islands Resort

Created when the gates of the Buford Dam were lowered in 1957, the Lake Lanier Islands are a very popular summertime destination for Atlanta families escaping the city. Recently privatized, the Lake Lanier Islands Resort (☎ 770-932-7200) offers a bit of everything.

Web site: www.lakelanierislands.com

Near the entrance to the islands, the Hospitality Center can give you basic information and rates. There's also an ATM here. Basic admission is $6 per car.

Once on the island, activities include a beach and water park, two golf courses, an equestrian center and a marina. The beach and water park are probably the most popular, but they aren't cheap: $24 for adults, $16 for anyone under 42 inches tall (free for toddlers under 2). Horse rides are $25 for 45 minutes; pony rides cost $8 for 30 minutes. Bikes can be rented at the equestrian center for $10 for four hours, $15 for all day. The cheapest boat rental is $129 for two hours; a Waverunner costs $138 for two hours.

Places to Stay The attractive *campground* (☎ 770-932-7270) has more than 300 sites for RVs and tents. Rates are $20 for tent sites without hookups, and $25 for sites with hookups. Premium lakefront sites cost $5 more.

Hilton Lake Lanier Island Resort (☎ 800-221-2424, 770-945-8787) is an attractive hotel with 216 rooms (some overlooking the lake), a business conference center, outdoor pool overlooking the lake, tennis courts, fitness center and a bar and grill.

GEORGIA

Rates start at $119 for a double room and breakfast for two.

Renaissance Pine Isle Hotel *(☎ 800-468-3571, 770-945-8921)* has a more isolated location, with 254 rooms, tennis courts and a golf course, heated swimming pool, hot tub, fitness center, private beach and conference and banquet facilities. Summer rates for doubles start at $119 weekdays without breakfast, $129 weekends without breakfast and $148 weekends with breakfast for two.

Getting There & Away From Atlanta, take I-85 north to I-985. Exit at Hwy 347 (Friendship Rd, exit 8), turn left and go 5 miles. This will take you up to the resort entrance.

Gainesville

Nearby Gainesville, on the northeast side of the lake, is the main town of the region. There's not much to see in Gainesville itself, but the local chamber of commerce runs a visitors center (☎ 770-532-6206), at the corner of EE Butler Parkway (US 129) and Brenau Ave, that is a good source for information on the Lake Lanier area and northeast Georgia in general. It's open 8:30 am to 5 pm weekdays. Take I-985, exit 22 to downtown Gainesville.

There's also a Northeast Georgia regional information center on I-985 just north of exit 12 that's open 9 am to 5 pm daily.

The Amtrak train *Crescent* passes through Gainesville on its way to New Orleans and New York. Appalachian Trail through-hikers can arrive here and take a shuttle to the trail. See the Dahlonega section for shuttle contacts. Call Amtrak at ☎ 800-872-7245 or see their Web site (www.amtrak.com) for more information.

North Georgia

North Georgia is the state's premier natural destination, featuring endless miles of hiking through national forests, up and down mountain ridges and across mountain streams full of trout. Cool mountain lakes provide opportunities for canoeing and swimming. The Chattooga River, on the Georgia–South Carolina border, is one of the best white-water rivers in the country. The spring wildflowers and colorful fall leaves are wondrous to see.

All of the North Georgia area is within the Appalachian Mountain range, from Lookout Mountain in the west to the Blue Ridge Mountains in the east. Northwest and Northeast Georgia are divided by the north-south Cartersville–Great Smoky Fault, located just east of Chatsworth and roughly paralleling Hwy 411. The Blue Ridge Mountains have a rich mixture of temperate climate plants, including many northern species at their southern limit. Many migrating birds fly through here on the Appalachian flyway. Within this area, the Chattahoochee National Forest covers 750,000 acres, incorporating protected wilderness areas, many camping facilities, beautiful waterfalls, wild caves, the beginning of the 2155-mile Appalachian Trail, full-service state parks and trout fishing.

Initially home to the Cherokee, the discovery of gold in Dahlonega in 1828 helped populate the region with settlers and was the final excuse needed to force the native Americans westward on the Trail of Tears in 1838. The area's mountain folk retain strong traditions of Appalachian culture – self-sufficiency; arts and crafts (baskets, pottery, quilts, weaving, woodworking); bluegrass and other traditional music; and clogging and square dancing. Depicted as malevolent in the book and movie *Deliverance* (filmed in northeast Georgia), mountain culture is now often celebrated in festivals and by organizations like *Foxfire,* in Mountain City.

The area is being changed by Atlanta dwellers seeking vacation homes, Georgia residents escaping the heat and humidity of the central and southern parts of the state and retirees looking for a more relaxed pace of life. The real estate market is booming, as indicated by the high number of realty offices in small towns.

The number of African Americans here is relatively low (5%) compared to the rest of the state, where they make up 30% of the population. Latinos are also moving into the area, as in many parts of Georgia, in huge numbers. For example, in Dalton – the 'Carpet Capital of the World' – the textile industry's demand for labor has helped increase the proportion of Hispanics from 6% in 1990 to 40% in 2000.

Accommodations include plenty of camping, the usual string of chain hotels, historic inns, cozy B&Bs and state parks with comfortable lodges and cabins. Hotels are often booked on weekends in October, when Georgians rush to see the marvelous

Highlights

- Hold onto your hat while navigating the white-water rapids on the Chattooga River.
- Hike, bike or fish for trout in the beautiful Blue Ridge Mountains.
- Begin the 2158-mile Appalachian Trail on Springer Mountain.

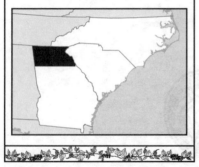

Monument to Baron Pierre de Coubertin, founder of the modern Olympics

The Reflecting Pool outside the Martin Luther King Jr National Historic Site, Atlanta

Cumberland Island, GA

Who knows what lurks in the swamp...

The best way to see the Okefenokee Swamp

Cypress forest in the swamp

Savannah waterfront

Cryptic sign at the Waycross entrance to the swamp

ANDRE JENNY

JOHN ELK III

LAWRENCE WORCESTER

LEE FOSTER

ANDRE JENNY

LEE FOSTER

TO FARGO
AND ALL
POINTS SOUTH
(IF YOU KNOW HOW)

fall foliage (aka 'leaf season'). Fall festivals are also huge draws. Advance hotel reservations are a must during these times, and prices skyrocket.

Georgia has a very strong state park system with several full-service parks in the North Georgia mountains. Here you'll finding mountain lakes, hiking trails (although not the most extensive), mountain biking, camping, lodges and cabins. For complete information, contact Georgia State Parks and Historic Sites (☎ 404-656-2770), 205 Butler St, Suite 1352E, Atlanta, GA 30334.
Web site: www.gastateparks.org

Getting around the area of the North Georgia mountains will be your biggest challenge. Amtrak stops in Atlanta, Gainesville (see the Around Atlanta section) and Toccoa on its way between New Orleans and New York. Local bus service is nonexistent; the closest stops are Gainesville and Anderson, South Carolina, just across the state border. Appalachian Trail through-hikers can find shuttle service from Gainesville (see the Dahlonega section). Otherwise, you pretty much need a car to get around between sites.

INFORMATION
The Georgia Welcome Center, at the second I-75 exit south of the Tennessee border, has a phenomenal quantity of brochures on things to see and do, parks and hotels throughout the state. It's open 8:30 am to 5:30 pm daily.

Many maps of the area are available, but some are nearly useless. One of the most useful general maps for outdoor recreation is *The Northeast Georgia Mountains*, by Fern Creek Press (☎ 706-782-5379), PO Box 1322, Clayton, GA 30525.

The *North Georgia Journal* is an informative quarterly magazine on regional history and the outdoors.

For information and maps on hiking, biking or fishing in the Chattahoochee National Forest, see the Forest Service's Web site (www.fs.fed.us/conf) or contact one of the regional offices in the following list.

Armuchee Ranger District – (☎ 706-638-1085), PO Box 465, 806 E Villanow St, Lafayette, GA 30728

Brasstown Ranger District – (☎ 706-745-6928), 1881 Hwy 515, PO Box 9, Blairsville, GA 30514

Chattooga Ranger District – (☎ 706-754-6221), PO Box 196, Hwy 197, N Burton Rd, Clarkesville, GA 30523

Cohutta Ranger District – (☎ 706-695-6736), 401 Old Ellijay Rd, Chatsworth, GA 30705

Dahlonega US Forest Service Information Center – (☎ 706-864-6173), Gold Mine Shopping Center, Hwy 19/60, Dahlonega, GA 30533

Tallulah Ranger District – (☎ 706-782-3320), PO Box 438, 825 Hwy 441 S, Clayton, GA 30525

Toccoa Ranger District – (☎ 706-632-3031), 990 E Main St, Suite 1, Blue Ridge, GA 30513

USDA Forest Service – Supervisor's Office (☎ 770-536-0541), 1755 Cleveland Hwy, Gainesville, GA 30501

Details on operating hours are given within each town's entry later in this section. Many of the Forest Service regional district offices are also excellent places to buy maps and specialized hiking or biking books.

SPECIAL EVENTS
Festivals celebrating mountain history, culture, food and arts and crafts are popular events in several North Georgia towns. Some of the most popular take place in the late summer and fall and include:

August
Georgia Mountain Fair, Hiawassee – 12 days of entertainment and crafts exhibits (☎ 706-896-4191), www.georgia-mountain-fair.com

September
Helen's Oktoberfest, Helen – German food and polkas, through early November (☎ 706-878-2181)

October
Apple Festival, Ellijay – crafts show in the middle of apple country (☎ 706-635-7400)

Fall Harvest Festival, Hiawassee – country music, arts and crafts (☎ 706-896-4191)

Gold Rush Days, Dahlonega – 3rd full weekend in October, arts and crafts, food, gold-panning contests (☎ 706-864-7247)

Sorghum Festival, Blairsville – syrup making and other mountain activities (☎ 706-745-5789)

NORTH GEORGIA

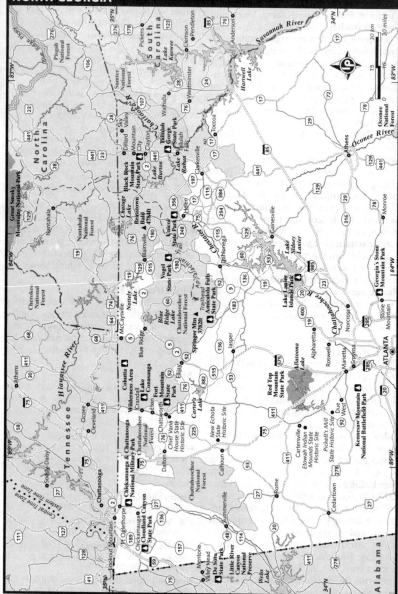

LOOKOUT MOUNTAIN

The dominant geologic feature of northwest Georgia is 84-mile-long Lookout Mountain, which spills into Tennessee and Alabama. The nearest metro area is Chattanooga, Tennessee right across the border, with several attractions convenient to northwest Georgia: Ruby Falls, the Incline Railway, the Tennessee Aquarium and the Tennessee portion of the Chickamauga & Chattanooga National Military Park.

Cloudland Canyon

This 2343-acre state park (☎ 706-657-4050, 800-864-7275 for reservations), on GA Hwy 136, is located on the western edge of Lookout Mountain. Sitton Gulch Creek cuts a deep gorge through the park, creating magnificent scenery and vistas. The best views are along the rim from the picnic area. A steep 0.3-mile trail leading down the canyon to two graceful waterfalls on Daniel Creek is well worth the effort. The 4.9-mile West Rim Loop Trail follows the canyon rim. Two- and 7-mile backcountry trails, with camping, are also available.

Accommodations here include 73 tent and trailer sites, 30 walk-in tent sites and 16 cottages. The cottages have a five-night minimum stay June through Labor Day, and a two-night minimum the rest of the year. Rates are $9 per site for walk-in camping, $15 to $17 per site for regular camping and $4 per person for backcountry camping. A two-bedroom cottage costs $80/90 weekdays/weekends during the peak season (Memorial through Labor Day, plus major holidays) and $85/95 during leaf season (October 1 through November 15).

Rock City

For years, travelers throughout the south couldn't ignore the huge signs painted on barns imploring them to 'See Rock City.' It was a masterful advertising campaign, in which Rock City painted barns for free in exchange for the right to paint their slogan on the roof. Advertising sign restrictions along the highways eventually ended the practice.

Rock City itself, near the Tennessee Border off Rte 157, combines a few interesting rock formations with a manmade fantasyland. Natural formations include a 1000-ton balanced rock, an overlook at Lover's Leap where you can (supposedly) see seven states, Fat Man's Squeeze and a waterfall. The Fairyland Caverns and Mother Goose Village contain almost proudly hokey dioramas depicting scenes from nursery rhymes. It's pleasant enough, but doesn't quite live up to the hype.

Admission to Rock City (☎ 706-820-2531) is a pricey $11/$6 adults/children; kids ages two and under are free. It's open 8:30 am to 8 pm Memorial Day to Labor Day, and closes earlier the rest of the year. A quick-service restaurant is located at the entrance, and a small snack bar is near Lover's Leap.

Hang Gliding

If you feel like jumping off a cliff, the western side of Lookout Mountain is a popular hang gliding spot. Updrafts along the 20 miles of ridge provide endless soaring for experienced gliders. There's a launch pad on state Hwy 189 north of Hwy 136; From there you can watch the intrepid ones run off the cliff, and then soar high above you. If you want to try it yourself, Lookout Mountain Flight Park (☎ 800-688-5637) certifies more hang glider pilots than any other school in the US. You can take a discovery tandem flight, which costs $129 for 12 to 20 minutes of feeling like a bird. A weekend package, where you actually learn to fly, is $399.

CHICKAMAUGA & CHATTANOOGA NATIONAL MILITARY PARK

During the Civil War, 58,000 Union soldiers met 66,000 Confederates in northwest Georgia and fought a bloody battle on September 19-20, 1863. The battle produced 34,000 casualties, including 4200 dead. The result was a Confederate victory, pushing the Union back to Chattanooga. But the battle of Chickamauga also marked the beginning of the end, as the Union troops eventually won in Chattanooga, marched and laid siege to Atlanta, then marched on to Savannah.

The battlefield is now part of the **Chickamauga & Chattanooga National Military Park,** designated in 1890 as the nation's first military park. More than 600 stone and bronze monuments were erected on the battlefield between 1890 and 1930. Plaques, cannons and pyramids of cannonballs show positions of fighting units, artillery batteries or where brigade commanders were killed. Three other sites are in Tennessee.

The park is located on US Hwy 27 about one mile south of GA Hwy 2 at Fort Oglethorpe. Start at the visitors center (☎ 706-866-9241), open 8 am to 4:45 pm, which has maps, a good Civil War bookstore and a dramatic, somewhat corny 24-minute sound, slide and video presentation shown every hour ($3/1.50 adults/children). A small museum has exhibits on the war's crucial issues and the vast Fuller Gun Collection, consisting of 355 weapons.
Web site: www.nps.gov/chch

A 7-mile, self-guided auto tour takes you by all the major sites and lasts perhaps 45 minutes. You can also rent a 2½-hour, 12-mile cassette tour at the bookstore. More than 60 miles of trails take you away from the main roads, through cedar glades and fields with pretty springtime wildflowers and unique prairie plants. Some of the back roads are suitable for bicycles, which are not permitted on the trails.

There's no charge for entering the park.

Places to Stay & Eat

A suitable place to stay when exploring the northwest Georgia area is the *Gordon-Lee Mansion Bed & Breakfast* (☎ *800-487-4728, 706-375-4728, 217 Cove Rd),* 2½ miles south of the park in the small town of Chickamauga, population 2400. Built in 1847, it served as the Union Army's headquarters and main hospital during the Battle of Chickamauga. Four rooms decorated in antiques rent from $75/85 single/double to $125; a modern apartment costs $65/75. A two-bedroom log house, with a completely furnished kitchen, is $90/100. Rates for the rooms (but not the log house) include a full breakfast.
Web site: www.fhc.org/gordon-lee

NEW ECHOTA STATE HISTORIC SITE

The independent Cherokee tribe established a capital here in 1825 and named it New Echota. The Cherokee learned English, operated mills and stores, wore European dress and individually owned farmsteads and plantations. In 1821, Sequoyah invented a written form of the Cherokee language consisting of 86 sounds. In 1828, from New Echota, the Cherokee published the newspaper the *Cherokee Phoenix* in English and Cherokee.

The state of Georgia, however, did not appreciate a sovereign nation residing within its boundaries. In 1828, gold was discovered in Dahlonega, on Cherokee land, adding pressure for white settlement. The state passed restrictive laws that the Cherokee fought through the court system. Although the Supreme Court ruled in their favor, President Andrew Jackson refused to enforce the ruling. These hostilities eventually resulted in the tragic removal of the Cherokee westward along the 'Trail of Tears' in 1838, along which more than 4,000 Cherokees died.

The historic site contains reconstructed buildings similar to those that populated the Cherokee town of New Echota, including a Supreme Courthouse, a tavern and a print shop. A small museum contains exhibits on Cherokee history and shows a 17-minute film.

The historic site (☎ 706-624-1321) is open 9 am to 5 pm Tuesday through Saturday and 2 pm to 5:30 pm Sunday; admission is $3/2 adults/children. From Atlanta, take I-75 north about 70 miles to exit 317 (GA Hwy 225), then go east 0.8 miles.

CHATSWORTH
pop 3500

Lying in the Great Valley at the intersection of GA Hwy 52 and US Hwy 411, between the Armuchee Ridges of northwest Georgia and the Cohutta Mountains (part of the

Blue Ridge Mountains), Chatsworth is an uninteresting town useful mainly as a point to collect information and stop over before heading farther east or into the wilderness.

The Forest Service office of the Cohutta Ranger District (☎ 706-695-6736) is located here on Hwy 52 at the intersection with Hwy 411. This office has an excellent selection of maps and guides to hiking, mountain biking and trout fishing in North Georgia. It's open 8 am to 4:30 pm weekdays, 9 am to 3:30 pm Saturday. When it's closed, the bulletin board outside lists other local places to purchase maps.
Web site: www.fs.fed.us/conf

Edna's, on Hwy 411 1.2 miles south of the turnoff to Fort Mountain State Park, serves up basic Southern cooking. Meals consisting of a meat, two or three vegetables and sweet tea cost less than $5. Service is quick and the food is decent.

Several roadside motels are in town, but none look very impressive or modern. A mid-price choice is the *Key West Inn* (☎ *800-833-0555, 706-517-1155, fax 706-517-1155, 510 GI Maddox Parkway/Hwy 52)*, near the Forest Service office. It has standard modern motel rooms for $45/49 singles/doubles, plus 9% tax.

Just east of Fort Mountain State Park, on GA Hwy 52, is *Cohutta Lodge & Restaurant* (☎ *706-695-9601)*, a pleasant, private lodge with large, comfortable rooms and good views for $79 to $149. Extras include a pool and a volleyball court. The restaurant here serves all three meals, with chicken, trout, catfish, steak or pasta costing $9 to $16. Special buffets are offered on weekends.
Web site: www.cohuttalodge.com

Chief Vann House

This state historic site (☎ 706-695-2598), at the intersection of GA Hwys 225 and 52A (a mile south of 52), is an 1804 Federal-style house built by James Vann, a wealthy Cherokee chief who owned 110 African-American slaves. Joseph Vann, his son, later inherited the plantation and house. Joseph Vann and his family were booted off the property in 1825 when Vann hired a white slave overseer, violating a new

Georgia law that made it illegal for whites to work for Indians. The house is a reminder that the Cherokee were settled here and owned houses and property before they were forcibly removed during the 1838 Trail of Tears. The house has been restored and furnished with period antiques. A new visitors center was under construction when we stopped by. It's open 9 am to 5 pm Tuesday through Saturday, and 2 pm to 5:30 pm Sunday; closed Monday. Admission is $2.50/1.50 adults/children.

FORT MOUNTAIN STATE PARK

This 3520-acre state park (☎ 706-695-2621, 800-864-7275 for reservations), 8 miles east of Chatsworth on GA Hwy 52, is one of Georgia's comprehensive recreational parks, with camping, cottages, hiking, mountain biking, a lake with swimming and a beach, miniature golf and backpacking possibilities. The park is named after an ancient 855-foot-long stone wall that historians figure to be a defensive structure built by prehistoric Indians (no one really knows).

Fourteen miles of hiking trails lead through rugged and diverse scenery of hardwood forests and blueberry thickets, giving some impressive vistas of the surrounding valley and towns. Some trails lead to a 400-foot cascade and an old gold mine. The 8-mile backpacking trail never really strays far from the park roads. There are also 30 miles of mountain bike trails and 37 miles of horse trails. The bike usage fee is $2 per day. Horses can be rented at the Fort Mountain Stables (☎ 706-517-8555), adjacent to the park on Hwy 52.

Camping is available for $8 for primitive sites, $16 for modern sites; showers and flush toilets are provided. Two- and three-bedroom cottages rent for $75 to $110 (plus 9% tax).

As with all Georgia state parks, you need a $2 ParkPass to enter.

COHUTTA WILDERNESS AREA

This area at the western edge of the Blue Ridge Mountains measures 36,977 acres;

combined with the 8082-acre Big Frog Wilderness area in Tennessee, this is the largest contiguous area of national forest wilderness east of the Mississippi. The Cohutta Mountains are steep, rugged and a hiker's delight – 93 miles of hiking trails wind through the beautiful hardwood forest crisscrossed by many mountain streams. Trout fishing is also considered very good in the area.

There are several access points to the wilderness: from Chatsworth and Ellijay to the south on Hwy 76/52; from the west at Eton and Crandall along Hwy 411; and from the town of Blue Ridge on the east via Hwy 5. Because there are a lot of turns in these routes, be sure to pick up maps from the Forest Service office (☎ 706-695-6736) in Chatsworth. Trails to consider include the **Beech Bottom Trail,** which goes 4 miles one-way through mountainous area down to Jacks River Falls; it's heavily used. The 13.1 **Conasauga River Trail** is also a popular trail through Eastern hemlock forest; it crosses the river 38 times. Hikers on this and other trails might have to wade across rivers and streams, some of which are dangerous and impassable after heavy rains – check with the Forest Service for trail conditions.

Mountain bikes are not allowed in the wilderness.

Backpackers can camp anywhere they can find a flat spot, which can be difficult. The camping at Beech Bottom is popular but overused.

The *Lake Conasauga Recreation Area*, 10 miles down a forest service road off US Hwy 411 4 miles north of Chatsworth, has 35 campsites, with flush toilets and cold water, close to a 17-acre lake. The cost is $8. The lake is stocked with trout, and has a small developed swimming area with a dock and pea-gravel bottom. Lake Conasauga is also a **Song Bird Management Area,** in which the vegetation is managed to provide good bird habitat. More than 100 species of birds have been recorded. For more information, maps and a list of songbirds, contact the Forest Service Cohutta Ranger District office in Chatsworth.

BLUE RIDGE
pop 1200
Downtown Blue Ridge is reminiscent of a mining town in the American West, with a railroad straight through the middle, surrounded by historic buildings and mountains. The historic buildings have been converted to tourist shops, which are worth a stroll if you've come to ride the train. The town makes a good stopping point for the Cohutta Wilderness Area to the west, or before heading east farther into the Blue Ridge Mountains.

The Chamber of Commerce Welcome Center (☎ 800-899-6867, 706-632-5680), on Hwy 2/76/515 behind the Burger King, is open 9 am to 5 pm Monday through Saturday and 1 to 5 pm Sunday.

The Forest Service Toccoa Ranger Station (☎ 706-632-3031), a couple of miles north of Blue Ridge on Hwy 2/76/515, is open 7:30 am to 4 pm weekdays. It has information, maps and books.

Aside from visiting the natural surroundings, the chief activity here is the **Blue Ridge Scenic Railway** (☎ 706-632-9833), downtown. The 26-mile, three-hour round-trip ride winds through rolling hills along the Toccoa River from Blue Ridge to McCaysville. The cost is $23/12 adults/children.

At Cycle South Blue Ridge (☎ 706-632-3533), on Old Hwy 76 (behind the Days Inn), you can rent mountain bikes to explore the surrounding areas for $35 per day. It's open 10 am to 6 pm Monday through Saturday.

Places to Stay
Several US Forest Service campgrounds are open March through October, including the *Lake Blue Ridge Campground* (☎ 706-632-3031). A couple of miles east of Blue Ridge off Old Hwy 76, this campground is set on a beautiful lake – the only one in the state where you can fish for muskie. The 58 campsites rent for $8, or $10 on the lakefront. There are bathrooms and cold-water showers. *Morganton Point*, on the eastern side of the lake near Morganton, has 43 campsites. It has flush toilets and hot showers.

The *Fannin Inn* (☎ 800-533-9834, 706-632-2005), on Hwy 515 south of Blue Ridge, has 32 overly deodorized rooms and an outdoor pool. Rates start at $45/50 singles/doubles. An on-site restaurant serves lunch and dinner.

Days Inn (☎ 800-325-2525, 706-632-2100), at Hwy 515 and the Hwy 76 connector, has 60 large, standard hotel rooms with outdoor pool and breakfast donuts from $46/$52 singles/doubles weekdays, $51/60 on weekends.
Web site: www.blueridgega.com/Daysinn

Douglas Inn & Suites (☎ 706-258-3600, 1192 Windy Ridge Rd), on the northeast side of town, are the fanciest digs in the area, with 20 comfortable rooms and rates from $69. Rooms with kitchenettes are available. The hotel opened in 2000.

Places to Eat
Several touristy restaurants are downtown near the Blue Ridge Scenic Railway. *The Deli Difference* offers sandwiches from $5. The *Village Restaurant*, next to the Piggly Wiggly shopping center on E Main St in the northeastern corner of town, has a $5 breakfast buffet and other inexpensive meals, but the food isn't very tasty.

About 6 miles east of Blue Ridge, on GA Hwy 515/US Hwy 76 (the Appalachian Hwy), just past Hwy 60, the *Forge Mill Crossing Restaurant* (☎ 888-374-5771), is better. Main dishes of mountain trout, chicken or steak cost $8 to $16; sandwiches and salads are available from about $6. It serves lunch and dinner daily, and breakfast on weekends (from $5).

AMICALOLA FALLS STATE PARK
The centerpiece of this gorgeous 2050-acre state park (☎ 706-265-4703, reservations 800-864-7275), 18 miles west of Dahlonega on Hwy 52, is 729-foot Amicalola Falls, the highest waterfall in Georgia. Appropriately, 'Amicalola' is a Cherokee word meaning 'tumbling water.' The falls can be viewed from several points, and a short trail leads to their base. A quiet mountain stream in the park offers trout fishing, and mountain laurel blooms here in late spring/early summer.

There are several **hiking trails** less than a mile long, plus a 2.6-mile nature trail. The 8.1-mile, strenuous **Appalachian Approach Trail** travels up and down the ridges of Amicalola Mountain and leads to 3782-foot Springer Mountain and the southern terminus of the Appalachian Trail (AT). From here, it's only 2155 more miles to Maine.

The visitors center has a small selection of books and gifts. A $2 per day ParkPass is required for park entry.

The Amicalola campground has 20 *campsites* starting at $15. Bathrooms, showers and a coin laundry are available. The park also rents 14 *cottages* for $95 to $165. Contact the park office for reservation information.

The 57-room *Amicalola Falls Lodge* (☎ 706-265-8888) sits atop a summit with a beautiful panorama of the surrounding mountains. The rooms are modern and comfortable. A restaurant serves three meals a day. Rates are $79 to $199.

One of Georgia's most unusual accommodations is the *Len Foote Hike Inn* (☎ 800-864-7275, 770-389-7275), which is reached only after a 4.9-mile (2½- to 3-hour) hike on an interpretive trail with patches of rhododendron and mountain laurel. The inn is fully stocked, so you only need to take hiking gear and whatever you need for the night. The 20 rooms are clean but tiny, with nothing but a bunk bed and plywood walls; they do not have heat or AC. But you won't be spending much time in your room, because the inn has marvelous public areas: decks that overlook the Dahlonega valley; a community room with games, a few books and wood burning stoves; and even a lovely outside spot to watch the sunrise. There are shared bathhouses with hot showers and odorless (really!) composting toilets. Hearty meals are served family style in the inn's cozy dining room. The staff is friendly, enthusiastic and partly made up of volunteers. No smoking, pets or electronic crap are allowed. Springer Mountain is only 4½ miles away.

Rates are $89/$130 singles/doubles, including dinner and breakfast. Sandwiches are available at lunch for a few dollars. This popular inn is often booked in the high season, especially October weekends. Tuesdays and Wednesdays are the most likely days the inn will have available rooms. Reservations must be made at least 48 hours in advance. The inn is owned by the Georgia Department of Natural Resources and operated by the nonprofit Appalachian Education & Recreation Services, which is affiliated with the Georgia Appalachian Trail Club. Profits are used for improvements at state parks or along the AT. Web site: www.hike-inn.com

Snacks can be bought from a private campground one mile west of the park entrance. Nearby, **Burt's Pumpkin Farm** sells huge pumpkins and snacks such as pumpkin pie and muffins; it's open only in September and October. Burt's hayrides are popular with families ($2 for 20 minutes).

DAHLONEGA
pop 3600
This quaint town is best known as the place where gold was discovered in 1828 – 21 years before California – beginning the nation's first gold rush. At the time, Dahlonega was Cherokee land; the discovery of gold and arrival of miners helped begin the final removal of the Cherokees from the region, culminating in the Trail of Tears in 1838.

A belt of gold extends 150 miles from Northeast Georgia to Southwest Alabama; the richest veins are around Dahlonega. Initially, gold lying in stream bottoms was easy to recover, and all you needed for a shot at riches was a pan. Gold veins were a lot harder to reach, and miners used water cannons to wash the mountains away and expose the gold; this harmful practice was eventually outlawed. Stamp mills were used to crush stone to get at the gold. Finally, shaft mining was used to dig tunnels through the rock in search of the ever more elusive metal. Larger companies with capital were needed to blast the tunnels. A US mint was established here to mint gold coins from 1838 to 1861, but it was closed in 1861 and the building later

burned. Sixty ounces of gold from Dahlonega were used in the dome of Atlanta's capitol building.

After the largest local mine closed in 1906, mining continued on a smaller scale until WWII, when miners went to war and mining equipment was sold for scrap. After the war, there were easier ways to make a living, and gold mining was over. Gold is still buried in the mountains, but it costs more to get it out than the metal is worth, though some people pursue recreational mining.

The boom these days is in tourism, not gold. Dahlonega offers a small town getaway at the edge of the Blue Ridge Mountains, with plenty of history, hokey tourist attractions and opportunities for natural recreation.

The Dahlonega-Lumpkin County Chamber of Commerce (☎ 800-231-5543, 706-864-3711) operates a **welcome center** on the square, open 9 am to 5:30 pm daily. Web site: www.dahlonega.org

Free Internet access is available at the public library (☎ 706-864-3668), 342 Courthouse Square, behind the courthouse.

Things to See & Do
Walking around the historic main square (at the center of which is the Gold Museum) is a major event by itself. Many offbeat shops compete for tourist dollars, and you can buy quilts, collectibles, jewelry, pottery, or antique and rare books. You can watch glassblown ornaments, candles and fudge being made. You can participate in a wine tasting, have your picture made posing as a cowboy or dance-hall girl, wander around the old-time general store, take a horse carriage ride or pan for gold.

The **Dahlonega Gold Museum** (☎ 706-864-2257), a state historic site, tells the fascinating story of gold mining in Dahlonega through an interesting film and exhibits. There's also a display of gold coins minted at Dahlonega now worth about a half million dollars. Hours are 9 am to 5 pm Monday through Saturday, 10 am to 5 pm Sunday; admission is $2.50. Web site: www.gastateparks.org

Consolidated Gold Mines (706-864-8473), next to the Gold Mine Shopping Center on Hwy 19/60 *(not* the route through town, known as Business 19/60), was the largest gold mine in the region for six years at the beginning of the 20th century. The high cost of getting to the gold prevented the mine from being successful. Forty-minute tours through the hole in the rock cover history, geology and mining techniques. At the end of the tour, you can try your hand at panning for gold; if you're careful you'll get a flake or two (every pan is spiked with gold). The tour plus panning takes about 90 minutes. Hours are 10 am to 4 pm weekdays, 10 am to 5 pm weekends; admission is $10/6 adults/children. Gold panning only costs $3 (so obviously, there will be less than $3 worth of gold in your pan).

Dahlonega's big festival is **Gold Rush Days** (☎ 706-864-7247), held the third full weekend in October. An estimated 200,000 visitors turn the streets through downtown into a big parking lot; traffic through the square itself is detoured. Besides 300 booths of arts, crafts and food, various contests are held for hog calling, lying, sawing, gold panning, pipe smoking, wrist wrestling and buffalo chip throwing.

The nearby Chestatee River offers opportunities for **canoeing, kayaking and tubing.** This calm Class I/II river is excellent for first-time canoeists and families. Appalachian Outfitters (☎ 706-864-7117, 24 N Park St), on the northeast corner of the courthouse square, rents canoes, recreational kayaks and tubes, and provides shuttle service to put-in and take-out points. Their most popular trip is 6.3 miles on the lower Chestatee, which lasts two to three hours and costs $40/25 canoe/kayak. These trips are offered on warm weekends in March and October, and daily April through September. The 30-minute 'Rapid Run' tubing trip is popular with families, and is not as crowded as the inner tube trips from nearby Helen. Rates are $6/4 adults/children, plus $2 each additional trip. Tubing is offered Memorial Day through Labor Day. Appalachian Outfitters also operates a well-stocked store with outdoor hiking supplies, regional travel books and maps of the Appalachian Trail and US Forest Service trails. They even provide shuttle service to the Appalachian Trail. Hours are 10 am to 3 pm weekdays, 9 am to 4 pm weekends. Web site: www.appoutga.com

The area offers several **mountain bike trails.** Bike rentals are provided by Mountain Adventures Cyclery (☎ 706-864-8525), just north of the intersection of Hwys 60 and 400. Rates are $25/day for a bike with front suspension, $35/day for full suspension, including a helmet, car rack and map of local trails. This is also a full-service bike repair shop. Its somewhat limited hours are 10 am to 3 pm Wednesday, 10 am to 6 pm Thursday, and 10 am to 5 pm Friday and Saturday. From Dahlonega, go south on Hwy 60 (Chestatee St) for about 5 miles; the shop is in a yellow house set back from the road on the left, a half mile before you reach Hwy 400.

The US Forest Service Information Center (☎ 706-864-6173), in the Gold Mine Shopping Center, has information on nearby hiking and camping options. A good selection of books and maps is sold here. **DeSoto Falls Recreation Area,** on US Hwy 129, has 2½ miles of hiking to two sets of waterfalls.

Places to Stay

The hotel tax rate is 12%.

Camping is available at the USFS's **Dockery Lake Recreation Area,** 11 miles north of Dahlonega off state Hwy 60. There are only 11 sites plus flush and chemical toilets, but no showers. Rates are $6. Trout fishing in Dockery Lake is popular.

Super 8 Motel *(☎ 800-800-8000, ☎/fax 706-864-4343),* 3/4 mile south of the main square on Business 19/60, is an adequate chain motel. Rates start at $55/60 singles/doubles, including a breakfast of cereal and donuts. ***EconoLodge*** *(☎ 800-553-2666, 706-864-6191),* a half mile north of the square on Business 19/60 (Grove St) is another simple chain. Rates start at $60 singles or doubles, and include cereal and donuts.

Worley Homestead Inn *(☎ 800-348-8094, 706-864-7002, worleyhomestead@alltel.net,*

168 Main St W), is two blocks southwest of the main square. This 1845 historic inn is furnished with antiques and has a dainty, eclectic Victorian decor. Each of the seven small but comfortable rooms is unique, and some have working fireplaces. Rates are $95 to $125, including a full breakfast.
Web site: www.bbonline.com/ga/worley

The *Smith House* (☎ 800-852-9577, 706-867-7000, 84 S Chestatee St), a block south of the main square, is a remodeled 1884 classic country inn decorated in a 19th-century style. It sits on a rich vein of gold that was never mined because of its proximity to the main public square. The wide verandas are good for relaxing, but the hordes of visitors headed for the restaurant make this a busy place. Its 16 rooms cost $60 to $178, depending on the room and the season.

The *Mountain Top Lodge* (☎ 706-864-5257), about 5 miles from Dahlonega on Old Ellijay Rd, is a rustic lodge with a perfect view of the Blue Ridge Mountains. A pleasant porch and balcony help you enjoy the views. The lodge is up a narrow, winding road; call for directions. Rates are $80 to $145.
Web site: www.mountaintoplodge.net

Places to Eat

The *Wagon Wheel Restaurant* (☎ 706-864-6677), a mile north of the town square on Business 19/60 (Grove St), is a basic, unpretentious, cafeteria-style restaurant that serves breakfast, lunch and dinner (except Tuesday dinner) at inexpensive prices. Friday and Saturday nights offer all-you-can-eat catfish.

It's easy to find a restaurant by walking around the square, where the pickin's range from sandwich shops to fancier, more expensive restaurants.

Caruso's Italian Restaurant (706-864-4664, 19B E Main St), on the square, serves decent Italian and also has some inexpensive choices. It offers basic subs, soups, salads, calzones, pizza ($9 for a 14-inch with two items) and pasta dishes ($5 to $13). The restaurant is open for lunch and dinner daily. Service is hit-and-miss.

The *Smith House* (☎ 706-867-7000, 84 S Chestatee St), a block south of the main square, is an institution. People come from miles around to eat unlimited quantities of fried chicken, catfish strips, fried okra, squash casserole and excellent creamed corn. The food is served family style (meaning you sit with strangers and pass the plates around). Perhaps this is as close to home-cooked as you can get with mass-cooked food. Unlike many buffets, the food here is top quality, but it still emphasizes gluttony – unless you eat until you hurt, you won't feel you've gotten a good value. The meal is a fixed $15 (aged 13 and above), $10 ages 10 to 12, and $7.50 ages 4 to 9, paid (oddly) in advance.

Rick's (☎ 706-864-9422, 47 S Park St), one block south of the square, is in a 1903 house with a relaxing atmosphere. It serves pastas, stuffed trout and smoked hen ($11 to $18), as well as salads, appetizers, gourmet sandwiches (like the grilled portobello mushroom sandwich with homemade chips) and burgers ($5 to $7). They're open for lunch and dinner, closed Tuesday. Rick's sometimes has live jazz at night.

Entertainment

Wylie's Restaurant (☎ 706-867-6324, 19 N Chestatee St) often has live music in the downstairs pub on weekend nights, starting about 9 pm.

VOGEL STATE PARK

This 238-acre park (☎ 706-745-2628, reservations 800-864-7275), 11 miles south of Blairsville via US Hwy 19/129, is one of the state's oldest, prettiest and most popular, drawing 500,000 visitors a year. At the base of Blood Mountain in the Chattahoochee National Forest, the park has 17 miles of hiking trails, with loops measuring 1, 4 or 13 miles, that offer excellent spring wildflowers, wildlife and trout fishing. Hikers can also reach the Appalachian Trail from here after a trek of 3½ steep miles. There are no mountain bike trails.

The park's main attraction is 20-acre Lake Trahlyta, which is stocked with trout and also has a swimming beach and paddle boats for rent. The visitors center has information and books.

The 103 campsites are set amidst nice plush trees and can fill up in the summertime. Rates are $8 for primitive walk-in sites, $15 for tent sites, and $17 for RVs, trailers, campers and pop-ups. The park also has 35 cottages that cost $55 to $115; a two-night minimum stay is required (seven nights in summer).

A $2 per day ParkPass is required for park entry.

WALASI-YI INTERPRETIVE CENTER AT NEEL'S GAP

At the gap where US Hwy 19/129 crosses the Appalachian Trail, this stone building was built in the 1930s by the Civilian Conservation Corps and is now on the National Register of Historic Places. The breezeway is the only place where the Appalachian Trail passes through a man-made structure. The center is now operated as an outfitting store and has an excellent selection of regional books on outdoor activities, hiking, the Appalachian Trail, history, Native Americans and nature. There are good views of the surrounding mountains from the center. It's open 9 am to 6 pm daily.

A 2-mile trail leads from Neel's Gap to Blood Mountain, the highest point on the Appalachian Trail in Georgia at 4458 feet. The trail is steep and rocky and leads to a summit with great views. It is the portion of the AT most often hiked in the state though

longer trails are also accessed from here. Parking for day hikers is about a half mile north of the Walasi-Yi Center.

BLAIRSVILLE

pop 660

This small town has no attractions other than a traditional courthouse square and a place to rest before heading out into the nearby mountains. The Blairsville Chamber of Commerce Welcome Center is on the Blue Ridge Highway west of the Hwy 76/19 intersection. Hours are 8:30 am to 4:30 pm weekdays. During June through October, it's also open 10 am to 1 pm Saturday. Brochures and lists of accommodations are available on the back porch even when it's closed.

The Brasstown Ranger District office (☎ 706-745-6928) of the US Forest Service is located 2 miles west of Blairsville on Hwy 515. It's open 7:30 am to 4:30 pm weekdays and 8:30 am to 5 pm weekends; it's the only one in the area open on Sunday.

Places to Stay & Eat

Seasons Inn (☎ 800-901-4422, 706-745-1631, fax 706-745-1334), on the downtown square, is an independent hotel with 26 clean, modern rooms with good beds and friendly, helpful owners. Prices start at $50, plus 12% tax.

The *Haralson House Bed & Breakfast* (☎ 706-745-9554, 3101 Kings Rd) is located on a rural, winding road 4 miles from Blairsville, and has large, relaxing grounds with inspirational mountain views and colorful gardens. The 1840 house was relocated from downtown, restored to its antebellum ambience, and decorated with antiques. Its five spacious rooms include three with a shared bath ($85), one with a private bath ($100), and one family suite ($140). Rates include a full breakfast and evening desserts. The minimum stay is two nights.

Web site: www.haralsonhouse.com

The *Blairsville Restaurant* (☎ 706-745-6921, 229 Earnest St), a half block south of Hwy 76/515, is popular with locals and has reasonably priced Southern cooking served cafeteria-style, or you can order off the menu. Lunch meals of a meat, three vegetables and tea are typically less than $5; dinner meals start around $7. Breakfast prices are also reasonable.

The *North Georgia Hole in the Wall Restaurant* (☎ 706-745-5888), on the square, serves cheap breakfast and lunch (under $5). This small, very smoky restaurant is open 6 am to 2:30 pm daily.

Monet's Café & Bakery (☎ 706-745-5305, 91 Blue Ridge St), one block north of the central square, is the best restaurant in town. It serves mostly Italian dishes from $9 to $14, and pizza from $12; the chicken Waldorf salad ($7.50) is a meal in itself. The desserts are excellent. Service, however, can be lackadaisical and very slow.

BRASSTOWN BALD

The highest point in Georgia, at 4784 feet, Brasstown Bald (☎ 706-896-3471) is 20 miles from Blairsville, reached from the very scenic GA Hwy 180. (A 'bald' is a summit without natural covering – in nature as in humans.) A steep half-mile-long trail leads up through mountain laurel and spring wildflowers to the top, where there's an interpretive center with exhibits on the natural and cultural history of the area and, best of all, a 360° view of the surrounding mountains. From here, three hiking trails 4½ to 6 miles long (one way) start at the parking area.

The parking fee is $3. A round-trip shuttle is also available from the parking lot for $2.

HELEN

pop 430

Helen, Georgia, is the sort of place you can only find in the USA: a faux Swiss-German mountain village filled with shops with names like 'Das Ist Leather.' Beginning in 1968, business leaders in this lumber town looked for ideas to transform the dull, dreary row of block structures into something that would attract tourists driving through to the mountains. Based on the pleasant memories of a businessman who

had been stationed in Bavaria 20 years earlier, the locals gradually added gable roofs, balconies and façade trim, details and colors intended to resemble a Bavarian village.

Somehow this place has become one of north Georgia's more popular tourist destinations. It may be a tourist trap, but the townspeople have managed to create a tourist-based economy that employs more people than most mills.

Helen lies 85 miles northeast of Atlanta and about 25 miles northeast of Dahlonega. The most common access highway is state Hwy 75.

Information

The **welcome center** (☎ 706-878-2181) is on Bruckenstrasse south of town. It has a 24-hour hotel reservation phone outside. Web site: www.helenga.org

Free Internet access is available at the library on Pete's Park Rd, north of Fest-Halle. It's open 9 am to 5 pm weekdays and 11 am to 2 pm Saturday.

There are public restrooms downtown.

Things to See & Do

Strolling around town is the major activity. There are lots of places that sell funnel cakes and strudel, and plenty of shops.

Oktoberfest is Helen's largest event, typically held from mid-September to early November. The main events are in the FestHalle, an open-air pavilion on the eastern side of town. Oompah bands play more German polkas and waltzes than you can shake a bratwurst at, while retirees wearing lederhosen and feathered hats move around the dance floor. Basic German food is served. The entry fee is $7; parking, if you can find it, is $3 more. The events are typically held on Thursday, Friday and Saturday in late September, and Monday through Saturday in October. Weekends are very crowded; weekdays will have fewer people and cheaper hotel rates.

A popular summertime activity for families is **Shooting the 'Hooch** – going down the relaxing Chattahoochee River in a large inner tube. Several companies offer rentals and shuttles; one is Cool River Tubing Co (☎ 706-878-2665), behind the Welcome Center. One- or 2½-hour floats are offered. The rates of $7/5 adults/children include a shuttle up to the put-in point; you float back down to the store. They're open Memorial Day through Labor Day. For a less crowded experience, see the Dahlonega section earlier in this chapter.

Parts of the river are also suitable for **kayaking, canoeing and rafting;** a few stretches of white water lie between the Hwy 115 and Hwy 384 bridges. Wildwood Outfitters (☎ 706-878-1700, paddling@ alltel.net), on Hwy 17/75 1.3 miles south of the Main St bridge, rents kayaks, canoes and rafts ($16 to $19 per person). A shuttle costs $5 more. They also have a complete range of outdoor supplies – backpacks, boots, hiking/biking guides, canoeing guides and canoe/kayak supplies. Wildwood provides shuttles to Appalachian Trail trailheads (starting at $10), and the company even ships supply drops for AT hikers.
Web site: www.wildwoodoutfitters.com

For **fly fishing gear,** go to Unicoi Outfitters (☎ 706-878-3083, 7280 S Main St), next to Wildwood Outfitters. A complete fly fishing outfitter, they offer rods, reels and other fishing paraphernalia, casting and fly tying lessons and a professional guide service.
Web site: www.unicoioutfitters.com

The **Sautee-Nacoochee Arts & Community Center** (☎ 706-878-3300), on Hwy 255 in the nearby arts community of Sautee-Nacoochee, presents plays and folk music throughout the year. Call or check their Web site (www.snca.org) for a schedule.

Nearby hiking opportunities include **Duke's Creek Falls,** 6½ miles north of Helen on Hwy 348, where a one-mile trail down a gorge leads to a mountain creek and 250-foot waterfall. A short distance up the road, **Raven Cliff Falls** has a popular 2½-mile trail that leads to a massive cliff, over which Dodd's Creek falls.

Woody's Mountain Bikes (☎ 706-878-3715), on Hwy 356 a mile north of Helen, next to Fred's Famous Peanuts, rents bicycles.

Places to Stay

The hotel tax is 12%. Hotel prices skyrocket during Oktoberfest, weekends and other popular times. A room that costs $45 in January might cost $60 to $80 in the summer, $60/$110 on September weekdays/weekends, and $140 during an Oktoberfest weekend.

There are many hotels in town with Bavarian names and decorations. These don't necessarily offer any better value than the more standard options.

Super 8 Motel (☎ 800-535-1251, 706-878-2191), on Main St just south of the Chattahoochee River, is in walking distance of both downtown and the FestHalle. It has some of the cheapest rooms in town, with rates from $29 to $129. Rooms are just OK. Next door, **Days Inn** (☎ 800-329-7466, 706-878-4079, 8288 S Main St) is a small step up, at $45 to $109, including continental breakfast.

A bit more south, **Best Western** (☎ 800-435-3642, 706-878-2111, 8220 Main St) has nice modern hotel rooms and a huge lobby for $35 to $119, including a continental breakfast. Rooms have a refrigerator and microwave.

The **Chattahoochee Riverfront Hotel** (☎ 800-830-3977, 706-878-2184, fax 706-878-1882, 8949 N Main St), within walking distance of downtown, is a family-owned motel with pleasant views of the river. Rates for the 35 so-so rooms are $40 to $165. There are no nonsmoking rooms, and the lobby can be quite smoky.

The **Bavarian Inn** (☎ 800-422-6355, 706-878-2840, 859 Edelweiss St) has a good location near the FestHalle and balconies overlooking the river. Summer rates for a room with a kitchen and fireplace start at $55 for doubles; Oktoberfest rates are higher.

The **Hampton Inn** (☎ 800-426-7866, 706-878-3310, fax 706-878-3566, 147 Unicoi St), on the northern side of town and western end of Spring St, is two blocks from downtown. More upmarket than the strip of chains, it features a plush lobby, large comfortable rooms and an outdoor pool. Rates are $105 for a standard room with two beds, more for suites or rooms with a view of the river; a continental breakfast is included.

Places to Eat

The **River Street Coffee Haus** (☎ 706-878-3292, 75 River St), overlooking the river downtown, is a good place to relax with a cappuccino and a muffin.

Sweetwater Coffeehouse, between Helen and Unicoi State Park at the intersection of Hwys 17 and 255, is a youngish, hip place where patrons from the nearby arts community of Sautee hang out. In addition to the usual lattes and espresso, they have good brownies, local crafts and sometimes live old-time music on Sunday afternoons. It's open Tuesday through Sunday.

Why not jump into the spirit of the place by eating at **Hofer's Bakery** (☎ 706-878-8200), on the northern side of town between Spring and White Sts? The German specialties include bratwurst with potato salad ($8), spaetzle (noodles) and *schweinebraten* (pork roast, $13). Sandwiches are also available from $6. Hofer's also has plenty of imported beer; if you need a *Spaten Franziskaner Weisse,* look no further. Delicious desserts include tortes, plum cake and strudel. Breakfast is also served. Sorry vegetarians, not much hope here.

The Wurst Haus, downtown, is a basic beer garden, with food served cafeteria-style and outdoor seating. Wurst sandwiches cost $3; platters are $6. There are plenty of domestic and imported beers. It's open until midnight during October weekends.

If you don't want to give in to the Bavarian hoopla, **West Family Restaurant**, 4 miles south of town, has the usual Southern buffet with fried chicken and okra, or you can order off the menu. Breakfast is $5 to $6, lunch and dinner are $7 to $8. Sandwiches are cheap ($3). Fancier choices include catfish, mountain trout and chicken livers ($8 to $16).

Shopping

Helen's shops sell a bit of everything, from kitsch to quality crafts and imports. There are dolls, music boxes, wooden shoes, jewelry, candy, handbags, country goods, toys, woodcrafts, candles and imported goods.

Tekakwitha (☎ 706-878-2938), 8047 S Main St, south of the main drag, specializes in authentic Native American goods from Canada to Mexico; over 60 different Indian nations are represented.

For the obligatory lederhosen or dirndl, head to the House of Tyrol (☎ 706-878-2264), 8641 Main St, on the main strip for more than 30 years. The shop sells authentic German/European ware such as cuckoo clocks, nutcrackers and hats; there are also English tea sets, Polish glassware, Matroyski nesting dolls, Italian music boxes and a wide range of music tapes.

Nora's Mill Granary (☎ 706-878-2375) is a water-powered grist mill a half mile south of town that sells stone-ground grits and flour, homemade preserves and jam. You can feed the fish in the river out back.

Fred's Famous Peanuts (☎ 706-878-3124), on Hwy 356 a mile north of Helen, sells boiled peanuts, peanut brittle and just about everything else made with peanuts.

The Gourd Place (☎ 706-865-4048), south of Helen on Hwy 384 2.3 miles from Hwy 75, features calabashes – hard-shelled fruits that are in the same family as pumpkins, cucumbers, squash and melons. Items for sale range from dried raw gourds to kitchen bowls, colanders, painted birdhouses, vases and the whimsical Gourdheads. A small museum here exhibits gourds from around the world – Nigerian milk bowls, Puerto Rican percussion instruments and African penis gourds; donations requested. There's even a nice lake and grounds for picnicking.

At Mark of the Potter (☎ 706-947-3440), the oldest craft shop in Georgia, you can watch pottery being made or buy homemade jams. In a very peaceful setting, you can also feed – but not catch – the dozens of trout in the river at the bottom of the falls. The shop is on Hwy 197 east of Helen, just south of Batesville.

UNICOI STATE PARK

Two miles north of Helen on GA Hwy 356, this 1023-acre park (☎ 706-878-3982) is one of the state's most popular. Unicoi is a Cherokee word meaning 'where the white

ATLANTA

NORTH GEORGIA

CENTRAL GEORGIA

SAVANNAH & THE COAST

Contents

Georgia & the Carolinas
1st edition – January 2002

Published by
Lonely Planet Publications Pty Ltd ABN 36 005 607 983
90 Maribyrnong St, Footscray, Victoria 3011, Australia

Lonely Planet Offices
Australia Locked Bag 1, Footscray, Victoria 3011
USA 150 Linden St, Oakland, CA 94607
UK 10a Spring Place, London NW5 3BH
France 1 rue du Dahomey, 75011 Paris

Photographs
Many of the images in this guide are available for licensing from
Lonely Planet Images.
email: lpi@lonelyplanet.com.au
Web site: www.lonelyplanetimages.com

Front cover photograph
Historic Savannah, Georgia, at sunset (Richard Cummins)

Title page photographs
Georgia (Richard Cummins)
South Carolina (Mark & Audrey Gibson)
North Carolina (Peter Ptschelinzew)

ISBN 1 86450 383 1

text & maps © Lonely Planet Publications Pty Ltd 2002
photos © photographers as indicated 2002

Printed by The Bookmaker International Ltd
Printed in China

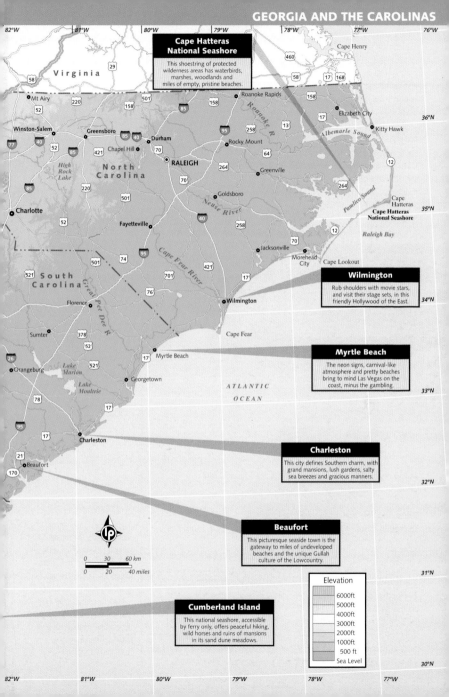

GEORGIA AND THE CAROLINAS

Cape Hatteras National Seashore

This shoestring of protected wilderness areas has waterbirds, marshes, woodlands and miles of empty, pristine beaches.

Wilmington

Rub shoulders with movie stars, and visit their stage sets, in this friendly Hollywood of the East.

Myrtle Beach

The neon signs, carnival-like atmosphere and pretty beaches bring to mind Las Vegas on the coast, minus the gambling.

Charleston

This city defines Southern charm, with grand mansions, lush gardens, salty sea breezes and gracious manners.

Beaufort

This picturesque seaside town is the gateway to miles of undeveloped beaches and the unique Gullah culture of the Lowcountry.

Cumberland Island

This national seashore, accessible by ferry only, offers peaceful hiking, wild horses and ruins of mansions in its sand dune meadows.

Virginia

North Carolina

South Carolina

Mt Airy
Winston-Salem
Greensboro
Durham
Chapel Hill
RALEIGH
Charlotte
Fayetteville
Florence
Sumter
Orangeburg
Georgetown
Charleston
Beaufort

Roanoke Rapids
Rocky Mount
Greenville
Goldsboro
Jacksonville
Morehead City
Wilmington
Myrtle Beach

Elizabeth City
Kitty Hawk
Cape Henry
Cape Hatteras
Cape Hatteras National Seashore
Cape Lookout
Cape Fear

High Rock Lake
Great Pee Dee R
Cape Fear River
Neuse River
Roanoke R
Albemarle Sound
Pamlico Sound
Raleigh Bay
Lake Marion
Lake Moultrie

ATLANTIC OCEAN

0   30   60 km
0   20   40 miles

Elevation

6000ft
5000ft
4000ft
3000ft
2000ft
1000ft
500 ft
Sea Level